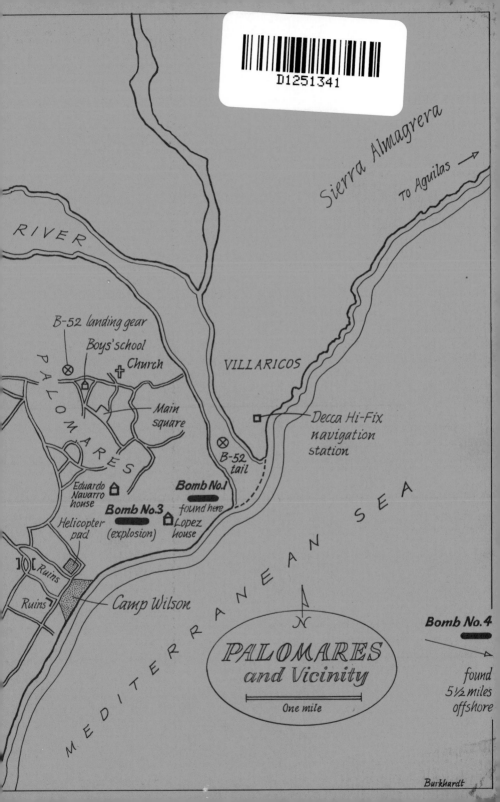

PALOMARES and Vicinity

One mile

N

Sierra Almagrera

To Aguilas

RIVER

PALOMARES

B-52 landing gear

Boys' school

Church

VILLARICOS

Main square

B-52 tail

Decca Hi-Fix navigation station

Eduardo Navarro house

Bomb No.3 (explosion)

Bomb No.1 found here

Lopez house

Helicopter pad

Ruins

Ruins

Camp Wilson

MEDITERRANEAN SEA

Bomb No. 4

found 5½ miles offshore

Burkhardt

The
Bombs
of
MARES

Tad Szulc

NEW YORK

The Viking Press

This book is for Babcia

A Note of Appreciation

In the most literal sense, the story of Palomares in its multiple aspects could not have been covered, reported, researched, understood, and written without the gift of help and time on the part of an impressive number of people, Americans and Spaniards. To them goes my appreciation. It is impossible to extend personal thanks here to all those who have patiently submitted to lengthy interviews, written letters and memoranda, opened their files, memories, and hearts, and in other direct or indirect ways contributed to this project. In no particular order of importance in terms of how much of their material has finally found its way to these pages, I would like to name some of them.

On the American side, members of the staff of the United States embassy in Madrid, starting with Ambassador Angier Biddle Duke, were of invaluable help. Among them: Information Attaché William Alexander Bell; Political Counselor Laurin B. Askew; Joseph L. Smith, then a member of the political section; and Timothy Towell, special assistant to the Ambassador.

Among the military, Major General Stanley J. Donovan, then head of the Joint United States–Spain Military Assistance Advisory Group and now Commander of the Sixteenth Air Force; Major General Delmar E. Wilson, former Commander of the Sixteenth Air Force; and the following officers of the Strategic Air Command and the Sixteenth Air Force at the Torrejón base who participated in the Palomares operation: Colonel Alton E. White; Lieutenant Colonel Henry R. Hirsch; Lieutenant Colonel Thomas B. Wright; Lieutenant Colonel L. C. Shepard; Major Ernest Moore, the Sixteenth Air Force director of information; and Captain Robert E. Finkel.

In the Defense Department in Washington, I wish to express high appreciation to Secretary of the Navy Paul H. Nitze for his assistance in making promptly available detailed records of the search and recovery operation of Task Force 65. At the SAC Headquarters at Offutt Air Force Base, Lieutenant Colonel Derrill deS. Trenholm, Jr., chief of media and liaison division in the Directorate of Information, provided vital research on the crew members of the lost aircraft.

Very special gratitude is offered to Dr. Wright H. Langham of the Los Alamos Scientific Laboratory of the Atomic Energy Commission for his brilliant explanation and interpretation of the contamination problems at Palomares and, even more, for his humanistic approach in outlining the village's drama.

My newspaper colleagues in Spain displayed extraordinary generosity in sharing their experiences and observations. They include Alvin Rosenfeld, Madrid Bureau Chief of the National Broadcasting Company and a frequent companion on Palomares news-gathering trips; Harold K. Milks, Spain Bureau Chief of The Associated Press; André del Amo, formerly a United Press International reporter in Madrid; Roy Ferguson, formerly a Reuters News Agency reporter in Madrid; and Robert Toth, *Los Angeles Times* Bureau Chief in London.

In Washington, Benjamin Welles of *The New York Times,* one-time correspondent in Spain, performed miracles in cutting through red tape to provide fast and accurate information. James Saylor, formerly librarian of the Washington Bureau of *The Times,* was a superb source of background data.

On the Spanish side, my thanks go to Dr. José María Otero Navascués, president of the Nuclear Energy Board (JEN), and his collaborator, Dr. Emilio Iranzo, for their technical advice on Palomares decontamination problems.

At the Ministry of the Air, Brigadier General Arturo Montel Touzet, the Spanish commander in Palomares, provided an extensive account of his experiences. At the Foreign Ministry, Angel Sagáz, formerly director of the North American Department and now Spanish Ambassador to the United Arab Republic, was of considerable assistance in reviewing the political aspects of the situation.

In Vera and Palomares, Captain Isidoro Calín Velasco of the Civil Guard was an outstanding eyewitness of the January events and an important source on the history, economics, and sociology of the region. Father Francisco Navarete Serrano, the parish priest of Palomares, contributed his narrative and insight into the events as they affected the village.

And then there were the scores of Palomares inhabitants, men, women, and children, who with unfailing courtesy and patience told over and over of their experiences when "the sky rained fire" and afterward. Airmen and sailors did likewise to cover their experiences.

In all, more than 120 separate interviews were conducted personally and by mail from the first week after the January 17 accident until months following the clean-up in the village and the bomb's recovery. Innumerable official and personal reports and accounts in the Spanish, American, and European press were studied. And, of course, technical books were devoured.

TAD SZULC

Madrid
November 1966

Contents

BOOK ONE *The Event*

i

Palomares is best reached from the sky.

Overland, the dusty village is just barely accessible to the rare visitor from the outside world. The loose collection of white-washed houses lies remote and forgotten under the ever-blue sky and ever-bright sun of Mediterranean Spain. The sandy, slag-covered tracks leading to it from three directions are like dead-end streets. For this village is not on the road to or from any-where and it is only natural that for a very long time the world bypassed it—until the startling morning of January 17, 1966, when history suddenly chose the sky as its gateway to Palomares. On that day it brought the dramatic reality of the nuclear age to this corner of the earth where Cro-Magnon cave men first trod and where Iberians, Phoenicians, Carthaginians, Romans, and Moors successively built their cultures. In Palomares, indeed, man's history has gone the full cycle.

Before that January morning, the traveler driving along the narrow black-topped Carretera Norte 340, the undulating national highway that skirts the coast of Almería province in southeastern Spain, would not have suspected the existence of Palomares. The village did not appear on most current maps. Tourist guidebooks mention most of the towns of the region, recording the presence of a Roman monument here or an especially interesting Moorish tower there. But Palomares has no shrines, relics, or architectural

3

points of interest. It offers only the leprous sight of scavenged ruins of old mining foundries, a pathetic reminder of happier times.

Motoring northeast from the city of Almería, the provincial capital 58 miles away, the traveler would cross the green and pungent orange groves between Tabernas and Sorbas. Then he would go through the desolate landscape of eroded yellowish hills behind Sierra Cabrera, which forms the mountainous northern wall of the coastal triangle that encompasses Palomares. Finally the visitor would reach the tree-lined straightaway taking him into Vera. That ancient town, founded by the Romans, was distinguished by Ferdinand and Isabella with the title "Very Noble and Loyal City" for serving as the bivouac for the Catholic Monarchs when they completed, in 1488, the reconquest of the Mediterranean coast from the Moors. From Vera, Ferdinand and Isabella swung west to take Granada four years later and thus end the 781 years of Moorish sway over Spain.

Once-proud Vera is now only a sleepy *comarca* (district) seat whose population has dropped from 8446 inhabitants at the turn of the twentieth century to somewhat over 6000 in 1966, accurately reflecting the state of affairs in the region and in the province of Almería as a whole. Because nothing meaningful has happened in Almería since the coastal mining industry—begun by the Phoenicians about the twelfth century B.C.—collapsed in the 1920s, the population of the province has remained virtually static in this century. It edged up from 359,013 inhabitants in 1900 to only 361,964 in 1964, a period in which Spain's population nearly doubled. For centuries Almeríans have fled their impoverished province.

One's first major impression of Vera is its gasoline station, known succinctly as "La Estación" because it is the only one in town. It is just off Norte 340, which then continues 79 miles northeast toward the city of Murcia, the quite prosperous capital of the adjacent and orange-rich province of Murcia. Immediately east of La Estación and directly behind it, two secondary highways join in a fork. The road going south merges with one of Vera's back streets, an unpaved stretch of potholes caught between two rows of two-story houses, leading to the highway, to the fishing port of Garrucha, and, beyond it, to the Moorish hilltop town of Mojácar. The road to the north is well paved and links Vera with Cuevas de Almanzora, another once-splendid *comarca* seat 3.5 miles away, and with towns on the Murcia coast. Sitting strategically astride this crossroads, La Estación controls, economically and socially, the region's traffic, which helps to explain why the station and the adjoining restaurant and its second-floor boarding house are Vera's most modern and roomy structures.

There is a tiny dark café with an old-fashioned marble-topped bar a few steps down the street from La Estación and across the street from La Ramona boarding house. But only Vera's old men go there to sip the bitter black coffee or down an occasional glass of inexpensive Spanish brandy. They have the dark, leathery faces of Andalusian peasants, and they sit at the little tables, silently staring into space, their black berets adding a touch of solemnity to their quiet demeanor. Sometimes a slow game of Tute, which resembles pinochle, or of La Baisca, in which each man holds three cards, starts in the evening to help the old men pass the empty hours.

It is La Estación, however, that functions as Vera's chief social center, attracting both the travelers who stop there to refuel and eat, and the town's leading citizens, who drop in for a drink and conversation.

Among the substantial citizens often found chatting at La Estación's bar-and-restaurant are: Captain Isidoro Calín Velasco, the articulate commander of the local detachment of the Guardia Civil (Spain's national gendarmerie) and a very important man in this whole area; Miguel Jiménez of the family that owns the shoe factory (which was the area's principal industry until the profitable aftermath of the January accident); and Dr. Jacinto Gonzáles, who runs the Vera clinic. These and other Vera men, and La Estación itself, were to play varyingly active roles in the events that were to unfold in Palomares and profoundly affect the neighboring towns and countryside.

Palomares men, the first-line performers in the nuclear accident, are also steady patrons of the gasoline station's social facilities. Farmers such as Miguel Castro Navarro and Antonio Saviote García, both owners of moderate-sized *fincas,* and Eduardo Navarro Portillo, an old man who owns so much land that not one but *two* hydrogen bombs were to crash on his property, seldom miss the Saturday market in Vera. This is where they supervise the sale of their tomatoes and beans and pigs, and where they buy their supplies and catch up with the latest gossip. Since people from the outside rarely have a reason for going to Palomares, the villagers regularly trek to the *comarca* seats of Vera and Cuevas de Almanzora. Guardia Civil Captain Calín, who is well acquainted with the population's habits after ten years of supervising the big police district that runs from Pulpi on the Murcia line to Los Gallardos south of Vera, says that the Palomares people "circulate all the time." It is one way to combat isolation.

The north highway to Cuevas de Almanzora reaches a barely discernible turn-off to the right, or east, less than a mile after leaving Vera. If it were not for the two arrow-shaped metal road signs pointing to the turn, one could easily miss it. The name on the signs is PALOMARES. Nowhere else is the way to the village marked.

This road to Palomares, really no more than a hard-beaten track, is known to people all around as the Vera Highway, presumably because it actually leads to Vera. This little fact makes the first point about Palomares: roads seem to lead away from it rather than to it. And as one starts up the road it is easy to see why. The roadbed here is sand kept in place with brownish slag from some long-forgotten foundry. The track is narrow— in spots just broad enough to let a large automobile squeeze through—and quite winding. It winds up and down around low, parched, yellowish hills dotted with the vegetation of the steppes. There are gray cacti, greenish, sparse shrubs with downy leaves known to botanists as *Salsolaceae,* and the tough esparto grass whose scientific name is *Macrochloa tenacissima,* and which is just that.

All together, the landscape is both North African and lunar in appearance. Arid, drought-punished, and inhospitable, it is the relic of the salt steppes that were left behind after the waters of the Mediterranean receded hundreds of centuries ago from the coastal triangle between the sierras, and of the more recent erosion of the old rocky hills. There is still salt in the soil outside Palomares, and less than one hundred years ago archaeologists could still dig up fossilized bone fragments of prehistoric mammals and sea creatures. The area of Palomares goes back to the Tertiary Age and the Neolithic era, and the link with that dim past has hardly been broken.

Crossing the hills, the track widens and suddenly dips into an oasis of orange groves. Here the soil, free of salt, is more fertile and the groves are lush, reddish and green. They run for more than half a mile, and for the first time since leaving Vera one sees signs of life. The Huerta del Viudo—the Widower's Grove—is the biggest one, and the manor house, the best in the neighborhood, in the middle of a walled flower garden, is ample and comfortable. But after the orange groves there is again the monotony of the moonscape. The rise of Cabezo Negro, the Black Head, 300 feet high, dominates the steppe-land about it. The lonely Palomares cemetery is here, one of the sites where the nuclear drama was to be enacted. Along the Black Head's northern rim, facing the village a mile away, four or five miserable houses nest in the dust. Their inhabitants, underpaid farm hands and their families, were to be the first Spanish actors in the drama.

A high irrigation wall, overgrown with cacti and esparto grass, forms the northern border of the village of Palomares. The Vera Highway traverses it through a cut at a point where three other tracks meet. One track comes up from the Quitapellejos beach, which later was to become world-famous under another name, and from the old iron foundry ruins known appropriately as the Fábrica del Hambre, the Factory of Hunger. The distance from the brown sand Mediterranean beach to the entrance to Palomares near the irrigation wall is about half a mile. The track crosses a field of slag between the beach and the Fábrica del Hambre, then rather abruptly enters green cultivated fields of wheat, fields of the large brown black-eyed beans known as *habas,* and long rows of tomato patches.

Beyond the fields is the village of Palomares, its whitewashed houses strung out in a ragged line from the edge of the wheat-planted area to an intersection adorned with a white-painted wooden chapel, the Palomares church, where many prayers of thankfulness would be offered after January 17. The boys' elementary school, a newly built low rectangle topped by a television antenna, stands nearby. Along the dusty street leading from the chapel to the uneven main square, and around the square itself, lies the central cluster of Palomares' houses. Most of the daily traffic is provided by herds of goats and sheep led to or from the village pastures.

It was slightly to the north of this cluster, perhaps half a mile away, that a Belgian archaeologist, Louis Siret, whose book on the Almería coast, published in 1887, remains the best study of the area, came upon a prehistoric burial ground filled with partly calcinated bones, funeral urns, and numerous artifacts. Among the artifacts were a crude bronze bracelet and two sections of a bronze collar. Siret, who refers to the site as Barranco Hondo (Deep Gulch), believed that his findings established that the tomb dates back to the Bronze Age or even the earlier Transition Period, also known as the Aëneolithic Period, or the Age of Copper. This would place the cultural origins of what today is the Palomares region at somewhere around 3500 B.C., fifty-five centuries before the arrival of the atomic age at this spot.

Another cluster of Palomares houses lies some five hundred yards to the east, between the beach and the wide, dry bed of the Almanzora River. These houses were built around the old structure of the Fábrica del Duro (coin factory), where *duros,* five-peseta pieces, were once minted from the region's metals. The *fábrica* is another link with Palomares' ancient history. It was one of the by-products of the immense riches of silver, lead, copper, and iron that were mined from the flanks and innards of Sierra Almagrera on the left bank of the Almanzora and from the low hills of Herrerías on the river's right bank. Siret established that the pre-Iberian tribes around the Palomares area were already mining copper and tin and making them into bronze at the dawn of recorded history. Other evidence, going back to Greek historians and later developed by Roman and Spanish scholars and by Siret, indicates that the mines of Herrerías and Almagrera were occupied by the Phoenicians between 100 and 21 B.C. The Phoenicians settled the zone stretching from Sierra Almagrera past Palomares to what today are the towns of Vera and Antas, naming the whole district Baria. Diodorus Siculus, a Sicilian-born historian who lived in Julius Caesar's time and traveled extensively around the rim of the Mediterranean producing chronicles that sound very much like the work of a care-free foreign correspondent of our age, recorded in his *Biblioteca Historica* the existence of Phoenician mines and settlements on the Almería coast. He described them vividly and colorfully, drawing on ancient Mediterranean legends and earlier chronicles for tales about mining pure silver. Siret confirms that remarkably pure silver, as well as argentiferous lead, was mined from the Almagrera's veins as recently as the middle of the nineteenth century.

But all that is left today of this opulence are the ruins of the foundries and the deep shafts, tunnels, and galleries in the body of Sierra Almagrera. The fishing village of Villaricos on the Almanzora's left bank was one of the principal Mediterranean ports in the Phoenician era. The Phoenicians called it Murgis, and the Greeks called it Urci. Pliny spoke of it in his *Geography*. It was then a prosperous mineral-exporting harbor for Phoenician, Carthaginian, and Greek trading fleets. Until the late 1920s it still served for the export of iron ore from the Herrerías mines. Nowadays it is a miserable and abandoned hamlet inhabited by dark-skinned gypsies and by descendants of the Moorish conquerors. The dusty track leading from Palomares to Villaricos and thence to Aguilas—the third way of reaching Palomares from the outside world—is all that remains of one of the great avenues of commerce in the forgotten centuries. Only an occasional farmer tills the parched land, and herds of sheep and brown-and-black goats graze on tufts of vegetation.

That Palomares wheat fields were green and tomatoes were ripening on their pole-supported vines in the midst of all this dryness during those January days was due to the miracle of water. The entire southeastern Spanish coastline, running from Murcia in the north to Motril at the foot of towering Sierra Nevada far to the southwest, is drought territory. Rain is a rare and precious commodity, and its chronic lack explains the heartrending appeals that cover the walls along the highways of Almería. FRANCO! . . . AGUA! ("Franco . . . water!") say these anonymously lettered signs addressed to Francisco Franco Bahamonde, the "Generalissimo of the Armies of Land, Sea, and Air and, by the Grace of God, the Caudillo of Spain." VICTORY IN WAR—WATER IN PEACE, cry the signs, as if to remind the ruler that twenty-seven years after his Civil War triumph, the province of Almería, much of which sided with his Republican opponents almost until the end, may finally deserve attention and water. The only people to capitalize on the drought—aside from the entrenched water monopolists in one *pueblo* or another—are American film-makers, for whom the Almería desert is an ideal location. It was across Almerían sand flats that Peter O'Toole galloped on his white horse as Lawrence of Arabia, and it was in Almería that *King of Kings, The Centurions,* and such Westerns as *The Finger on the Trigger* were filmed. So in Almería not only the past and the present blend, but also the real and the illusory.

In Palomares, as drought-beaten as the rest of the province, the last measurable rain before the events of January 1966 had fallen on October 18 of the preceding year. The last rain of any value to farming had come in January 1964, when 41.5 liters per square meter (11 gallons per 1.196 square yards) fell on Palomares. This was a grudging gift because the bare minimum of rain for farming without irrigation is 40 liters (10.56 gallons) per square meter. The rainfall on that last October 18 had been a frustrating 15 liters. Records of this melancholy state of affairs are kept by Julio Ponce Navarro, whose duties as hired hand for his boss—a Vera pharmacist who doubles as a Palomares landlord—include measuring the level of rainfall in a barrel on the roof of his modest rented farmhouse at the foot of the Black Head hills. After each infrequent rain, Julio brings out his well-thumbed blue copybook to enter the pathetic figures that only emphasize the magnitude of the relentless drought.

Because of this dryness, the farmers of Palomares went to the depths of their baked earth to wrest the water that the skies would not spare them. And therein lies the water miracle of the village. Some eleven years ago a group of enterprising businessmen and land operators from Valencia persuaded the people of Palomares that they should start growing tomatoes, which thrive in dry top-soil and require relatively little water for their roots. This seemed a solution to the misery and unemployment that had followed the closing in 1945 of the last lead and iron mines and foundries in Herrerías. (The only iron mine still operating in the region is west of Vera, and the ore is moved on overhead conveyor belts to the little port of Garrucha for shipment.)

Palomares decided that it must dig wells to survive. In the ensuing years a village cooperative formed by 103 men sank nearly 100 wells. The three bank agencies in Vera and the Palomares branch of the Almería Savings Association have earmarked most of their rural loans for the well-digging. In the village's elementary but highly effective irrigation method, water is brought out of deep wells—in some of them gasoline-engine pumps are used—and a network of ditches then distributes the water to the fields. Under the cooperative system members hold shares in the available water supply and each share is equivalent to one hour of the water flow, which averages 6.6 gallons a second from each well. A member is free to sell his unused shares for 25 pesetas—nearly 42 cents—each.

The new irrigation system, combined with the use of chemical fertilizers and the basic fertility of the land—the latter resulting from organic and alluvial clay deposits left behind by the long-receded sea—has recently brought a measure of prosperity to the big and small landowners of this isolated village, if not always to its farmhands.

About 65 per cent of the 250-odd families of Palomares are land-owning. The Spanish national census counts noses in munici- palities or *comarcas,* such as Cuevas de Almanzora, but not in its component *barriadas* (hamlets), such as Palomares. For this reason nobody is quite certain of the Palomares population. Cap- tain Calín estimated the number of adult inhabitants in 1966 at 756. With children, the total population was in excess of 2000 persons.

The village's land lots range from the half-acre of Juan Zamora, a taciturn and hermit-like farmer who lives near the dry bed of the Almanzora River, to the scores of acres owned by old Eduardo Navarro, stretching from one end of Palomares to the other. All in all, between the big owners and the small landholders, Palomares produced and sold six million pounds of fat, juicy tomatoes from its two 1965 crops. Most of the tomatoes went to such big Spanish cities as Barcelona and Madrid, and many shipments found their way to Germany and England. These tomatoes brought Palomares nearly 15 million pesetas ($250,000) in 1965, which is quite a bit of money as things go in southeastern Spain. The village also harvested a lot of alfalfa, two wheat crops, beans, and a bit of cotton.

All these revenues, swollen by the rising price of tomatoes in recent years, permitted the installation of an electric-power genera- tor in 1958—the last memorable event in Palomares before the sudden coming of the nuclear age—and the lighting of many of the village's 140 houses, particularly those bunched together around the main square.

The new prosperity encouraged Antonio Saez Martínez—the owner of one of Palomares' two tobacco stores and one of its three bars and the local representative of the Almería Savings Association—to open a movie house in 1964, and at this Capri Cinema pictures are now shown two or three times a week. The extra money in the Palomares farmers' jeans (American-style jeans have become popular in Spain) has also guaranteed sound business for seven general stores and the three taverns. One of the bars, probably the most popular gathering place in Palomares, belongs to Tomás Mula. Nearly as busy is the café of Tomás Alarcón La Torre, behind the unpaved and rutted main square.

Affluence and standing in the community are measured by the ownership of motor vehicles and modern appliances. Fourteen men own small passenger cars or panel trucks. Antonio Saez, the local Croesus, has a car as well as one of the village's two big trucks. José Manuel Gonzáles Fernandez, landowner and politician, who acts as the mayor of Palomares one day a week, drives a *deux chevaux* Renault pickup truck. The Renault came in handy after January 17, when Manuel Gonzáles had to serve as full-time mayor for long weeks. Eight tractors are owned in Palomares and seventy-two men, mainly young ones, drive their own motor scooters or motorcycles. There are eight television sets in the village—three of them in the bars—and most of the houses have radios, a fact that was to have considerable significance in the days to come.

Captain Calín, who is something of an amateur sociologist, believes that Palomares is well above the social and economic average for hamlets and villages in Almería, though this may not be saying very much in a province that ranks forty-ninth of Spain's fifty provinces in per-capita income. In 1962 Almería's annual per-capita income was merely the equivalent of $200 as compared with the Spanish national figure of $408.

An illustration of this basic poverty in Almería is that a Palomares day laborer, a man such as rain-recorder Julio Ponce, may earn 100 to 175 pesetas daily ($1.33 to $2.91), but chances are that he will work less than 120 days a year in the fields. To support the family (and pay his pharmacist boss 125 pesetas, or $2.08, monthly as rent for his house), Julio Ponce and his wife, Esperanza ("Hope"), raise chickens, goats, and rabbits, all of which share both the yard and the inside of the house with them.

For Julio Ponce and the other day-laboring families of Palomares the life problem, then, was one of plain and dull survival. It was so as well for small farmers such as Miguel Castro Navarro and Antonio Saviote García, whose concern was irrigation and the prices for their tomatoes at the Vera market. And it was so even for the rich men of Palomares such as Antonio Saez and José Manuel Gonzáles Fernandez, whose fortunes too were tied to the water and the tomatoes and the money in the villagers' jeans. They paid little heed to the outside world and its violent politics because since the end of the Spanish Civil War nearly twenty-seven years earlier none of these problems had touched them directly. If they knew about the Cold War, they were not personally concerned with it. For men who had to worry about water and tomatoes, this outside world was too remote.

And then, with awesome impact, the world invaded them from the blue Palomares skies.

The nuclear age came to Palomares, Spain, precisely at 10:22 a.m., local time, on Monday, January 17, 1966.

It came as a loud explosion high in the sky northeast of the village and over the bluish serrated ridges of Sierra Almagrera, from which the Phoenicians once mined absolutely pure silver and fashioned it into glittering anchors for their ships.

This explosion, feared but only half expected for nearly thirteen years, was heard without comprehension in Palomares by Señora Esperanza Ponce as she fed her chickens and by virtually every other inhabitant of the village as he or she was going about the routine Monday-morning chores. But it was almost at the same time and quite chillingly heard thousands of miles away in the deep underground command post of the United States Strategic Air Command at the Offutt Air Force Base near Omaha, Nebraska, and in Washington, D.C.

Some twenty-three hours earlier Captain Charles J. Wendorf, a blue-eyed, blond United States Air Force pilot who was just twenty-eight days short of his thirtieth birthday, gently lifted the nose of his heavily laden B-52G jet bomber from the darkened runway of the Seymour Johnson Air Force Base near Goldsboro in North Carolina. It was around five o'clock in the morning on Sunday, January 16, a cold winter day in the eastern United States. In southern Spain, where Januaries are springlike, it was already about eleven in the morning.

At the big joint United States and Spanish Air Force base of Morón, near Seville, a United States Air Force major, two captains, and a master sergeant were resting on what was to be their last day alive.

In Palomares, 224 miles southeast of Morón, as the crow flies, the villagers were enjoying a quiet Sunday. The next day promised to be busy, what with the winter tomato crop ready to be picked and the festivities in Cuevas de Almanzora celebrating the day of Saint Anthony the Abbot, the patron of farmers and animals. Since Palomares belongs to the Cuevas parish, many people from the village would try to make the noon mass—with music—at the church of La Encarnación, and later the procession and the bullfight.

Although three of the seven men aboard Captain Wendorf's huge aircraft would also be dead within twenty-four hours, none of them had reasons to give any special thought to Spain in general and to Morón and Palomares in particular as they busied themselves with the complex take-off procedures. Spain was incidental in their secret flight plan, Morón was an aerial refueling base that they would not even overfly, and Palomares was a meaningless name, though on earlier trips they might have noticed from high above its cluster of glimmering white houses near the Mediterranean coast.

On this Sunday morning Captain Wendorf was at the start of what was to be a routine mission for his aircraft and a companion B-52 of the 68th Bomber Wing from Seymour Johnson. The flight was part of the around-the-clock airborne alert flown by jet bombers of the Strategic Air Command over the Atlantic, the Mediterranean, and the Pacific and as close to Soviet and Chinese borders as discretion and caution would allow. SAC, whose motto is "Peace is our profession," flies the alert on the long-standing theory that United States bombers should be in the air at all times to be able to retaliate instantly if an enemy deals a sudden blow to America or her allies.

These SAC flights are fully armed. Locked inside the bomb bays of Captain Wendorf's B-52 were four plutonium-uranium-235 hydrogen bombs of the most modern United States design, each with the tremendous destructive power of 1.5 megatons. The 5000-pound bombs were of the fission-fusion-fission type—capable of a triple reaction, in effect, in which the atoms split, fuse, and split again to produce maximum blast and radioactivity yields. They were the latest nuclear weapons in the United States arsenal and a considerable advance on the early models of the hydrogen bomb. The 1.5 megatons represent 75 times the power of the Hiroshima bomb. (On some missions the B-52s also carry fastened under their wings two nuclear-warhead Hound Dog missiles designed to neutralize air and ground defenses. Captain Wendorf's bomber did not carry them, however, on this particular mission.)

In January 1966 one-half of SAC's total of 680 B-52s were permanently flying the airborne alert with nuclear weapons or standing by on "strip alert," ready to be in the air in little more than ten minutes after the order was given. Although the airborne-alert operations were to be sharply cut in mid-1966, because of progress in military technology and because of the Palomares events, in January they still represented—along with the land-based and Polaris submarine hydrogen-warhead missiles—the striking arm of the United States' Cold War strategic deterrent policy.

Thus Captain Wendorf was taking off in that wintry North Carolina dawn on another monotonous and routine alert flight, just like dozens of others that he and his crew had made before. Yet this particular take-off was the beginning of a journey that would bring a taste of the nuclear age to Spain and Palomares, cause immense problems, embarrassment, and expense to the United States government, and turn the harsh spotlight of attention on the propriety and wisdom of flying with lethal cargoes of hydrogen bombs over a world relatively at peace.

Once in the air, the B-52's crew settled down for the long trans-atlantic flight that would take them over Spain, then over the full length of the Mediterranean, and finally to their assigned alert station in the general vicinity of the Soviet Union's western borders. After nine or ten hours in the air on station, the huge bomber would again cross the Mediterranean and Spain and then head home over the Atlantic.

The men in the B-52 were all experienced in their aerial trades. A stocky Ohioan, Charlie Wendorf had been flying airplanes ever since he graduated from Duke University in 1958. Before enrolling at Duke, Wendorf attended high school in New Orleans, where his family had moved from Kenton, Ohio. A born pilot in the opinion of his Air Force superiors, Wendorf started flying F-86 Sabrejet fighters, then moved on to bombers, breezing through the B-52 Combat Crew Training School and the Central Flight Instructor Course. The giant B-52s, in fact, became his life. Out of his total of 2500 hours in the air, he had spent in the last five and a half years 2109 hours behind the controls of B-52s. He became a staff pilot and command post controller—a ground assignment on which many top SAC pilots alternate with flying— and in 1964 was made aircraft commander. At the time, Wendorf was not quite twenty-eight years old, and the promotion is considered a distinction at such an age.

Since his assignment to the 68th Bomber Wing at Seymour Johnson, Wendorf had lived in a one-family house on Goldsboro's Chandler Road on the base, with his wife, Betty Jean, his five-year-old and three-year-old daughters, Kristie and Laurie, and his year-old son, Charles James IV. Like all the SAC fliers' families, the Wendorfs had to live on base because of the "strip alert" requirements. And like all Goldsboro families, the Wendorfs were intimately associated with the nuclear age: not only were the men in the business of flying hydrogen bombs; four years earlier a B-52 laden with the missiles had crashed right outside of town. It had been quite a scare.

In the cockpit with Captain Wendorf were Major Larry G. Messinger, his staff pilot, and First Lieutenant Michael L. Rooney, the copilot. The B-52s normally carry a crew of six, but an extra pilot is added to the airborne alert missions so that the nuclear bombers may stay aloft longer without risking pilot fatigue.

Major Messinger, Canadian-born and California-educated, was

an "old man" in the business of flying heavy bombers. He had flown them for nearly a quarter of a century, first in Europe in World War II, then in Korea, and finally on the globe-girdling SAC missions. In his forty-four years, more than one-half of which he had spent in the Air Force, Major Messinger had flown 4800 hours, including 3300 hours of jet time, on bombers that ranged from the old B-17 Flying Fortress to the B-29 Superfortress and then, in the jet age, from the B-47 to the B-52 Stratofortress. He had been aircraft commander on all four of them; for the last six years he had flown as aircraft commander on the B-52s. Like all top pilots, Major Messinger alternated missions as staff pilot and as aircraft commander. Like Captain Wendorf, he also acted on occasions as SAC command post controller. But his B-52 flying time was actually less than Wendorf's, only 1255 hours.

A much-decorated aviator (his Air Medal carries seven Oak Leaf Clusters), Larry Messinger had been wounded in Europe after thirty-five combat missions in the B-17s. In Korea his B-29 earned the distinction of shooting down the first Soviet-built MIG jet fighter to be destroyed by an American bomber. A slim brown-haired man, Major Messinger also lived on base at Seymour Johnson. As he took off on the January 16 mission, his wife, Marian, his two sons—ten-year-old Gary Niell and seven-year-old Geoffrey Curtis—and his five-year-old daughter, Melissa, were left behind at their Goldsboro home.

Twenty-five-year-old Lieutenant Rooney, the copilot, was too young to have flown operationally any aircraft other than jets. A New Yorker, he had joined the Air Force in 1962, immediately after graduating from the University of North Carolina.

Major Ivens Buchanan, a burly thirty-four-year-old Virginian, and First Lieutenant George J. Glesner, a twenty-six-year-old New Yorker, performed key missions on the B-52. Major Buchanan, as radar-navigator officer, had the primary responsibility for plotting the nuclear bomber's attack course. If the crew received orders from the United States to drop on an enemy target the four hydrogen bombs nesting in the huge aircraft's two bomb bays, it would be Major Buchanan who would advise the plane's commander of the coordinates, working them out from the combination of secret instructions carried aboard and radioed from home. As it turned out, Major Buchanan was to terminate his mission in a most peculiar and unexpected set of circumstances.

As for Lieutenant Glesner, the electronic-warfare officer, his job was a rather awesome one. If orders should come for a nuclear attack, this young man would be expected to provide the finishing touches in the complex procedure of arming the four hydrogen bombs aboard the B-52. Hydrogen bombs carried by SAC are unarmed when they are loaded on the aircraft, and they are rendered capable of a nuclear reaction—thus becoming operational nuclear weapons—only when a series of carefully guarded steps are taken. One of the final steps in preparing the bombs for nuclear reaction—and explosion—is the insertion of a Top Secret arming mechanism. This was what Lieutenant Glesner would have done on a real combat mission.

The two remaining members of Wendorf's crew were First Lieutenant Stephen S. Montanus, the twenty-three-year-old aircraft navigator from Ohio, and Technical Sergeant Ronald P. Snyder, a twenty-eight-year-old Pennsylvanian who served as the B-52's gunner.

The first half of the flight was uneventful. Some six hours after leaving North Carolina, the bomber approached the Spanish coast from the northwest and proceeded over Spanish territory on an easterly course. Past Zaragoza in northern Spain, the B-52 and its companion aircraft prepared for the refueling rendezvous with a pair of KC-135 tankers that had come up from the joint United States–Spanish Air Force base at Torrejón del Ardoz, nineteen miles from Madrid. The refueling operation was accomplished smoothly high over Spanish territory between Zaragoza and the Mediterranean coast. It was nearly five o'clock in the afternoon, and the winter dusk was already spreading over Spain, when the refueling was completed and the B-52 headed east for its alert station.

It was night when Captain Wendorf's plane reached its assigned alert area, probably somewhere between the eastern Mediterranean

and the Turkish-Soviet border. Because the B-52s can fly only
over international waters and over the territory of friendly nations
—in this case Turkey and Greece—the crews must engage in
intricate navigation to avoid invading the air space of other nations. At jet speeds of between 500 and 600 miles an
hour (the B-52's top speed is 650 m.p.h.) and at night at an
altitude close to 50,000 feet, operations on airborne alert station call for the utmost care and attention. The station area was
thus quite confining as Captain Wendorf's B-52 flew in a roughly
circular pattern, waiting to be relieved at first light by SAC's
next nuclear detachment. Circling so close to Soviet and Bulgarian
borders that it would take the B-52 just a few minutes to invade
Communist territory and head for its preassigned targets, Charlie
Wendorf and his crew assumed that they were being tracked by
Soviet radar and that the slightest error in navigation would bring
out MIG jet fighters and a barrage from the SAM surface-to-air
missile emplacements. In the nuclear age the shooting is done first
and questions, if any, are asked later when a potentially hostile
bomber suddenly enters a nation's air space. United States defenses would react in the same instantaneously lethal manner if a
Soviet bomber crossed into North American air space from Siberia.

As the pink dawn rose over Russia in the east, Captain Wendorf's bomber was relieved and headed home. In nine or ten
hours it should be landing at Seymour Johnson in North Carolina,
in time for the crewmen to be debriefed and make it for lunch at
their homes along Chandler Road, Westover Road, and Carswell
Lane in Goldsboro. The pilots took a southwesterly heading that
would lead the plane over the southeastern coast of Spain en route
to the United States.

Just as Captain Wendorf swung the B-52 away from the airborne alert station near the Soviet border, four other American
fliers were preparing to intercept the bomber over Spain. They
were the crewmen of a KC-135 aerial tanker whose daily mission
was to take off from the joint United States–Spanish Air Force base
at Morón in order to refuel the SAC bombers returning from airborne alert missions in the east. Although the B-52s of the

G model, such as the aircraft flown by Captain Wendorf, have an unrefueled range of more than 7500 miles, the long airborne alert flights would not be feasible without aerial refueling. To demonstrate, on the other hand, what air fueling can accomplish to lengthen the missions, three B-52s flew 24,325 miles around the world in 45 hours without landing during a 1957 exercise. Aerial tankers, stationed strategically along the B-52s' globe-circling route, fed them five times in the course of the flight.

Now, after twice traveling the length of the Mediterranean and spending the long night on station flying a circular and highly fuel-consuming pattern, the eight turbojet engines of Captain Wendorf's B-52 would be thirsting for jet kerosene. It had been more than twelve hours since the bomber was last refueled in the air as it flew east over Spain, and another full load of kerosene would be necessary for a safe return to North Carolina as well as for unforeseen emergencies. For the four tanker crewmen at Morón it was time to be aloft once more with their volatile and explosive cargo.

Refueling over Spain, at fixed points east of Zaragoza in the north and over the Almería coast in the southeast, has been a standard daily procedure since 1953, when the United States and Spanish governments signed their first military agreements. The main feature of the agreements, renewed and expanded in 1963, called for the use by the United States of a series of air and naval facilities to be operated jointly with the Spaniards. In practice, it meant a grant to the United States of military bases that it could administer and operate in virtually any way it chose. In exchange, the United States undertook to train and equip the highly obsolete Spanish military establishment and to provide direct and indirect aid to what in 1953 was a collapsing Spanish economy. For the Franco regime, until then almost completely ostracized by the West, the military agreement was a spectacular boost in every field, including the political.

The publicly released text of the 1953 agreement stipulated that the United States could establish "joint" air bases at Torrejón near Madrid, at Morón near Seville, at Zaragoza, and at several other points in Spanish territory. But a secret annex also gave Washington overflight rights for the nuclear bombers, the permission to station SAC attack aircraft and tanker planes on the new bases, and authorization for refueling the bombers over Spanish territory. This part of the agreement was not made public at the time on the theory that it pertained to the highly secret SAC operations. The subsequent installation of the base at Rota, near Cádiz, for the Polaris submarine was the first public acknowledgment that the United States and Spain had embarked on a nuclear partnership of sorts. So long as the Polaris submarines were stationed at Rota, their nuclear warheads had to be stored there too.

It was, then, under the provisions of the pact between the United States and Spain that KC-135 tankers of the 910th Air Refueling Squadron, normally attached to the Bergstrom Air Force Base near Austin, Texas, were stationed at Morón on temporary duty on that January morning. These Stratotankers, which are a special version of the Boeing 707 transport jet, had been refueling the SAC bombers over Spain since 1957, when they replaced the earlier KC-97 tankers. The KC-97s had worked with SAC's smaller B-47 bombers until the new combination of the B-52s and KC-135s was placed in operation for airborne alert duty. Air refueling of nuclear bombers over Spain had been going on in one shape or another for nearly thirteen years prior to the morning of January 17, 1966.

On this morning two KC-135s were being prepared to meet and refuel the two B-52s returning from Eastern airborne alert duty. As a matter of operational expediency, refueling is always done in pairs, two bombers and two tankers rendezvousing in the same area. The two sweptwing tankers, each carrying a full load of 30,103 gallons of kerosene jet fuel, took off from Morón about 9 a.m., Spanish time.

At the controls of the second of the pair of tankers was Major Emil J. Chapla, a veteran bomber pilot who was just sixteen days away from his forty-third birthday. A rail-thin, dark-haired six-footer, he was a native of Ohio, like Captain Wendorf. After having flown B-24 bombers in the Pacific during much of World

War II, he had been discharged from the Army Air Force in 1945. Four and a half years later, eight days before the eruption of the Korean war, he was recalled to active duty, and he never left the Air Force again. He flew B-29s, then shifted to jets and SAC, and finally was assigned to the refueling squadron at Bergstrom. When he went to Morón on temporary duty, his wife, Joan, and his three children—Mary Jo, nineteen, Christopher John, fifteen, and Mark James, twelve—remained behind at their small house on Daugherty Road in Austin. It was to be just another routine separation for an Air Force pilot's family.

Major Chapla's copilot was thirty-one-year-old Captain Paul R. Lane, a powerfully built six-footer. He too had been born in Ohio and, oddly enough, had gone to high school in Lorain, Ohio, Major Chapla's home town. He had been flying for less than five years. With his wife, Ellie, Paul Lane lived on base at Bergstrom. They had no children at the time.

The navigator on the tanker was Captain Leo E. Simmons, a twenty-seven-year-old Oklahoman who had been in the Air Force since he graduated from the Ponca City High School. All his flying experience had been on refueling aircraft, first the KC-97s and then the KC-135s. A wife and two daughters awaited him in Austin.

The fourth member of the crew was Master Sergeant Lloyd Potolicchio, the boom operator. The actual refueling in flight was his job. A forty-one-year-old native of New Brighton, New York, Sergeant Potolicchio had been a gunner in bombers during World War II, then left the service to graduate from Georgetown University. He returned to the Air Force in 1950, just in time to go to Korea as a B-29 gunner. Later he became a specialist in aerial refueling and was assigned to SAC's worldwide operations. Back in Austin, his wife, two sons, and a daughter waited for him to return from temporary duty in Spain.

Taking off from Morón, Major Chapla swung his heavy aircraft to the southeast, following the lead KC-135 toward the fixed rendezvous point with the two B-52s flying back from alert station. It was a clear and sunny morning over southern Spain, and Major Chapla could easily make out in the distance the massive shape of the Mulhacén in the snow-capped Sierra Nevada. After his weeks of commuting between Morón and the Almería coast, it was a familiar but always beautiful sight.

In Palomares the morning was bright and, at 62 degrees, unusually warm for January, even in the eternal spring of the
Almería coast. But it was quite windy, with a northwester blowing
steadily to ripple the waters of the Mediterranean and agitate the
branches of the village's few palm trees. Despite the anticipation
of the fiesta at Cuevas later in the day, this Monday morning of
January 17 was like any other winter morning.

Behind the village meeting hall, the Salón de Pueblo, Tomás
Alarcón La Torre was serving his powerful cognac to early cus-
tomers in need of a bracing shot before the day's work. Eduardo
Navarro Portillo, the elderly landowner, was back for his first
morning drink, after having spent most of Sunday evening at
Tomás's bar. Miguel Castro Navarro, a stocky thirty-seven-year-
old farmer who owns tomato land and six cows, was in the shed
next to his house near the main square, tinkering with his red
tractor. Pedro de la Torre Flores, a cousin of Tomás and, at the
age of eighty-three, the second oldest inhabitant of Palomares,
stepped into the front yard of his little house between the Fábrica
del Duro and Eduardo Navarro's big compound. He stared idly
at a terraced embankment some one hundred yards away, wondering if Navarro would do any plowing there. At the girls' elementary
school past the village square, Conchita Fernandez de Arellano,
a bright and pretty twenty-five-year-old teacher, was reading from
a book on Spanish geography to her class, which included twelve-

26

year-old Maria Ponce, the daughter of Julio Ponce the keeper of rain records. Back in his yard, Julio looked up to the sky for signs that it was close to 10:30 a.m., a time-keeping system that had worked perfectly in Palomares for the preceding nine years.

At this time a fishing boat from Aguilas, a small port twenty-four miles away, was trolling for shrimp directly in front of Villaricos and Palomares, about five miles offshore. She was the forty-four-ton *Manuela Orts* with six crewmen and a dashing captain, thirty-eight-year-old Francisco Simó Orts, who was about to embark on a startling new career. Another fishing boat, the *Dorita,* was at anchor in the Aguilas harbor. Her captain, Bartolomé Roldán, was to remain the forgotten man in days to come.

High above the southern end of the Gulf of Mazarrón, catching up with the *Manuela Orts,* a light helicopter of the Spanish Navy, Number 001/2, was flying west at an altitude of 3000 feet on a trip by easy stages from the naval base of Santa Ana de Cartagena to the joint United States–Spanish base at Rota, where the nuclear Polaris submarines are berthed. The helicopter carried two young naval lieutenants, Emilio Erades Pina and José Antonio Balbas. The two pilots noticed the fishing boat and, farther ahead of them, the Spanish Navy's hydrographic ship *Juan de la Cosa* moving slowly in front of the little port of Carboneras. There were wind-driven whitecaps on the sea, but otherwise the Mediterranean was as blue and peaceful as it could be.

At 10:20 a.m. Captain Charles Wendorf started the B-52 on the final approach to the refueling area over the Almanzora River and the hills between Cuevas and Palomares. This location, noted on SAC maps as the Saddle Rock Refueling Area (though the Air Force maps did not show Palomares), was one of the best in the world for aerial rendezvous operations. With invariably clear weather, Saddle Rock was perfect for visual navigational pinpointing. It was removed from major population centers and was easily reached from the Morón tankers' base. And to refuel over Palomares the nuclear bombers did not have to deviate from their route between the eastern Mediterranean and the eastern seaboard of the United States. The arrangement was immensely convenient for the Air Force, and another contribution of the Franco regime to Western defenses. But the people of Palomares, like the rest of the Spaniards, had never been told about it.

The refueling over Saddle Rock of the two B-52s was expected to be a purely routine operation. A SAC bomber is refueled in the air somewhere over the world every six minutes day and night as the command's B-52 Stratofortresses and supersonic B-58 Hustlers are continually met in the air by the seven-hundred-plane fleet of KC-135 tankers. Since 1959 more than 750,000 aerial refueling hookups had been carried out with only one known accident. That was on October 15, 1962, when a B-52 and a KC-135 collided over Kentucky, spilling two nuclear bombs. But the weapons were recovered quickly, causing no special problems. On January 17, 1966, however, the law of averages—or fate— was about to intervene with a vengeance.

Flying at 30,500 feet and beginning to reduce speed from his cruising 600 miles an hour, Captain Wendorf had crossed into Spain near the port of Cartagena and now was following the coastline toward the Saddle Rock Refueling Area, and Palomares, on a true 256-degree southwestern heading. Below his B-52 laden with four hydrogen bombs were the jagged peaks of Sierra Alma- grera and an occasional mountain farmhouse, just a white dot among the bluish-gray rock outcroppings. The town of Cuevas was immediately ahead and to the aircraft's right, a tree-surrounded splotch of white and gray shapes. To the left and on the far side of the Almanzora River, whose sandy bed was now coming into sight, lay a disorderly collection of white dots that looked from the air like building blocks carelessly scattered by a child. It was Palomares.

A few minutes earlier Major Emil Chapla had cut speed and lowered his KC-135 tanker to enter a left-hand "racetrack" orbit 21 miles ahead of the approaching B-52. To hook up for refueling over the 70-mile track, the bomber must gradually edge up behind and slightly below the tanker, whose fuel boom is then lowered and connected to the B-52's nose. It is a highly delicate operation calling for split-second timing and extraordinary flying precision. But it is also a completely routine maneuver with which both bomber and tanker pilots and crews are utterly familiar. The bomber need not change basic course, regardless of wind conditions, and the principal advantage of this technique is that little extra time or fuel is wasted during the refueling.

The two circling aircraft had now been in direct radio contact for a number of minutes. When they were a half-mile from each other, Sergeant Potolicchio, the tanker's boom operator, took over the task of talking Captain Wendorf into configuration for the actual hookup. Their crisp dialogue was being recorded on tape.

Looking down from the KC-135's tail section, the sergeant could see the B-52's nose moving up nearer and nearer. Below, in the bomber's cockpit, Captain Wendorf listened to Potolicchio's radioed instructions as he kept closing in. At 200 feet, the two men could almost see each other's tense faces.

"Closer and the nose higher up," Sergeant Potolicchio called out calmly.

Captain Wendorf made a minute correction as the two planes roared one below the other at 275 miles an hour. In the KC-135's tail, Potolicchio prepared to lower the 42-foot-long boom whose nozzle was to fit into the B-52's nose.

"Okay," said Potolicchio. "Now just a bit closer and—"

The B-52 was 150 feet below the tanker when Major Messinger, the veteran staff pilot, suddenly noticed from his cockpit jump seat that the bomber's closure rate—the speed of approach to the KC-135—was excessive.

"Hey, watch it, you're coming in too fast!" Potolicchio yelled into his microphone, his voice rising in alarm. "You're too fast—"

In the cockpit of the KC-135, Major Chapla and Captain Lane, the copilot, heard Potolicchio's anguished warning over their intercoms. So did Captain Simmons, the navigator, in his seat behind the pilots. But there was no time for evasive action.

In the B-52, Captain Wendorf, his left hand grasping the controls and his right hand feverishly working the engines' power throttles to adjust the speed, saw the backswept starboard wing of the tanker suddenly rush in front of his cockpit window. Then he felt a powerful thud and the aircraft shook and buckled. The huge B-52—a missile made up of more than 400,000 pounds of airframe metal, engines, and nuclear weapons, hurtling through space at 275 miles an hour—had underrun the KC-135 and rammed it with the top of its fuselage. The two planes were directly above the Almanzora River, past the sharp bend east of Cuevas.

For a few seconds after the collision the B-52 and the KC-135 continued to fly—or just move through the air from sheer momentum—on their southwest course. Then an orange flame enveloped the 300,000-pound tanker as the equivalent of three railroad tank cars of jet fuel caught fire. There was the deep booming sound of an explosion shaking the Almería skies. The bomber and the tanker, now tangled up together over the sandy hills south of the Almanzora and a mile or so northeast of Palomares, began breaking up into hundreds of fragments, huge and tiny. In the forward section of the disintegrating B-52, Major Buchanan, the radar navigator, instinctively pressed a button he had never expected to touch. In the bomber's smoke-filled cockpit there was a smaller explosion, and all went black for the three pilots and their radar navigator. It was 10:22 a.m.

BOOK TWO *The Aftermath*

i

"Jesus Christ," the boom operator of the lead KC-135 yelled into his intercom. "The other B-52 is on fire!" The young sergeant had been on the point of calling the first bomber into refueling position when he saw the explosion.

His pilot looked out of his left cockpit window just in time to see the orange ball of fire in the sky, one or two miles away. Like the boom operator, he automatically assumed that only the B-52 had caught fire—the two men did not immediately realize that a collision had occurred because they could not see their fellow tanker—and he twisted a UHF radio dial to tune in the frequency of the control tower at the Morón air base. But Morón was out of his range, and the disaster call had to be relayed through another United States aircraft in the vicinity. The pilot repeated his boom operator's report: "The other B-52 is on fire." He thus gave his base, and the world, the first word of the unfolding tragedy.

The Morón tower controller calmly acknowledged the message and instructed the KC-135 pilot through the air relay to remain in contact for additional reports. Meanwhile the Morón command post passed the message to the headquarters of the Sixteenth Air Force at Madrid's Torrejón base, thereby setting in motion what was to become a transatlantic emergency lasting months.

The SAC controllers in Spain instantly grasped the gravity of the situation: they were aware that the burning aircraft was carry-

33

ing four hydrogen bombs. Anything might happen, they realized with horror.

Two minutes later the tanker over Almería was relaying to Morón the boom operator's second terse message. "The B-52 is in a spin," it said.

This message too was immediately sent on to Torrejón, and the SAC controllers at both bases then knew with utter finality that the accident the United States had feared had happened at last. An aircraft loaded with nuclear weapons was crashing on the territory of a foreign nation. It was a replay, under immeasurably worse circumstances, of the 1962 collision over Kentucky between a B-52 and a KC-135. At this early stage, however, nobody could assess the magnitude of the accident and foresee its immense consequences and ramifications.

Yet it still had to be business as usual for the other SAC aircraft: the lead tanker proceeded to refuel his B-52 just half a mile away from the collision point and along the track running seventy miles inland from the coast. The KC-135 then flew back to Morón for a routine landing.

In their helicopter over the Gulf of Mazarrón, Lieutenant Erades and Lieutenant Balbas also heard the explosion. Looking up ahead of them, they saw the orange ball of fire high in the sky above Palomares. Lieutenant Erades shouted, *"Por Dios!"* and radioed the Spanish Air Force base at San Javier, near Murcia, that a plane had blown up somewhere over Almería. Then the two naval pilots headed along the coast toward the spot where they thought the accident was occurring. They were to become the first rescue team on the scene, and their presence was one of the many lucky, if not nearly miraculous, ingredients of the developing situation.

Aboard the *Manuela Orts,* the old fishing boat named after his mother, Captain Francisco Simó Orts observed the aerial collision directly in front of him and above the coastline. He had been waiting five miles offshore, roughly between Villaricos and

Palomares, for the raising of his shrimp nets after two hours' trolling in the Mediterranean. Simó, a handsome, cool, and quick-thinking Catalonian from Tarragona, had been going to sea for twenty-seven years—since he was eleven years old—and his reactions were sharp and professional.

A 60-knot northwesterly gale was blowing from the land to the sea, and presently Simó noticed six parachutes, one of them gray, floating down from the sky amidst the falling debris of the two aircraft. One of the parachutes seemed to be on fire and descended faster than the others. Simó followed it with his eyes until it disappeared ashore behind the coastal dunes. Three other parachutes floated high over the *Manuela Orts* and vanished far out to sea. But two billowing parachutes headed straight for Simó's boat. He watched them go past and hit the water, the first one 80 feet and the second 260 feet behind his boat, as pieces of the planes rained down all around the *Manuela Orts*.

As Francisco Simó was to recall later, "From one of the parachutes hung something that looked to me like a half-man and on the other parachute a dead weight that looked like a man." The "half-man" was the one that splashed down closest to the fishing boat. The manlike "dead weight" went into the water farther out. Simó, who navigates mainly by the peaks of the coastal sierras and other familiar shore points, calculated quickly that the two parachutes had sunk roughly five and a half miles from the beach. This, Simó realized, was in the area of a wide underwater gully known to fishermen as the Hoyo de Villaricos, the Villaricos Gulch. The water there was 3000 feet deep and more, and the bottom was a submerged mountain chain.

Simó made a cross on his depth-soundings chart to mark the spot—37 degrees 12 minutes north latitude and 01 degrees 41 minutes west longitude—where he saw the two parachutes sink. This presence of mind was to turn Francisco Simó, a man with highly developed nautical as well as business instincts, into a key and controversial personality in events that were now to move with immense speed. Simó had no way of knowing at that moment that the "half-man" on the gray parachute was a 10-foot-long hydrogen bomb partially hidden by its harnesses, and that the other weight was a secret piece of the disintegrating bomber's equipment. As he told it days later, "I thought that what was hanging at the end of the parachute was a dead man. It did not move."

The other thing Francisco Simó did was to hurry down to his old radio transmitter to flash a disaster call to the Spanish Navy's shore station at Alicante, a hundred miles up the coast.

Glancing toward shore as he emerged from the radio shack, Simó could see black smoke curl up here and there among the white houses of Palomares, which shimmered in the sun, and amidst the bare hills on either side of the village.

Palomares in Spanish means "dovecotes." That morning fire and twisted steel and dead men and hydrogen bombs fell on Palomares.

Many of the villagers actually saw the explosion high over the river, some of them because of their habit of many years of watching the daily refueling operation—the sight of the four tiny dots moving through the skies had become in an odd way a reassuring sign of normality to them—and others because they looked up, startled, when they heard the tremendous boom of the collision. Then, as the B-52 and the KC-135 began breaking up over the hills northeast of the village, a sudden inferno descended on Palomares. In a wide, sweeping arc from the lonely cemetery in the Cabezo Negro hills, across the village itself, and then over the Almanzora's dry bed and for miles into the Mediterranean, huge chunks of flaming metal rained and rained from the sky.

"It is the end of the world," nearly every man and woman of Palomares thought or yelled as the inhabitants rushed in all directions, seeking safety and an understanding of what was happening. As they spoke afterward of their emotions, this seemed to be the first idea in everybody's mind. The idea of a nuclear attack did not occur to any of the villagers.

The main section of the B-52's landing gear—tons of metal and one huge wheel with its rubber tire—and the plane's aft bomb bay crashed together in a field off the road leading into Palomares from the Vera Highway and 80 yards from the boys' elementary school.

The B-52's 85-foot-long right wing landed without its engine pods in a tomato field across the same road and 150 yards from the crossroads chapel. The fuel trapped in the wing and the rubber from several other wheels still attached to it burst out in a gruesome bonfire.

José Molinero, twenty-five-year-old teacher at the boys' school, was at the blackboard, explaining the construction of words to his fifty-one pupils, aged six to eleven, when the chunks of the bomber crashed around them. Molinero and the children rushed to the windows to see the twisted shape of the landing gear in the adjoining field and, in the distance, the fall of other flaming pieces of the aircraft. Some of the boys began crying; others shouted in excitement. José Molinero quickly made his decision. "Nobody may leave the classroom," he ordered. "All of you are to stay here."

Fifty yards away, María Badillo, whose husband, Manuel, is a tomato farmer and well-digger, was in her house preparing the noon meal when the B-52's gear came down at the edge of her vegetable garden. Her five-year-old daughter ran into the house, screaming, "Mama, the sky is raining fire!" María Badillo, a plump thirty-eight-year-old woman in a black skirt and crimson blouse, with a black kerchief on her head, grabbed her daughter and two of her infants by their hands to drag them behind the concrete railing of the porch. They hid there, crouching, waiting for the sky to stop raining fire.

The flaming debris was pouring all over the village—in the streets, in the back yards, in the gardens, and in the fields. But miraculously it kept missing the houses, the people, and the animals. It was, indeed, as if God had directed the fall of the two planes' fragments to spare Palomares death, injury, and serious damage. Only the main electric cable was severed, cutting the power supply. Father Francisco Navarete Serrano, the young priest from Cuevas who is in charge of the Palomares church, was to insist later that it had to be "the hand of God" that had saved the village from what seemed like inevitable destruction.

In the girls' elementary school on the far side of the main square, Conchita Fernandez de Arellano, the pretty teacher, made the same decision as had José Molinero at the boys' school. She forbade her thirty-six little girls to leave the classroom.

But at the foot of Cabezo Negro, west of the village, fear for the children gripped three families living in two miserable little houses facing each other across the highway to Vera. With an earth-shaking thud, the number one engine of the KC-135 had just buried itself in the parched soil and was burning brightly 65 feet behind the house of Julio Ponce Navarro. The tanker's three other jet engines crashed in the hills in a semicircular pattern a few hundred feet away. The cockpit of the KC-135 landed nearby, also behind the Ponce house. Orange fires were burning strongly, and black smoke was rising toward the blue sky. Although the 30,103 gallons of jet fuel carried by the tanker had evaporated in the air after the collision at 30,500 feet with the bomber, the kerosene-filled engines were on fire when they plummeted to the ground. (It was this evaporation of the tanker's own load and of the 250,000 pounds of fuel still in the B-52's tanks that helped to save Palomares.) A muted explosion and another column of smoke followed by a small black-brown cloud of dustlike particles then came from the Cabezo Negro hills, some 1500 feet away, adding to the families' fears.

Esperanza Ponce's first reaction was to think, as others were doing, that she was witnessing the end of the world. But her second thought was for María Ponce Navarro, her twelve-year-old daughter, who was at the girls' school in the village. Abandoning her cooking, she ran screaming into the front yard, where her tender care had made it possible for red and white flowers to defy the long years of drought. In the yard she ran into her sister-in-law, María Ponce Serrano, who was also terrified. Her eight-year-old son was at the boys' school. The two tough peasant women, whose families share the crowded house, stood helplessly crossing themselves and watching the planes' debris steadily fall over the village in the distance.

"I didn't know where to go, where to run," Esperanza Ponce said later, still shivering at the memories of that morning. "All my thoughts were on the children."

On the far side of Palomares, in the direction of the Almanzora River, Pedro de la Torre Flores had been idly contemplating the fields of Eduardo Navarro Portillo, the rich landowner next door along the Fábrica del Duro road, when the two American planes collided almost over his head. Pedro, who at eighty-three is not easily excitable, stared with interest at the debris that was beginning to shower down as far as he could see. Just as he started to say something to his two little grand-nephews, who had been chatting with him on the doorstep, a dark shape whooshed down from the sky and there was a loud explosion. Fire broke out on the side of a plowed knoll terraced with low brick walls some 330 feet away, and acrid smoke and a black-brown cloud rose and floated in the Cabezo Negro hills. The shock waves from the blast seemed to lift Pedro in the air, and then the wizened old man sprawled on the ground, on his stomach, the wind knocked out of him. The two little boys were also thrown down. From the house where Pedro lives and which belongs to his nephew José López Flores, there came the crackling sound of shattered window panes.

At Eduardo Navarro's spacious farmhouse, which is separated by the terraced hillock from José López's home, the explosion's waves tore a heavy iron lock from a door. Eduardo was away at the time of the accident—he was having his morning brandy in a Palomares bar—but his wife, Ana, was home tending her brown rabbits. The blast literally scared her out of her wits. The petite woman in her late fifties was speechless and trembling for many minutes afterward.

Four engines and the inboard section of the left wing of the B-52 came to rest 120 feet from the farm of Antonio Saviote in a valley across the highway from Eduardo Navarro's house.

Antonio was in the village, but his wife and three small children were at home when the big sections of incandescent metal dropped in his field, near the water cistern. Two other B-52 engines—numbers 7 and 8 from the right wing that fell near the school—crashed in the general area of the Navarro property, close to the Fábrica del Duro, the old minthouse.

With havoc and confusion spreading all over Palomares, only a few persons were aware of the two explosions that occurred almost simultaneously on both sides of the village. The Ponces and their relatives heard the explosion in the Cabezo Negro hills behind their houses but they quickly forgot about it in their preoccupation with the safety of their children at school. The octogenarian Pedro de la Torre Flores was, of course, aware of the blast that knocked him to the ground. The old man, however, was too dazed to try to understand what had happened to him. José López Flores, his nephew, also heard the explosion and saw the dark cloud and, in fact, was to undertake a unique inspection of this occurrence. But he too was incapable of comprehending what he had witnessed and certainly unable to realize the great perils involved.

Yet these explosions, sounding like giant firecrackers going off at a village fiesta, and the strange little clouds became the most important and bewildering events to affect Palomares in the wake of the aerial collision.

At sea the rescue operation was under way within moments of the accident. The Spaniards wasted no time in going after possible survivors. Again luck—or "the hand of God"—and Spanish courage and fast thinking played a decisive role.

After radioing the San Javier base that an air collision had taken place over the Almería coast, Lieutenant Erades and Lieutenant Balbas gunned their little helicopter's engine and raced toward what they thought to be the scene of the accident. Like Francisco Simó, the two naval pilots saw a number of parachutes fluttering down into the water and they headed their chopper in that direction. As they flew out to sea they kept radioing their observations back to San Javier.

When Colonel Emiliano José Alfaro, commander of the Spanish Air Force Academy at the San Javier base, received word of the accident he quickly checked his map against the tentative fix radioed by the chopper pilots. He concluded that the fishing port of Aguilas, just inside the Murcia province line, would be the closest and most convenient point for coordinating sea rescue operations. Accordingly, he ordered an emergency telephone call to the ensign in charge of the Spanish Navy's small detachment in Aguilas. This was the first of Colonel Alfaro's uncounted efforts to support and facilitate the immensely complex Palomares operations that were then beginning to unfold.

The naval ensign at Aguilas moved equally fast. After checking on the availability of seagoing craft in the port, he ordered the fishing boats *Dorita* under Captain Bartolomé Roldán and *Agustín y Rosa* under Captain Alfonso Simó, a cousin of Francisco Simó, to sail at once to the Gulf of Vera to try to pick up any survivors. The ensign knew that Francisco Simó's *Manuela Orts* was somewhere near the scene.

Acting independently, the hydrographic ship *Juan de la Cosa,* which also observed the descending parachutes, steamed at full speed from the vicinity of Carboneras to the Palomares area. Three Spanish merchant ships that were steaming past the site— *Cabo San Vicente, Sac Badalona,* and *Campoverde*—did likewise. Thus a full-fledged sea and air rescue operation was in progress a few minutes after the collision.

But it was the smooth teamwork between the helicopter and the fishing boats that produced the results. Recklessly exceeding their helicopter's range, Emilio Erades and José Antonio Balbas flew far away from the shore—much farther than a two-seat chopper running low on gas should venture over the sea—until, eight miles out, they spotted a rubber raft with a man on it. Then they flew back to lead Francisco Simó's *Manuela Orts* to the raft. On another low pass over the Mediterranean, the helicopter spotted two more rafts bobbing close to each other on the wavelets, five or six miles from the coast. The two Spaniards again swung back, this time to lead the *Dorita* to the two rafts.

The *Dorita* picked up the first two survivors thirty minutes after they splashed. They were Captain Wendorf, the B-52 aircraft commander, who had been at the controls at the time of the collision, and Lieutenant Rooney, the copilot. Both were in a state of shock as Bartolomé Roldán and his crew gently lifted them aboard. Charlie Wendorf had been unconscious until he hit the water and his raft inflated automatically, and now his face was so pale and drained of blood that it reminded Captain Roldán of a whitewashed wall. His upper arm seemed broken. He did not say a word to his rescuers, just lay on the deck of the *Dorita* as the fishermen covered him with blankets. Lieutenant Rooney had a deep gash on his lower back, but he quickly regained his faculties. As Bartolomé Roldán was to remark in Aguilas, it was a miracle the two pilots were alive. Indeed, few men survive a 30,500-foot drop from an exploding bomber and into the sea. Their parachutes deployed automatically at 14,000 feet after they had plummeted, unconscious, for 16,500 feet.

A few minutes later Francisco Simó took aboard the *Manuela Orts* the man who had been seen floating in his raft eight miles from the coast. He was Major Larry Messinger, the staff pilot. The forty-four-year-old flier seemed to have survived the accident best of all. He had been able to pull his ripcord immediately after ejection and drifted for twenty minutes with the strong wind before landing in the sea.

But rescuing Larry Messinger was not the end of Simó's activities that morning. After lifting the pilot onto his boat, the fishing captain noticed an extra parachute floating in the water. Assuming that either another survivor or a body was in the folds of the chute, he started to hoist it to the deck. However, the weight was so great that the *Manuela Orts* could not lift the parachute out of the water. Having dented the bottom of his boat against the submerged object, Simó reluctantly gave up his effort, wondering whether he had left a man to sink to the bottom. He never found out what the weight was that he had so desperately tried to bring aboard. He argued later that he had nearly fished out the bomb, but nobody could be sure. While all the nuclear weapons carried parachutes, certain pieces of classified equipment were also secured to silks.

With the rescued men aboard, the two boats headed straight for Aguilas, where an ambulance waited at dockside to take the pilots to the local hospital. So nervous and tense were Simó and Roldán that they gashed their vessels as they moored at the dock. "We made a mooring that the worst apprentice would not make," Simó was to say later. "I won't forget that day as long as I live," he added.

Only when the fishing boats sailed home with the survivors did

Emilio Erades and José Antonio Balbas terminate their search mission. Then they put down their helicopter on the brown sand of the beach facing Palomares. The fuel gauge at that moment stood at less than two gallons.

After the first shock of the collision and of the fire-raining sky wore off, the people of Palomares and people from Vera and Cuevas rushed to look for survivors and put out the burning fires, blissfully unaware of the immense and invisible dangers they were running.

From the houses at the foot of the Cabezo Negro, Julio Ponce, his seventeen-year-old carpenter son Martín, his cousin Alfonso Flores, and several men from the Jorda Paredes farm across the road raced uphill toward the fires. They were joined by Baltasar Flores Gonzáles and a dozen other neighbors from houses down the road. "We wanted to save those poor *Americanos*," Mrs. Ponce said later.

Near a hilltop in the middle of a desolate area of empty land known as Las Algarrobinas the men came upon three fiercely burning engines of the KC-135. Jet fuel, spilled on the ground in a wide circle, was feeding grass fires. To put them out—while wondering whether any crewmen were trapped in the flaming debris—the villagers began hurling sand and earth with their bare hands. But the fires kept burning. A few of the men stayed around the engines to continue the firefighting, while others rushed four hundred yards toward the cemetery, where they had spotted another pillar of black smoke.

There, five human bodies were burning in jet fuel. They were carbonized beyond recognition when the gasping, horrified villagers reached the scene. Crossing themselves, the men came as close to the bodies as they dared in the intense heat and, crying from the smoke and frustration, they threw fistfuls of earth in a brave, pathetic attempt to save the Americans' remains from further destruction. Julio Ponce was not to forget the sight of one of the bodies: its limbs were completely burned away and its head had shrunk to the size of a six-year-old's. Several villagers turned away to retch. The sight and the smell were unbearable.

Baltasar Flores walked a hundred yards away from the furiously burning pyre and came upon the body of a flier who had plummeted to earth after his parachute either failed to open or burned in the air. All his bones were smashed and his eyes were out of their sockets. Baltasar Flores thought the dead American had "all the horrors of the world mirrored in his face."

A few steps uphill another flier lay smashed and dead, still strapped to his ejection seat.

It occurred later to Julio Ponce that it was a grisly irony that the seven dead men had found their resting place within a stone's throw of Palomares' ancient cemetery. How the seven, all the victims of the collision, came together in the same spot of Las Algarrobinas remains something of a mystery.

Four of the five carbonized bodies were the full crew of the KC-135. Since the tankers, unlike B-52s, are not equipped with automatic ejection seats, three crewmen were trapped in their plane's flaming nose section, which crashed close to the engines. They must have died instantly when the KC-135 blew up. The bodies of Major Chapla, Captain Lane, and Captain Simmons were then thrown clear of the wreckage and into the fuel-fed fires. How Sergeant Potolicchio happened to rejoin his fellow crewmen in death was inexplicable. The KC-135's tail section, in which he was riding, had crashed several hundred yards south of the nose section. It is possible, but unlikely, that he had time to bail out when he realized that the B-52 was about to ram the tanker. If he did bail out, his parachute must have burned in the air.

The fifth carbonized body belonged to one of three B-52 crewmen in the bomber's aft section. All of them—Lieutenant Montanus, the navigator; Lieutenant Glesner, the electronic warfare officer; and Sergeant Snyder, the tail gunner—were killed in the accident, though the four fliers in the forward section were ejected or thrown out to safety. (Of these, the first three were picked out of the water by the Aguilas fishermen and the fourth was to be found ashore later.) But it was unclear just how the deaths of the three men in the back of the B-52 had occurred and, again, how their bodies had been thrown together with the remains of the KC-135 crewmen.

The bomber's tail section, for example, had crashed in the dry bed of the Almanzora River, almost two miles away from the cockpits of both the B-52 and the KC-135. To be sure, a part of the B-52 fuselage was found not far from the tanker's engines, but this did not fully explain the location of the bodies of the three men who rode in the bomber's aft compartment. This pattern of dispersal of the bodies became crucial in the ensuing days, when experts began their studies to determine where vital components of the two planes and the bomber's important cargo had fallen.

It is assumed that the B-52's carbonized crewman had been ejected from the bomber, as had some of his companions, but that his parachute immediately caught fire from the burning fuel, causing a dead-weight fall in a nearly direct trajectory. Chances are that this crewman was carbonized in the air. In the case of the remaining two fliers who plummeted to earth without burning, the assumption is that their parachutes simply failed to open for mechanical reasons after ejection.

And now the seven Americans' bodies lay in the parched Spanish hills under the hot morning sun. The old Palomares cemetery, a lonely plot of land so near the scene of the tragedy, displayed the only signs of life in the midst of the desolate landscape. Behind its yellow walls fruit trees were casting a cool, pleasant shade. Birds were singing. At the foot of another nearby hill, where several villagers had gone to put out a small brush fire, a silvery cylindrical shape protruded menacingly from a crater. Alfonso Flores Serrano thought the long cylinder was cracked open, but he felt uneasy and went away without inspecting it any further.

The little dark cloud had drifted away with the wind toward the road.

At the other end of Palomares, a forty-seven-year-old grocer decided to investigate matters more thoroughly. He was José López Flores, the nephew of the octogenarian who was hurled to the ground by the shock waves of the sudden explosion a few minutes after the aircraft collision. Pepé López, a bespectacled and naturally inquisitive man, heard the blast and ran out of his house just in time to see his uncle lying in the dust. He helped the old man to his feet and led him back into the house. Then he decided to go and take a look at whatever had exploded practically in his front yard.

López first saw the burned shreds of a large parachute draped over the brick wall on the side of a terraced hill known as Rabbit's Rise. A small brush fire was burning around the remains of the parachute. Despite a strong wind blowing out to sea, Pepé smelled the acrid smoke. It smelled the way a gun smells after a shot has been fired. He also noticed specks of dark dust drifting in the air. Pepé assumed they were bits of something that had burned there. Edging closer, the shopkeeper noticed a shape under the strips of the silk. He thought it could be one of the pilots from the collision and he rushed forward to try to save what he feared was a man.

Stamping out the fire with his feet, Pepé López tore away at the cloth. Instead of a man, he found a long silvery bomb. It was identical in appearance with the big cylinder that Alfonso Flores had seen in Las Algarrobinas hills. The bomb's metal casing was cracked, and, inside, López could see what he thought was black powder. He pulled back instinctively but steadied himself and with reckless courage resumed stamping out the brush fire around it. As he was to tell his friends later, "Of course I knew it was not safe to have a fire around a bomb."

Pepé thinks that in his excitement he may have kicked the bomb, but he is no longer positive. If he did, he is probably the only man in the world ever to have kicked this kind of bomb. Just then his wife Luisa came out of the house. Seeing her husband jumping up and down on the fire, she shouted, "What in the name of God are you doing, Pepé? Get away from there! This could be dangerous."

Luisa and Pepé López had no way of knowing, of course, just how terribly dangerous his find really was, and how lethal this danger could be, even though the dark cloud was no longer visible. To see what was happening in the village and whether any of their many relatives had been hurt, the couple set out for the center of Palomares.

At this stage only four persons in the area had actually noticed that bombs might have fallen from the skies around the village. One was Francisco Simó, who had seen the parachute with "a dead weight that looked like a man" sink behind his boat. Another was Alfonso Flores Serrano, who came upon the cracked cylinder in the Cabezo Negro hills. And, finally, there were Pepé and Luisa López, Alfonso's second cousins, who had a bomb virtually on their doorstep.

None of them, naturally, shared the others' knowledge. In fact, none of these four persons gave much thought that day to the bombs they had seen, since they were completely unaware of their real nature. And, curiously, none of them mentioned the bombs or the little dark clouds to anyone else until questions started to be asked.

The two men representing rural Spain's two principal pillars of authority, the Guardia Civil and the Roman Catholic Church, also reacted with speed when the B-52 and the KC-135 collided over the village in their care. Within minutes of hearing the shattering sound of the explosion in the air, these two men were converging on Palomares from two directions with aides and volunteers.

In Vera, Guardia Civil Captain Isidoro Calín heard the blast as he sat in his ground-floor office at the headquarters of his detachment, located on the town's outskirts along the highway leading to the fishing port of Garrucha. It was a routine Monday morning for Captain Calín, a deeply tanned forty-eight-year-old Galician from the Atlantic shores but equipped with a completely Mediterranean personality. The Guardia commander was drinking coffee and reading his mail and the orders from the provincial headquarters at Almería when the explosion came. Calín ran out into the street to find out what had blown up. Looking toward Palomares, a few miles away, he saw "balls of fire" falling from the sky. He also noticed a parachute floating down in the distance, and this made him realize that it was some sort of air mishap and that the pilot was probably safe. Then the parachute caught fire, turned into another ball of fire, and vanished from sight in a trail of smoke.

All Vera was brought to an anxious standstill by the air blast. Shopkeepers ran out of their stores to stare at the sky. At La Estación's bar conversations were frozen in mid-sentence. In the streets the brown-and-black goats that are led from house to house to be milked every morning before each housewife's watchful eyes started bucking in alarm and the goatherds could barely keep them from stampeding. Vera had been completely destroyed by an earthquake in 1518 (it was rebuilt fifty years later by King Carlos I, who then died insane at the age of twenty-three), and some inhabitants may have wondered what new disaster was facing the town after 448 years.

Knowing only that something extremely serious was occurring around Palomares, Captain Calín phoned the Guardia command in Almería at 10:25 a.m. to report the explosion three minutes earlier and then ordered his troopers to start for the site. He took eight men with him in a police Land Rover, while seven others followed on motorcycles. They roared through Vera, cut diagonally over mule tracks, and, guiding themselves by the smoke rising from Cabezo Negro, reached the fires in fourteen minutes.

The *guardias* joined Julio Ponce, Alfonso Flores, and the others in covering the fliers' burning bodies with earth, but still the fires would not go out. Captain Calín strode over to the spot where the broken bodies of the two other Americans lay in the sun. He bent down and glanced at the watches still strapped to their wrists. Both were stopped at 10:22 a.m.

Just then the priests arrived.

Father Francisco Navarete Serrano, the twenty-five-year-old priest coadjutor of Cuevas, was preparing himself for the noon mass at La Encarnación church in celebration of the day of Saint Anthony the Abbot, the desert hermit saint who is the town's patron, when the American aircraft collided overhead. The accident was so close that windows shook in all the houses and Pablo Muñoz, a retired artillery officer who owns a local store, remarked to his stockboy that it sounded like a direct howitzer hit on a building next door.

Father Francisco grabbed his rosary and, instinctively, the sacramental oils and ran out into the narrow street, where the Cuevas post office faces his house. Around the corner troopers from the Guardia Civil post were already in the street, their lieutenant talking excitedly to officials from the adjoining courthouse. There were sounds of other explosions high in the air, and beyond the Cuevas roofs Father Francisco could see smoke already rising from the direction of Palomares. Palomares was his personal responsibility, and the priest asked the secretary of the Cuevas Investigations Magistrate if he could go along in his car to the scene of whatever accident had occurred.

As coadjutor under Cuevas priest Enrique Arriaga Aguera, the young Father was in charge of three villages belonging to the seven-parish church district. Cuevas was the seat of the district, and Father Francisco officiated at Palomares, Villaricos, and Herrerías. Ordained just eight months before, he was a circuit priest and drove daily on his scooter to one or another of his villages. He normally made four weekly visits to Palomares, on Sundays and on alternate days of the week. On Friday evenings he taught catechism to children at Palomares' Saint Francis Xavier crossroads church. In addition to Sunday mass, he attended to weddings, baptisms, deaths, and whatever social work was required among the village's impoverished families. Like many young Spanish priests, Father Francisco also encouraged the socially minded work of the Spanish Catholic Action, and in Palomares he had seven members of the fairly progressive Catholic Labor

Youth and the Workers' Brotherhood of Catholic Action. Father Francisco thus was one of those active young priests who are very much involved in their communities and who provide a good example of how the Spanish church is shifting away from its traditional, conservative, and passive ways. Speaking of Palomares, he once remarked that the village had had an old priest for so long that the people, except for women, had almost entirely lost interest in going to church. Faced with the traditional Andalusian anticlericalism, Father Francisco—along with many young priests—was engaged in an effort to make the Catholic Church meaningful to the new generations.

Now, peering anxiously from behind his dark-tinted eyeglasses, he was rushing toward Palomares in the magistrate's secretary's 4-L Renault with the Guardia lieutenant and two troopers. Looking for "smoke and sound," as the priest put it, the secretary's car quickly reached Las Algarrobinas hills. Another car was pulling up at about the same time. In it were Father Fernando Peinado, the rector of the Minor Seminary of Saint Tarsicio in Cuevas, and several philosophy students. (In minor seminaries, only philosophy is taught; theology is given in the major seminaries.)

The priests' immediate concern on the hill was to give the dead fliers absolution and the last sacrament, in case they were Catholics. Father Francisco gave conditional absolution to the two bodies that had escaped being carbonized. "They needed it if they were Catholics," he said later. "If they weren't, it wouldn't do them any harm anyway."

Father Fernando, an older man, rushed into the fire to reach the burning bodies. The bottom of his cassock caught fire and some men tried to pull the priest out of the pyre. Father Fernando turned on them and barked, "Just put out the fire on my cassock!" And he proceeded with the sacrament.

Captain Calín's next concern was to look for other possible survivors and to try to calm down the awe-stricken village. The people were visibly stunned, reluctant to go to their fields, where the tomatoes were waiting to be picked but where the planes' debris was now smoking, or to return to other jobs. They stood in little knots in front of their houses and in the streets, chatting nervously, wondering what had happened.

Touring the beach area, the captain saw the Navy helicopter hovering over the blue waters as it busily directed the fishing boats in the rescue operations. A transport aircraft with Spanish Air Force markings flew low overhead. Shortly before noon a *guardia* on a motorcycle drew up at Captain Calín's Land Rover to report that a survivor had been found in the valley beyond the Fábrica del Duro, not far away from the beach. The captain rushed there.

There was indeed a survivor, and he lay on the ground, moaning weakly. He was Major Ivens Buchanan, the radar navigator. A *guardia* corporal from Herrerías had found him half conscious under his overturned ejection seat. He was still strapped to both the seat and the parachute. The corporal cut him loose from the harnesses with a straight razor he had in his pocket. Captain Calín sent a motorcycle trooper to fetch a private car. Two *guardias* gently placed the thirty-four-year-old flier on the back seat of the vehicle, careful not to aggravate the pain from his burns, and drove him to Dr. Jacinto Gonzáles' clinic in Vera.

As Major Buchanan recounted his frightening experience later, his seat did not eject properly when the B-52 broke up, and the automatic parachute mechanism failed him altogether. Pulling desperately at the ripcord as he fell to earth from 30,000 feet, he finally succeeded in opening the parachute just before he hit the ground.

With additional Guardia Civil units streaming to Palomares from all the towns and villages in the Vera police district and beyond, Captain Calín could now organize his men into patrols to continue the search for what he hoped would be more survivors and to guard what seemed to him important sections of the broken-up planes.

At this time, less than two hours after the collision, Captain Calín knew only that two United States military aircraft had fallen over Palomares. Nobody had yet reported to him the presence in the area of two cracked bombs. But the police officer was more disturbed than the mere fact of the collision would seem to warrant. "I've been thinking of hydrogen bombs ever since the Cuban missile crisis in 1962," he said later. So, with curious prescience, he sent word to the *guardias* not to let any villagers approach the planes' debris or the still burning fires.

iv

The first word of the aerial collision over Almería reached the headquarters of the United States Sixteenth Air Force at the Torrejón del Ardóz base, near Madrid, at 10:25 a.m., three minutes after the accident. It came from the Morón base, which had just received the flash from the lead KC-135's boom operator that "the other B-52 is on fire."

Major General Delmar E. Wilson, the fifty-four-year-old commander of the Sixteenth Air Force—a SAC unit—was at his second-floor office in the sprawling red-brick headquarters building of the base, which oddly resembles a modern college campus. General Wilson had just finished conducting his daily morning meeting—the "Standupper"—with his staff when one of the phones by his desk began jingling insistently. It was the SAC controller at the Torrejón command post, passing on the initial Morón report that a B-52 was on fire.

General Wilson, a veteran bomber pilot, calmly asked the controller to request clarification and additional details from Morón. He wanted to know what the first report meant, whether the B-52 had an engine on fire or what. He told the controller to call him back as soon as any new information was available. Six minutes later, at 10:31, the command post rang him again. Now it had Morón's second report from the lead tanker's boom operator, that the B-52 was on fire and "in a spin." This was

enough to send General Wilson bouncing out of his office to the
command post at the other end of the building.

He knew that the B-52 must be one of SAC's aircraft on airborne alert and that it must be carrying nuclear weapons. From
the preliminary and sketchy information from Morón he also
surmised that the bomber had been 'over the air-refueling control
point in southern Spain. The suspicion of an aerial collision between the B-52 and a tanker began shaping in General Wilson's
mind. In any case, he had already heard enough to realize that
an accident involving nuclear weapons was in progress over
Spanish territory.

Accidents with nuclear weapons carry the designation "Broken
Arrow" in the SAC codes. Instantly General Wilson ordered
Broken Arrow emergency procedures to be set in motion. His
first step was to order Lieutenant Colonel Leland C. Shepard, the
commander of the command post and Torrejón's senior controller, to assemble the base's disaster control team and the Aircraft Accident Board.

General Wilson's second move was to pick up the emergency
red telephone in the command post to call the headquarters of
the Strategic Air Command at the Offutt Air Force Base near
Omaha, Nebraska. Torrejón's red telephones are a part of SAC's
worldwide communications network, the "SAC net," which through
special operators provides instantaneous contacts among the
Strategic Air Command's bases, aircraft, and headquarters. It
was 10:35 a.m., Spanish time, when General Wilson told the
Torrejón operator to get him SAC at Offutt.

At Offutt the local time was 3:35 a.m. when General Wilson
was put through to Major General Charles M. Eisenhart, SAC's
Chief of Staff. General Eisenhart was asleep when his phone rang,
but Wilson's first words shook him into instant awakening. Wilson
reported that an accident with a B-52 and a KC-135 had just occurred in the Saddle Rock refueling area on the Spanish coast
somewhere in the vicinity of a town named Vera, possibly fifteen
miles northeast of it, and that the bomber carried nuclear weapons.

His first words to Eisenhart, as he remembered later, were, "Broken Arrow in Spain." He added that he was leaving for the scene within the hour, as soon as he could assemble his disaster control and investigation teams. Palomares was not mentioned because it did not appear on General Wilson's maps and because nobody had ever heard of it.

Eisenhart said he agreed that Wilson should proceed immediately to the accident area and asked for continual reports on the developments. Then he awoke General John D. Ryan, the SAC Commander-in-Chief, to inform him of Wilson's report. He called Major General A. J. Beck, SAC Director of Matériel and chief of SAC's main disaster control team, and directed him to prepare an immediate deployment to Spain. At 4:06 a.m., as the cold winter night still lay heavily over Offutt, General Beck issued orders to prepare for the flight to Torrejón. General Ryan flashed Washington to advise the Pentagon of the emergency. On the Potomac planning began at once for support operations that were to involve United States military outposts in Western Europe, Britain, and North Africa. Forty-four minutes had elapsed since the B-52 and the KC-135 collided over Spain, and the worldwide emergency mechanism of the United States armed forces was already in full swing.

In Madrid the immediate need was to notify the Spanish government of the accident and its implications. The Spanish Air Force and Navy were learning at the same time from their own commands that an aerial collision involving United States aircraft had taken place over Almería—the first information had come from the San Javier base and from the Guardia Civil—but the Spaniards lacked the ominous knowledge that four hydrogen bombs might have fallen on their territory. They had to be apprised at once, and some form of coordination with the Spanish government had to be worked out instantly.

The obvious channels for notifying Spanish officials were the United States military representatives in Madrid and the American embassy there.

Within minutes of the receipt of the first Morón flash, the duty officer at the Torrejón command post phoned the office of Major General Stanley Joseph Donovan, chief of the Joint United States Military Group and Military Assistance Advisory Group, Spain (JUSMAAG), at the Spanish Air Ministry on Madrid's wide Calle Princesa. JUSMAAG—and General Donovan, as its head—coordinated all the military relationships with Spain under the provisions of the 1953 and 1963 agreements, including the operations of the joint air and naval bases and the SAC overflights. In this sense, JUSMAAG's role was both military and political.

General Donovan, a bomber pilot and staff officer, fifty-five years old, known to friends and acquaintances by his old West Point nickname of "Moose," was well suited personally for his over-all assignment, and for the immensely delicate task, on this particular morning, of informing his Spanish colleagues that American nuclear weapons might be on the loose in Almería. Having first served in Spain as the deputy to the JUSMAAG chief between 1955 and 1960, Moose Donovan had returned to Madrid in 1963 as head of the mission. A gregarious man with blue eyes and a toothbrush mustache, he spoke Spanish fluently and had wide-ranging friendships among officers in Spain's armed forces.

His most important friendship was with Captain General Agustín Muñoz Grandes, the seventy-year-old chief of the Spanish High Staff and Vice President of the Spanish government. In this twin capacity Muñoz Grandes was Spain's ranking military officer and civilian official after Generalissimo Franco. It was on Muñoz Grandes that Moose Donovan made his first emergency call that morning.

After requesting an urgent appointment by telephone, Donovan drove to the High Staff with Lieutenant Colonel John McCleary, his assistant. He told the old captain general all that was known at the time of the Almería accident, emphasizing the fact that the B-52 carried four nuclear bombs and that the American command simply had no knowledge at this juncture of what had happened to them or where they were.

Muñoz Grandes took the news calmly. He showed no excitement, except to express his regret that the United States had lost two aircraft and that there might be dead and injured among the American crewmen. One of the most pro-American of Spain's top officials, he made it clear to Donovan that in his view the possibility of accident was a risk inherent in the alliance with the United States, which his country had to accept. This reaction, at least for the duration of the emergency, was to color the attitude of most Spanish officials.

After spending fifteen minutes with Muñoz Grandes and touching on various aspects of the accident, Donovan drove back to the Air Ministry to make the same report to the Spanish Air Minister, Lieutenant General José Maria Lacalle Larriaga. General Lacalle reacted essentially in the same manner as had Muñoz Grandes. He placed all the Spanish air facilities, and notably the San Javier base in Murcia, at the Americans' disposal to assist in the rescue and search operations, and said he was naming Brigadier General Antonio Llob Lamarca, the commander of the Gibraltar Straits Air Zone, as the Spanish coordinator on the site for Broken Arrow.

Donovan rushed home to pack an overnight bag, and then on to Torrejón to fly to San Javier aboard his C-54 plane. The coordination with local authorities in Almería in a situation of still unforeseeable risks and problems would be his immediate responsibility.

At the American embassy, a modernistic six-story building on tree-shaded Calle Serrano, the first call on the accident came at 11:05 a.m. to Second Secretary Joseph Smith, the young officer in charge of military-political affairs. The call was from General Donovan's JUSMAAG office and it told Joe Smith that there had been an accident involving a B-52 nuclear bomber and a KC-135 tanker somewhere near the Gulf of Mazarrón, west of Cartagena. The information, coming both from the Sixteenth Air Force and from the Spanish Air Force, indicated that the two planes had crashed, that there were several survivors floating in the Mediterranean, and that the B-52 had "unarmed nuclear weapons aboard." Since the call was over an open line, the Air Force officer at JUSMAAG was reluctant to go into further details. But this was enough to launch Joe Smith into immediate action.

He walked across the fifth-floor hall to the office of Laurin B. Askew, chief of the embassy's political section, to pass on the JUSMAAG report and seek instructions. This was Askew's first day in his job—he had just been transferred to Madrid after a year at the Imperial Defence College in London—and after a brief discussion he told Smith to inform Ambassador Angier Biddle Duke.

In the outer office Smith found Timothy Towell, the Ambassador's special assistant. Towell told him the Ambassador had gone downtown to deliver a speech before a meeting of the American Management Association on the problems of the gold outflow from the United States. The embassy's Minister-Counselor, William W. Walker, was away in Washington on temporary assignment with a State Department task force. Smith and Towell felt it was urgent to notify Ambassador Duke so that he, in turn, could communicate with the Spanish Foreign Ministry. But the number of the building where the Ambassador was speaking that morning was not in the telephone directory. There was no time to be wasted, and the two young men decided to find Duke at all costs. Joe Smith typed out on two slips of paper the message about the Almería crash and the fact that "nuclear weapons were involved." He gave one to Towell, in case the Ambassador returned to the office, and took the other one with him. Commandeering Walker's limousine, Smith set out for downtown Madrid.

It took him fifteen minutes through the heavy midmorning traffic to reach the building where the Management Association was holding its sessions. An attendant directed him upstairs. At the door to the meeting room, Smith came upon an American with a badge on his lapel.

"I'd like to see the American Ambassador," Smith told him.

"He's in a conference now," the man replied. "Are you a member of the association or a delegate?"

"No. I'm from the embassy," Smith said. "I want to see the Ambassador on urgent business."

"Oh, damn it," the man said with prescience, opening the door. "I bet he'll have to leave now."

Inside the room Smith spotted Ambassador Duke sitting with five other men on the dais, listening to a speech by Spanish Industry Minister Gregório López Bravo. Smith stood by the door to the right of the dais, hoping the Ambassador would glance at him. In fact, he stared as hard as he could at the Ambassador to force him by sheer will-power to turn his head. Finally Duke did look at Smith and the young man raised his hand to signal him. The Ambassador said something to the men on either side, got up, and pushed his way off the dais. At the door Joe Smith said, "I have some information I have to give you. It's important. Let's step out."

In the corridor Smith gave the Ambassador the typed slip of paper. Duke read it and asked if there was any additional information on survivors. Smith said there was none. He told the Ambassador that General Wilson was already en route to the disaster area and General Donovan was about to take off for the south. Duke paced up and down for a minute or so, then said, "Let's go back to the embassy."

Downstairs the Ambassador and Smith got into a limousine and told Fausto, the Ambassador's driver, to hurry up to the embassy. But half a block down the street Duke changed his mind. "Let's go to the Foreign Ministry," he said.

Ten minutes later they reached the ministry, a lovely old palace next to the Plaza Mayor, which once served as a prison for the kingdom's nobles. On the ground floor Duke and Smith went straight to the office of Angel Sagáz, then the ministry's director of North American Affairs. Sagáz handled most of the business with the American embassy, but that morning he was away from the ministry. The Ambassador asked a uniformed usher for Sagáz's deputy, but he too was away. Duke then decided to see at once Foreign Minister Fernando María Castiella y Maíz. He and Smith ran up the carpeted stairs to the second floor, but the Minister's outer office was empty. A phone was ringing insistently with no-body there to answer it.

Stepping outside, Duke spotted another usher. He asked where the Minister was.

"He has gone to the funeral, sir," the usher replied.

He asked Duke if he wished to see the Chief of Protocol, the Marquis of Jurareal. Ambassador Duke, who had served as President Kennedy's and President Johnson's Chief of Protocol before coming to Spain ten months earlier, said he would. The Marquis appeared a few moments later and the Ambassador told him he was anxious to see the Foreign Minister. The Chief of Protocol explained that the Minister, along with many ministry officials, was attending the funeral of the mother of one of his colleagues.

"Well," Duke said impatiently, "I came to inform him that there has been an accident with a B-52 and a tanker in the south near Cartagena, and to tell him that—"

The Marquis did not let him finish. "Would you like to see Cortina?" he asked.

Adolfo Cortina was the Under Secretary of Foreign Affairs, and Duke said, "Yes, yes."

When Cortina entered the room, the Ambassador read to him from his slip of paper about the accident. Cortina shook his head regretfully. Then Duke said, "The bomber was carrying nuclear weapons"—the Spaniard looked up sharply—"but there was no explosion," the Ambassador went on.

Cortina interrupted him. "Just wait a minute, please," he said. "I'd like to make a call."

Presently Ramón Sedó, the other Under Secretary, joined them. The four men discussed the situation for a few minutes. The Spaniards were concerned that the accident might have occurred in a populated area. Before leaving, Duke told the Spanish officials that the embassy would keep the ministry informed of all developments. Then he made a remark expressing a wish that would long go unfulfilled by both governments.

"We should coordinate the handling of public information," he said.

At Torrejón the Broken Arrow alert procedures were now fully in motion. The disaster control team and the Aircraft Accident Board members were assembling at the base command post to be briefed by General Wilson on the situation while aircraft were being made ready to fly them to San Javier, the airfield believed to be the nearest to the accident area. The exact location of the crash was still unknown, and none of the Torrejón officers had ever been to San Javier. The planning then under way at the command post was, therefore, a combination of well-rehearsed emergency procedures and deft improvisations. It included telephoning San Javier over an uncertain line to say that United States aircraft would soon begin landing there and to request help in arranging ground transportation to the accident site.

Lieutenant Colonel Thomas B. Wright, the chief of the Torrejón disaster control section, happened to walk into the command post at 10:25 a.m., just as the first flash came in from Morón. He remained there, making mental preparations for action he instantly sensed to be impending, until General Wilson arrived and the first orders began to be issued. Even before Wilson ordered the assembling of the disaster team, Colonel Wright telephoned Technical Sergeant Joe Martin, his top clerk, to come running over from his daily Spanish-language class. Within two minutes Wright and Martin, using two telephones, had a "pyramid alert" going— each man receiving a call phoned another member of the team— and by eleven the whole group was gathered in the command post. Lieutenant Colonel Carl Paine, the disaster control team leader, was one of the first to reach the CP. The officers of the Aircraft Accident Board with Lieutenant Colonel George Paine, its president, presently joined the group.

General Wilson, a tall blue-eyed, white-haired officer, proceeded to outline the situation. A B-52 and a KC-135 had collided over the Saddle Rock area. Both planes crashed. The B-52 carried four unarmed hydrogen bombs. It was not known where the weapons had gone, whether they were intact or damaged. If one or more of the weapons were damaged, there was danger of radioactive contamination in some degree. The immediate tasks ahead of the disaster control team were to locate the weapons, determine their condition, and, if necessary, proceed to contain the contamination.

Both SAC and General Wilson had long prepared for the contingency that now faced them. The disaster teams at all SAC bases around the world continually went through simulated nuclear-accident exercises, including radioactivity detection and decontamination tests. In a typical exercise involving both pilots and disaster teams, a nuclear bomber would come in with several of its eight engines out two or three minutes before landing. The teams then had to react on the assumption that nuclear weapons would spill out or be damaged.

General Wilson was an old hand with bombers as well as with nuclear weapons. After flying bombers in World War II in Europe and the Pacific—he flew some of the first B-29 missions against Japan from Taipan—he became command liaison officer for General Curtis E. LeMay on the Atom Bomb Project on Kwajalein Island in the South Pacific in May 1946. With the gradual advent of the Cold War, the United States was again exploding nuclear weapons, for the first time since the Hiroshima and Nagasaki attacks ten months earlier. Present during the Kwajalein tests, but then unknown to General Wilson, was another expert in nuclear problems who was soon to play a key role in the Spanish events.

For nearly eleven years now, General Wilson had been associated with SAC—and nuclear deliveries—commanding bases and air units in the United States and England. Late in 1964 he went to Spain to take over the Sixteenth Air Force. On this January Monday in 1966 he was at the start of the most exacting and bewildering mission of his long Air Force career.

As General Wilson was to remark later, no exercise ever held by SAC involved an accident at such a great distance from a base and, to boot, on foreign territory. Palomares, indeed, had never been quite rehearsed.

His briefing completed, Wilson drove from the command post to the Torrejón strip. The general and four aides boarded his

twin-engined command T-39 jet—a North American Sabrejetliner
—for the flight to San Javier and the beginning of their unpredict-
able assignment. Flying the fast jet was Lieutenant Colonel Henry
R. Hirsch, a tough, lean pilot who was the Sixteenth Air Force's
Director of Operations and Training. The others were Colonel
George Paine of the Aircraft Accident Board, Lieutenant Colonel
Barnett B. Young, the Sixteenth's Director of Information, and
"Pete" Correjeda, General Wilson's Spanish civilian adviser.

The T-39 roared off Torrejón strip at 12:36 p.m. Seven
minutes later a turboprop C-97 transport took off with twenty-
eight members of the disaster control team—including Colonels
Wright and Carl Paine—and twelve members of the Aircraft Accident Board. The men on the disaster team represented every
specialty that might be required in a nuclear situation, including
nuclear safety, radiation, and munitions experts, and communications, security, engineering, biological environment, supply, procurement, and legal specialists. Also aboard was Captain Fritz
Byrum, a flight surgeon.

The men on the Aircraft Accident Board were experts in problems of flight, aircraft structure, and human factors. Their job
was to determine what had caused the collision and what could
be learned from it for the future. Some of the officers and men
who lived on base had time to pack overnight bags. Others left
for San Javier as they were: in blue winter uniforms, fatigues, or
flight suits. But the C-97 took along all the emergency equipment
that might be needed to start controlling a radioactively contaminated disaster area. There were radiation suits, face masks,
and gloves. And most important, as it turned out later, there
were several PAC-1S survey meters for measuring alpha radiation.
These were commonly known as alpha oscillator counters. The
aircraft also carried a single-sideband radio transmitter and receiver for emergency communications between the accident site
and the Torrejón command post.

General Wilson's T-39 and the disaster control team's C-97
were the first aircraft of Broken Arrow, the vanguard of what

was to become a massive airlift of men and equipment from the United States, Europe, and North Africa.

A KC-135 took off from Offutt Air Force Base in Nebraska for Torrejón thirty-eight minutes after the C-97's departure from Madrid for San Javier. It was 6:21 a.m. and still dark in Omaha when the big plane left with General Beck and his main disaster control team. Accompanying them were Colonel C. W. Rhodes, SAC's chief of Ordnance Disposal, and Colonel J. A. Norcross from the Directorate of Nuclear Safety in the Air Force's Nuclear Medicine Division.

General Ryan, the SAC Commander-in-Chief, was taking no chances with the Spanish situation and he wanted to make sure that the best talent and equipment were available on the scene. No actual nuclear explosions, obviously, had occurred in Almería, but there were many other grim possibilities that could not be discarded.

By mid-afternoon another KC-135 was en route to Spain from Albuquerque, New Mexico, where the Air Force has its Nuclear Safety Office, bringing military experts and civilian scientists from the Atomic Energy Commission's scientific laboratory at Los Alamos and from the Sandia Corporation's laboratory in Albuquerque. An additional SAC disaster control team was simultaneously flying to Torrejón from Wiesbaden, Germany, with more of the precious PAC-1S radiation meters. Air Force and Army men were being alerted to move to Spain at United States bases ranging from Toul and Metz in France to Wheelus in Libya. And, as the Pentagon in Washington swung into action, word to stand by for support operations went out to the headquarters of the United States Naval Striking and Support Forces Southern Europe in Naples, Italy.

There Rear Admiral William S. Guest, the deputy commander, heard of the Spanish accident without any inkling that within days he would be staking his career on its outcome.

The world learned of the midair collision over the Spanish coast, but not immediately of its tremendous implications, from a bulletin filed from the Madrid office of the Associated Press at 11:55 a.m., one hour and thirty-three minutes after the accident. In sending his bulletin, AP Bureau Chief Harold Milks scored a clean forty-five-minute beat over his rivals at the Reuters News Agency and a sixty-six-minute beat over United Press International. In the highly competitive wire-service business, a forty-five-minute lead over another agency on a major story is an achievement that brings bouquets and congratulations. But the UPI was to have its day too, as the Almería story promptly turned into a nightmare of confusion and contradictions in the hands of the Pentagon's information policy-makers.

Milks, a veteran of international reporting in China, Russia, India, and Cuba, scored his scoop almost by chance, the way so many great stories are obtained. Shortly after the two planes collided in the south, with no idea that an accident had occurred, he happened to call Torrejón on another matter. But the man whom Milks was telephoning shouted that he was just going out the door and that he might have something to tell him later. This puzzled Milks, and he proceeded to call other sources at Torrejón. Mysteriously, nobody was available. Increasingly suspicious, Milks called several of his Spanish news sources. Within two minutes a Spanish friend called back to say that an American plane had crashed near Almería. Milks had barely finished typing a two-paragraph bulletin when his source called back with additional details of the crash.

Hearing that a B-52 was involved, Milks, who is an Air Force reserve officer, quickly concluded that nuclear weapons might be involved. Caught between caution and instinct, he compromised on this wording in his 11:55 a.m. bulletin:

MADRID, Jan. 17 (AP)—Spanish sources said today that a giant United States B-52 *nuclear* bomber and a KC-135 tanker crashed near Almería on the southeast coast of Spain, apparently after a midair collision while refueling.

While his Reuters and UPI rivals were still to put out their first bulletins on the accident, Milks decided to pursue the nuclear angle. He phoned Torrejón again and, at 12:30 p.m., wired this bulletin to London:

> The headquarters of the United States Sixteenth Air Force would *not* say whether or not the B-52 carried nuclear arms on today's flight. Normally such bombers are armed on such transoceanic training flights.

What Milks and the rest of the press corps in Madrid were up against that day—and for days and weeks to come—was the Pentagon's standing policy of refusing comment on situations touching upon nuclear weapons. Working from SAC's black-covered manual of instructions on information policies to be followed in nuclear accidents, the Sixteenth Air Force at Torrejón refused for days to confirm, or even discuss, the possibility that hydrogen bombs were aboard the B-52.

After acknowledging in the early afternoon that an accident had occurred, the Sixteenth Air Force finally issued a communiqué as newsmen's pressures mounted. But the communiqué told them considerably less than they already knew. It said:

> A B-52 bomber from the 68th Bomb Wing at Seymour Johnson Air Force Base, North Carolina, and a KC-135 tanker from the 910th air refueling squadron at Bergstrom Air Force Base, Texas, crashed today southwest of Cartagena, Spain, during scheduled air operations. There are reports of some survivors from the crews of the aircraft. An Air Force accident investigation team has been dispatched to the scene. Additional details will be available as the investigation progresses.

That was all the Air Force had to say publicly on January 17. But its discretion did not deter the reporters from digging and speculating. At the Associated Press office, Milks went on raising the nuclear possibility in his night leads. At the UPI, Harry J. Stathos, the young bureau chief, filed the same report on Torrejón's refusal to comment on the B-52's weapons. In his night leads, Stathos wrote that the SAC bomber was "possibly carrying a nuclear weapon." And his final story of the evening said:

> The Air Force has slapped a curtain of secrecy on the incident. . . . The possibility that a nuclear device was aboard the B-52

was raised by observers when it was learned that General Wilson had flown to the scene with his top information officer, Col. Barnett B. Young. . . .

Stathos's deduction was obviously sound. A commanding general does not rush to the scene of an aircraft accident unless there are special and overriding reasons for it. And additional information was streaming in from shot-in-the-dark telephone calls to the area and from the Spanish news agencies, Cifra and Mencheta. Among other facts, it included the word that four crewmen had survived and that seven had perished.

A UPI reporter located Captain Wendorf by phone at the Aguilas hospital and held a brief conversation with him. Wendorf said he had not yet talked to anyone from the Air Force and therefore could not comment on the accident. "All I know is I have a broken arm and it's killing me," Wendorf said and hung up. And the Reuter News Agency forced out of a Torrejón spokesman an admission—though it was partly inaccurate—that the B-52 was about to refuel in the air "to continue a routine nonstop mission to an Eastern country." The truth, of course, was that the B-52 was returning from just such a mission.

All in all, the Madrid correspondents had a reasonably clear picture of the situation at the day's end, despite the Air Force's continuing reticence. It is just possible that without the newsmen's dogged pursuit of the story the Palomares accident would not have reached its subsequent magnitude and forced the United States government into the vast search and recovery effort that was to ensue.

V

This search effort began in earnest when General Wilson reached the southeastern coast of Spain in his T-39 and decided to investigate the situation from the air. He felt that an immediate aerial reconnaissance of the Almería coast might help to identify the area of wreckage and therefore speed up land operations. Taking the jet's controls from Colonel Hirsch, the general veered southwest from San Javier toward Vera. The T-39 circled for about fifteen minutes at a few thousand feet over the Almería hills. Presently Wilson spotted a wisp of smoke in what appeared to be a valley near the coast. Banking even lower for a better look, he observed the tail section of the B-52 in the sand in the dry bed of the Almanzora River. The houses of Palomares were strung out directly south of the bomber's tail. General Wilson and his companions were still unaware of the existence of Palomares, but now they knew what the accident site looked like. It looked extremely difficult for conducting a search for four missing hydrogen bombs. Wilson landed his jet at San Javier at exactly 2 p.m.

The C-97 with the disaster control team from Torrejón had arrived fifteen minutes earlier, and now the Spanish Air Force Academy was the scene of intense activity. Colonel Alfaro, the academy's commander, and a United States Navy lieutenant in charge of a communications station at the Cartagena naval base were on hand to meet Wilson and his staff. They also had made some preliminary arrangements to start moving the SAC teams to

70

the crash site. A bus, several panel trucks, sedans, and taxis were waiting to take them there.

Wilson conferred briefly with the Spanish colonel about additional arrangements. Learning that three of the survivors were at the Aguilas hospital, he decided to drive there first. He ordered the rest of his party to assemble at the B-52's tail section in the Almanzora's dry bed and wait for him there. Then he left in the American Navy lieutenant's car with Colonel George Paine, Flight Surgeon Byrum, and his Spanish adviser, Correjeda.

The drive through the winding highways of Murcia province, first through orange groves and then through a landscape of sandy hills, took nearly two hours. At Lorca, a town famous for its rug factories, the party left the main highway, Norte 340, to take the secondary road to Aguilas.

The little fishing town with a population of some 15,000 inhabitants was tingling with excitement. Aguilas fishermen had rescued the three American fliers from the morning's crash, and now the town was bursting with civic pride. As the Wilson party drove through the streets toward the hospital, men were standing in little knots at intersections and in cafés, discussing the events.

At the Central Hospital, Wilson found Captain Wendorf, Major Messinger, and Lieutenant Rooney in the same room. Though they had suffered shock and exposure and Captain Wendorf had a broken arm, all three were "very rational." While Flight Surgeon Byrum discussed their condition with the Spanish doctors, Wilson and Colonel George Paine questioned the pilots about the collision.

All three agreed that they were not aware of any malfunction in the B-52 prior to the collision. But Major Messinger, who had not been occupied with the actual flying and could better observe the events, recalled noticing that the closure rate was "excessive" as the bomber edged in under the tanker's tail. The normal procedure for a B-52 preparing to refuel is to approach the tanker at 275 miles per hour, then stabilize the airspeed at some 500 feet away, and, finally, start moving up slowly, increasing the speed at a rate of about 2 miles per hour, until the boom can be lowered into the bomber's nose.

But Major Messinger remembered seeing the underside of the KC-135's wings at a distance of 150 feet before feeling a thud and realizing the two aircraft were on fire and exploding. Messinger and Rooney ejected themselves at that point, while Wendorf was thrown clear of the plane. Subsequently the B-52's wings snapped off under the stress, and the tail shuddered and broke off.

The three pilots said they bailed out over land and were carried out to sea by the strong northwestern wind. Major Messinger said he had seen other parachutes in the air and he anxiously inquired how many of them had been blown over the Mediterranean.

General Wilson left the hospital room suspecting that the collision might have been due to pilot error. But it was up to his Aircraft Accident Board and to other experts to come up with the final conclusions. Presently a helicopter from Morón landed in Aguilas to lift the three pilots to San Javier, from where they would be flown to the hospital at Torrejón.

From Aguilas the Wilson party drove back to Lorca and then to Vera. At La Estación they were given directions on how to proceed to Palomares over the rutted Vera Highway. In ten more minutes they were crossing the stunned little village and reaching the B-52 tail in the soft sand of the Almanzora riverbed. There General Wilson established his first command post in Palomares.

Earlier that afternoon the Guardia Civil's Captain Calín had decided to drive back to Vera to check on Major Buchanan's condition and request further instructions from the provincial command in Almería.

Buchanan was in bed at Dr. Jacinto Gonzáles' clinic. He was in pain from his broken shoulder and from body burns. Calín thought Buchanan was still in "nervous shock" after his experience. Their conversation was further complicated because Buchanan spoke no Spanish and Calín no English. In the end, Buchanan managed to ask the Spanish officer whether the collision had caused any damage and whether any of the planes' fragments had fallen on top of people.

"No," Calín told him, "there was no damage—only what you have suffered."

A few minutes later a Spanish Air Force ambulance arrived to take Buchanan to San Javier.

Stopping by his office at the Guardia headquarters at 4 p.m., Calín received a telephone call from Major Francisco Martín Meca, his chief in Almería. Major Martín informed him on the basis of information from Madrid that "it is possible that this plane may have carried missiles with nuclear warheads." Then he instructed Calín to use the Guardia to cordon off tightly the whole area and not to allow anyone to touch the planes' debris. Calín nodded. He had already given out essentially the same orders several hours earlier.

One man, however, had eluded the Guardia's vigilance. He was Roberto Puig Alvárez, a Madrid architect who was engaged in building apartments in the hilltop town of Mojácar near Palomares. Puig drove to Palomares immediately after the collision to see what had happened, and somehow came upon the bomb next to Pepé López's house. He peered down and knelt at the edge of the shallow crater to examine more leisurely the still smoldering bomb. His curiosity was later to create serious problems for the United States.

Now the early winter dusk was settling over Palomares, and candles and kerosene lamps were being lit in the village's houses. It had not yet been possible to repair the power cables broken in the morning by the falling pieces of the planes.

Just about that time two Guardia Civil troopers patrolling the beach area at the mouth of the Almanzora River made a startling discovery. They rushed a few hundred feet to the B-52 tail section where the Americans were setting up camp and motioned to them to come over. At a point 400 yards from the coast a slightly dented but otherwise undamaged hydrogen bomb lay under its white-gray parachute. It was reposing horizontally at the foot of a low embankment, from which it had slid after its fall, on the border between the riverbed's sand and a tomato field. Curiously, the bomb had come to rest close to an old watchtower on the river's bank that in Phoenician days marked the end of the flourishing Mediterranean Betic region which stretched west all the way to the rock of Gibraltar. The Greeks called this tower Murgis Akra, the hill of Murgis.

The bomb, designated as Weapon No. 1, was positively identified at 4:44 p.m. Men from SAC's explosives ordnance disposal team proceeded to defuse it by disconnecting the forty electric detonators for the TNT charge that surrounds the nuclear material like a jacket. When an armed hydrogen bomb is being set off, the TNT explodes toward the center—or creates an implosion —acting as the first trigger in a nuclear reaction by rendering the compressed plutonium and uranium supercritical. Although the bombs dropped from the B-52 were not armed for nuclear reaction—a separate system of security locks had not been actuated— an accidental TNT blast can scatter plutonium particles around, in itself a potentially dangerous development. The ordnance experts completed their task shortly after 10:30 p.m., working with flashlights and portable lights. The next morning the 5000-pound hydrogen bomb would be loaded aboard a flatbed truck from the Morón base with the aid of improvised winches and dispatched by road to San Javier, from where it would be flown to Torrejón and on to the United States. But the location of the first bomb and the plans for its evacuation overland were a deep secret that night. The world had not yet been officially told that nuclear weapons had been lost in Palomares.

Encouraged by the finding of Weapon No. 1, General Wilson ordered three search teams formed to survey the countryside around the area where the first bomb had been discovered. Colonel Young, a pilot and weapons expert currently assigned to public-information duties, took one team. Colonel Carl Paine, head of the disaster control team, took the second team. Colonel Hirsch, the Sixteenth Air Force chief of operations, took the third group.

The three teams communicated by walkie-talkie. But the search in falling darkness proved fruitless and it was abandoned.

Meanwhile Colonel Wright was in the hills of Cabezo Negro, surveying the area where most wreckage had fallen and where the seven bodies had been found. Aircraft debris and vegetation were still smoldering. Colonel Wright turned on his alpha oscillator counter—the PAC-1S—on the chance that he might get a reading. Strangely, he did not record any significant radiation, just the standard background radiation from the soil.

For all practical purposes, the day had ended. One bomb had been found, but three others were still missing. General Wilson correctly concluded that a long and complex operation lay ahead. Calling Colonel Ralph Jenkins, his executive officer, at Torrejón on the single-sideband radio, General Wilson requested the immediate dispatch of at least three hundred airmen to Palomares from the Madrid base and from Morón.

Because single-sideband transmissions could be easily monitored, the two men began using code names for a minimum of privacy. General Wilson became "Warner" and Colonel Jenkins was "Baleful."

At Cuevas' La Encarnación church, noted for its Doric columns, Father Francisco Navarete officiated at the noon high mass in honor of Saint Anthony the Abbot. But because of the accident there was no music at the church and Father Francisco's sermon dealt not with Saint Anthony but with the terrible things he had witnessed up on the Cabezo Negro hills that morning. Saint Anthony's mass thus became a service for the eternal rest of the American fliers and, as Father Francisco told the faithful of Cuevas, for "Christian resignation for their families."

In the late afternoon the bodies were brought from Palomares to Cuevas by the townfolk and Guardia Civil men. Inexplicably, eight coffins were prepared for the seven bodies. The coffins were laid out among burning candles in the reception room of the Cuevas *ayuntamiento,* the town hall. General Wilson, who drove up from his riverbed camp in Palomares to claim the bodies, had the duty of examining the charred and smashed remains of the fliers. Then Father Enrique Arriaga Aguera, the elderly Cuevas parish priest, said the prayers for the Americans' eternal rest. All that was left for General Wilson to do was to sign the receipts for the bodies. Late that night an Air Force truck drove them to San Javier for shipment to Torrejón to be identified and embalmed. The ghastly task of identifying them from their dental configurations fell to the base dentist. Then the bodies were flown home to North Carolina and Texas.

In the darkened village General Donovan, the head of JUSMAAG in Spain, conferred by the light of a butane gas lamp with José Manuel Gonzáles Fernandez, the bulky man who is the part-time mayor of Palomares. Because Palomares depends administratively upon Cuevas, it does not require a full-time mayor, and Gonzáles normally acts as an occasional delegate of the municipality to the village where he lives. But now Gonzáles had emerged as the only legal authority in Palomares, aside from the Guardia Civil corporal commanding the local six-man detachment, and General Donovan was reviewing with him the situation created by the morning's accident.

The two men were talking in a small room atop a combination bar and grocery on Palomares' main square. Gonzáles had made the room available to Donovan as a temporary command post pending the setting up of a more permanent camp by the Americans the following day. Donovan and Wilson had talked earlier with Captain Calín to hear his impressions and make communications and other arrangements, but the JUSMAAG chief was anxious to know how the villagers were reacting to the sudden crisis.

Gonzáles told Donovan that the villagers were still scared and upset. They were worried that some of their crops might have been damaged by the flaming debris of the aircraft and they were becoming alarmed over the fact that the Guardia Civil was cordoning off large areas of the Palomares fields. And there were rumors that mysterious weapons had been lost in or around the village. Gonzáles knew of several instances in which women had refused to sleep that night in homes near where big chunks of the planes had fallen and in which children had been sent away to stay with relatives in nearby towns and villages. Could the general, Gonzáles asked, tell him what had really happened?

Unable, because of official secrecy, to tell the anxious mayor the truth about the missing nuclear weapons, Donovan sought to assure Gonzáles that there was no danger to the village and its inhabitants. Everything would be cleaned up quickly, he said, and the United States would surely indemnify Palomares for whatever damages it might have suffered. They parted on this note.

Donovan and several Air Force officers then drove to a beachside tourist hotel, the Maricielo, near the paved highway from Vera to Garrucha. The hotel, a brand-new structure, had closed down the day before after the long Christmas holiday season, but Donovan persuaded the woman in charge and a young boy to reopen it for his group. Wilson had only a limited number of tents at his temporary camp in the riverbed, and Donovan's exhausted officers desperately needed some sleep before the dawning of the second day of the search for the lost hydrogen bombs.

BOOK THREE *The Search*

i

At first light of the second day, Tuesday, January 18, Air Force search parties fanned out over the Palomares fields to resume their quest for the three missing hydrogen bombs. It was still half dark, as in January day does not break until nearly seven o'clock. It was also chilly, what with the strong wind blowing from the Mediterranean and slashing through the men's inadequate clothing. Some of the officers and airmen had brought along fur-lined flight jackets, but most of them shivered in their fatigues.

The search problem facing General Wilson and his improvised search teams was staggering, to say the least. They were to locate, with the greatest possible dispatch, three tubular objects measuring 10 feet in length and 20 inches in diameter that could have dropped almost anywhere in an area of many square miles— either ashore or in the sea. The terrain was unspeakably rough: there were valleys, gullies, and gulches, and there were hills, boulders, and knolls. And, worst of all, the fields were overgrown with tomato vines, bean patches, cacti, and esparto grass. Finally, nobody really had any idea where to look and for what, exactly, to look.

That the first bomb had been found the previous afternoon in the riverbed did not assure that the three other weapons would be in the same area. The dispersion pattern of the aircraft debris over several miles from the Cabezo Negro hills to the Almanzora suggested that the bombs also might have been scattered across a wide range.

As General Wilson knew, gravitational acceleration forces of at least 8 Gs, produced by the impact of the planes' collision, would be required to tear the bombs loose from their racks in the bomb bays; the same forces could have projected the weapons in any direction and for quite a distance. Each bomb, once separated from the bomb bay by the G forces, no longer had to follow the same fall pattern.

Furthermore, nobody knew whether the B-52's electronic-warfare officer—one of the dead crewmen—had had time to eject the weapons at the moment of the collision, whether the plane's computers had taken over, or whether the bombs had simply been torn out of the bays. Since a SAC bomber had accidentally dropped parts of a nuclear weapon over Florence, South Carolina, on March 11, 1958, the Air Force had ordered crews to "lock in" the weapons in flight. This meant they could not be jettisoned easily or quickly in an emergency such as the Palomares explosion.

If a controlled ejection had occurred, however, chances were that each bomb could have floated down on one or both of the parachutes with which it was equipped. One of the parachutes was a tactical one, designed to stabilize the bomb for a midair burst at a predetermined altitude. The other chute was intended to ease the bomb down to earth in the event of an accident. But, of course, nobody knew whether either of the parachutes had opened and whether or not they had caught fire from the flaming fuel.

To compound matters even further, General Wilson could not rule out the possibility that one or all of the three missing bombs had been damaged during the collision or suffered a TNT explosion in midair. In such an event, the weapons would have disintegrated wholly or partially in the air, and the search then would become an impossible job of looking for tiny pieces of casings, control mechanisms, and nuclear materials in the midst of tomato vines. A TNT explosion on impact with the ground also could have scattered fragments of the bombs far and wide. And if any of the bombs had fallen in the sea, the search could go on forever, particularly if the weapons had been torn asunder before hitting the water. The searchers, of course, had not been told of the two bombs at Cabezo Negro and near Pepé López's house. In short, then, it was a nightmarish proposition which General Wilson and his men were facing on that morning after the Palomares collision.

As the search resumed at daybreak, General Wilson was still grievously short of men and specialized equipment. He had only the teams that had arrived with him from Torrejón and San Javier the previous afternoon and a handful of additional experts and airmen who had driven in during the night from Madrid and Morón. The reinforcements, including the high-level SAC team from Offutt and the teams from Germany and France, would not reach Palomares until later in the day.

Five slightly wayward Air Force buses carrying some of the reinforcements were hurtling down dusty Spanish roads from Torrejón to Palomares just as the searchers began recombing the Almería countryside. Like General Wilson's advance echelon that had flown to San Javier Monday afternoon, this contingent had only a vague idea of where it was going and even less of a notion of what it was to do.

The 240 men and 8 officers had departed from Torrejón at 3 a.m. on Tuesday in response to General Wilson's radioed request for troops to expand his bomb-search operations. Almost simultaneously, 3 other buses with 125 troops aboard left the Morón base near Seville for an overland crossing of Spain's south, over some of the country's worst mountain roads.

At Torrejón and Morón the men had been called out of bed at 1 a.m. after the local commanders had drawn up plans to deplete the two bases of all personnel who were not absolutely essential to maintain skeleton operations. Clerks, cooks, bakers, and all other airmen who could be spared for Palomares were alerted by telephone at their base and off-base quarters.

At Torrejón calls to six officers were made by Major W. M. Tooke, Sr., who normally is responsible for the three dependents' schools at the base. Major Tooke ordered them to report immediately at the Torrejón Service Club. He said he could not tell them much of their mission except that they were designated to lead search teams somewhere in the south of Spain. He also told them to alert and assemble their troops for the trip.

Captain Robert E. Finkel, the twenty-nine-year-old commander of the Sixteenth Air Force's headquarters squadron, received Major Tooke's call at his home at the Royal Oaks housing quarters thirty minutes away from Torrejón. Emerging from deep sleep, Bob Finkel was apprised that he was being assigned to Operation Broken Arrow, a move he thought to be immensely appropriate, considering that he had once lived in Broken Arrow, Ohio.

When he arrived at the service club forty-five minutes later, a briefing was in progress. Lieutenant Colonel Vaughn Brock, the Torrejón base controller, gave each officer the command of a bus and forty men for the trip to Palomares. The next hour had to be spent procuring supplies and water. Water containers were the biggest problem. Most of the big jerry cans at Torrejón were used for storing gasoline, and now men had to drain them and wash them out before pouring in the water. Blankets and in-flight meals had to be assembled.

Finally the six blue Air Force buses got under way, with Colonel Brock leading the convoy in his station wagon. Each bus commander was given a "map of sorts," as Bob Finkel put it, and told to proceed to Palomares. Airman First Class John S. Chipouras, a twenty-two-year-old New Yorker, summed up the troops' reactions by asking loudly, "What the hell is Palomares, anyway?"

Aboard bus number four, Captain Finkel told his men as much as he knew of the accident, explaining that they were being sent to Palomares to support General Wilson. In any case, he said reassuringly, this would be a new experience and "a hell of a good way to see Spain."

They started seeing Spain by getting lost ninety minutes out of Torrejón. Crossing a darkened little *pueblo* on the main highway to Albacete, three buses made a wrong turn. By the time they found the highway again, Colonel Brock's car and the first three buses had vanished in the night. Shortly thereafter, one of the buses broke down and forty men had to be reloaded aboard two other buses. Two overcrowded buses, with men sitting and sleeping on the floor, continued their journey through the night. With two more stops en route, one for coffee and one for lunch, Captain Finkel's bus finally reached Palomares at 5 p.m., fourteen hours later, as the dusk was falling over the camp in the riverbed. The caravan from Morón arrived about the same time.

General Wilson now had close to four hundred men on the scene, but the day's startling developments made it painfully clear that at least twice as many troops would be required to cope with the problems of Palomares.

The day's work had started with the small search teams accompanied by Guardias Civiles moving out from the camp around the B-52 tail section and checking the immediate area in the faint hope that the other bombs might have fallen near Weapon No. 1. To mark the ground already covered, the men laid out lengths of twine from one point to another, sometimes one or two miles long. Areas visited by the searchers, who were spotting aircraft wreckage as well as looking for the bombs, were also marked with long garlands of white toilet paper fluttering in the wind from bushes and poles. Everything was still highly improvised, but at least no time was being wasted.

Several helicopters had arrived from Morón early in the morning, and about 9 a.m. General Wilson and General Donovan went up in a chopper for a low-level reconnaissance flight. They hovered over the village, where the inhabitants anxiously peered up at them, and over the tomato fields and the brown sand coastline. The helicopter swung over the Cabezo Negro hills, where the debris was still sending up wisps of smoke, and then toward the pocked sides of Sierra Almagrera. The flight gave the two generals a fair idea of the location of the main pieces of wreckage and impressed upon them even more the extraordinary difficulties of the terrain where their men were searching for the lost bombs.

In Palomares, the villagers faced the new day with growing anxiety and alarm. It was already obvious to them that the invasion of their long-isolated lives by the aerial collision of the day before had not ended with the accident itself—and with their luck in surviving it unscathed—but that new and awesome problems beyond their understanding were only beginning to bedevil them.

The Americans' cars and trucks were rushing through the village and up and down the roads leading to the fields. The men in them looked grim and preoccupied and they spoke no Spanish. In fact, they seemed unaware of the villagers they passed on their way to wherever they were going. Overhead, helicopters were flying low, scaring the sheep and goats out of their wits. They raised clouds of dust when they landed or took off at one spot or another. But what worried the people of Palomares most was the Guardia Civil, blocking access to the fields.

Early in the morning a laborer employed during the harvest by Miguel Castro Navarro walked over to a field outside the village to start picking the ripening tomatoes. But two green-uniformed *guardias* in black patent-leather hats rose from their resting place by the roadside to tell the laborer, gently but firmly, that he could not enter the field.

"But why?" asked the man. "I work for Don Miguel and I have to pick the tomatoes."

"I know you work for Don Miguel," the trooper said. He belonged to the Palomares detachment and knew everybody in the village. "But even so I cannot let you into the field," he added. "These are my orders and nobody told *me* the reason for them."

The laborer walked back to the village and reported to Miguel Castro what had happened. A few minutes earlier Antonio Saviote García had come to Palomares to spread the word that *guardias* had just prevented him from going to his own fields. Miguel Castro Navarro had no choice but to tell his farmhand that if he could not work in the fields he would not get paid his daily wage. It was not that Castro Navarro was a heartless landowner: the economics of Palomares were such that if a man did not work, for whatever reason, he could not get paid. The laborer knew this, but he was stunned. The tomatoes were there to be picked, he had a job, and yet he was not allowed to work and nobody could tell him just why. The economic impact of the Monday collision on Palomares had begun.

Everywhere in the Palomares area the same thing was happening. The patrols of the Guardia had now established a tight cordon around the fields, and nobody was allowed to enter. The sun had not yet risen high in the sky when all economic activity in Palomares ceased. There was no work to be done and no place to go. So the men stood in the village streets, wondering what would happen to their unpicked crops and what would happen to them. And the worst of the Palomares truth was not yet known.

At 10 a.m. an Army helicopter from Morón was hovering over the Cabezo Negro to survey the wreckage-strewn hills. General Wilson had ordered the choppers to overfly the countryside on the theory that it might be possible to spot the bombs or their parachutes from the air. It was a long shot, but Wilson thought it certainly worth trying. And indeed it paid off almost immediately —in one case, at least.

Banking low over the hills south of the cemetery, the pilots noticed a long shiny object protruding from what seemed like a shallow crater at the foot of a hill. The object shimmered in the sun. This was what caught the pilots' attention. The helicopter sat down for a better look. There could be no question that the tubular shape was a hydrogen bomb. It lay on its side in a crater 4 feet deep and 10 feet in diameter. Then the pilots saw that the casing and the warhead were completely split open as if by an explosion. There was no parachute in sight. The pilots radioed the camp that they had located a weapon.

General Wilson immediately jumped into his car to rush to the bomb site with several aides and specialists. As Wilson was racing two miles from his command post to the Cabezo Negro hills, an airman with a search party a half-mile west of the camp stopped to relieve himself by a stone wall at the foot of the terraced knoll known as Rabbit's Rise. He looked to the left, in the direction of Pepé López's house, and saw a bomb protruding from a crater under the embankment. The burned shreds of a parachute lay alongside the missile. The casing was split open. It was 10:30 a.m.

In a sense, the search was progressing unexpectedly well. Three out of four missing hydrogen bombs had been located within twenty-four hours of the accident. Now hopes were soaring that the fourth weapon would be found just as expeditiously.

But no sooner had the Air Force experts had their first good look at the cracked remains of the two hydrogen bombs after they were transported to the riverbed camp than they knew that the United States was facing in Palomares a situation vastly more disturbing than the mere fact that one bomb remained lost.

The situation, briefly, was that the two bombs had suffered explosions of their conventional TNT trigger charges when they hit the ground. The blasts were set off by the action of several of the electrically controlled detonating caps that circle the TNT jacket. When all the caps are triggered electrically—some of the new thermonuclear weapons have as many as forty caps—a TNT implosion, or inward blast, takes place. The implosion serves to compress the plutonium inside the warhead to the point where it becomes critical, and a nuclear reaction starts if the weapon is already armed for it. In a modern plutonium-uranium bomb, the plutonium acts as the trigger, or match, to light the uranium mass and set the fusion phenomenon in motion. But an implosion will not occur, at least in theory, unless all the detonating caps go off simultaneously, which scientists believe to be impossible in an accident. The action by only some caps produces an outward blast. This is what happened with Weapons No. 2 and No. 3 in Palomares.

The outward TNT blasts ruptured the casings around the missiles' warheads. In contact with the air, the exposed radioactive isotopes of uranium-235 (or uranium-238) and of the plutonium-239 trigger became oxidized in the form of tiny particles that were scattered by the wind over wide areas of Palomares. Because particles of both uranium and plutonium oxide emit alpha radiation even in the absence of a nuclear reaction, the Air Force's experts instantly discovered the grim truth that Palomares had been under radioactive contamination for the past twenty-four hours.

What they did not know for the moment, however, was the actual extent of the alpha contamination caused by the TNT explosions inside the two bombs. They did not know the intensity of radiation that still remained in and around Palomares. And, most important, they did not know whether any persons had been exposed to alpha radiation immediately after the accident. If there had been such exposure, then it was urgent to find these people and try to determine the degree of their contamination. Preliminary monitoring with the few PAC-1S instruments that General Wilson had available at that time did confirm the existence of intense alpha radiations around the impact areas of Weapon No. 2 and Weapon No. 3. In the very "hot" areas near the craters, the instruments registered 2 million alpha emission counts per minute, which is as far as the needle on a PAC-1S will go. Weapon No. 1, which fell in the riverbed, did not crack and therefore offered no radioactive danger.

Since no nuclear explosions had evidently occurred, the United States did not have to be concerned with contamination by potentially lethal beta and gamma rays. These forms of radiation resulting from nuclear fission or fusion were responsible for the radiological deaths and sickness after the 1945 atomic attacks on Hiroshima and Nagasaki. Among other effects, they may lower the body's leucocyte—white blood cell—count below survival levels, cause genetic mutations, and induce sterility. An immediate check with Geiger counters established that none of this easily detectable radiation was present around Palomares. But even alpha radiation presented quite a problem and quite a danger to the population.

The chief danger to the village came from the bombs' plutonium, which is one of the most toxic substances known to man. It oxidizes quickly in the air, turning into fine particles which do not readily cling to a surface as is the case with uranium. Instead, plutonium particles tend to travel through the air.

Because of this peculiarity, particles of plutonium may be easily inhaled by persons who find themselves in its path. This is plutonium's greatest single hazard. While Pu-239 will not penetrate unbroken skin and has limited effects through ingestion into the stomach, it may well produce plutonium poisoning and then various types of sarcoma—cancer—as a result of inhalation. It may also be dangerous if it enters the body through cuts or open wounds.

In the twenty-six years of studies of plutonium—the substance was discovered in 1940—it has been established that from the lungs it moves to the respiratory lymph nodes and then deposits itself predominantly in the skeleton and the liver. Because plutonium's biological half-life is about 200 years (its radiological half-life is 24,400 years), a person inhaling it in doses equal to, or exceeding, the maximum permissible body burden would retain 90 per cent of it in his skeleton fifty years later. In other words, the plutonium lodged in a person's skeleton would emit cancer-causing alpha radiations indefinitely.

But this is where current knowledge ends. Inasmuch as only twenty-two years have elapsed since plutonium came into industrial use for the production of the first atomic bombs during World War II, it is not yet known what may really happen to persons who have inhaled more than the maximum permissible amount of three-fifths of a microgram (three-fifths of one millionth part of a gram). Because plutonium's radioactive poisoning effects are similar to those of radium, scientists accept a twelve- to thirty-year delay between actual exposure and the appearance of the first symptoms of chronic radiation damage, presumably cancer. For this reason, scientists think, no case of plutonium poisoning has thus far been registered among the fifty-odd persons in the Western world who are suspected of having accumulated three-fifths of a microgram or more of plutonium in the course of industrial or weapon-handling work.

This, then, was the state of affairs facing the United States in Palomares when it became apparent that two of the hydrogen bombs had cracked and spewed radioactive plutonium about the countryside. It was fraught with still unknown and unmeasured dangers for the population and it carried staggering psychological and political implications for the United States in its relations with Spain and the rest of the world.

The stark fact was that the United States had accidentally spilled a load of hydrogen bombs over the territory of a friendly nation and, in the process, had radioactively contaminated a Spanish village. Although the long spectacular search for a missing bomb was to overshadow the village's radioactivity problem in public opinion, the contamination was in reality the most significant nuclear-age situation to emerge from the whole Palomares experience.

In fact, Palomares was the second nuclear-age experience in which civilians have been collectively exposed to radiation since the first atomic bombs were dropped on Hiroshima and Nagasaki in 1945.

There have been industrial and laboratory radiation accidents involving individuals exposed to plutonium, such as the one at the Chalk River facility of the Canadian Atomic Energy Establishment in 1950 and another at the Harwell plant of the British Atomic Energy Authority in 1952.

In the crash of parts of a nuclear weapon on top of a house in Florence, South Carolina, in 1958, the TNT exploded, causing damage and injuring six persons. But, as far as is known, there was no plutonium or any other form of contamination. For one thing, it is not certain that the Florence weapon was a thermonuclear bomb with a plutonium trigger. In the accidents in Georgia and North Carolina in 1958 and 1961, in which SAC bombers crashed, spilling their nuclear weapons, there were no known explosions and thus there was no radiological contamination. No radioactive mishap developed when a SAC bomber laden with nuclear bombs burned on the runway of an air base in Morocco. Other publicly unreported nuclear accidents occurred harmlessly throughout the United States and in the Arctic. While there was radioactive leakage in connection with a Palomares-type weapon accident in Wichita, Kansas, it was promptly controlled by the SAC crews on base and no outsiders were exposed. And during 1965 there were thirty-eight cases of misplaced radioactive materials, mainly for industrial use, but, according to the AEC, no significant radiation hazards arose.

But prior to Palomares one major instance in the Western world of group exposure to radiation, a tragic one, had occurred in the two decades of the nuclear age. Cynical—or realistic—scientists say that this is an excellent batting average when one considers the tremendous proliferation of nuclear weapons and installations in the intervening years.

This first instance was the deep contamination of the Japanese tuna-fishing boat *Daigo Fukuryu Maru—Lucky Dragon No. 5—* by the radioactive-ash fallout from a United States thermonuclear test detonation in the Pacific on March 1, 1954. The *Lucky Dragon* and its 23 crewmen found themselves 87 miles from the Bikini atoll, apparently just outside the restricted area, just as a 15-megaton hydrogen weapon burst on the surface in the Bravo test of the Castle series. It was the second hydrogen "superbomb" explosion ever staged by the United States—the first was the Mike 10.4-megaton test blast of the Ivy series on Eniwetok on October 31, 1952—and its yield was the highest that Washington has ever admitted obtaining in any test. The Soviet Union detonated an incredibly powerful 58-megaton thermonuclear bomb over Novaya Zemlya on October 30, 1961, but the United States never disclosed the power of any of the 73 devices it blew up in the Pacific between the Bravo test and August 1963, when the test-ban treaty was signed.

Not only did the 15 megatons of the Bravo explosion represent 750 times the power of each of the bombs dropped on Hiroshima and Nagasaki but something evidently went wrong in terms of fallout and radioactivity. President Eisenhower told a press conference three weeks later that scientists were surprised and astonished at the results of the blast and that "something must have happened that we never had experienced in previous tests."

Thus, 28 United States government personnel and 236 civilian residents of the Marshall Islands were exposed to varying degrees of radiation, though apparently without serious consequences.

And when the *Lucky Dragon* reached its home port of Yaizu in southern Japan on March 14, its entire crew was suffering from various types of radiation sickness. Most of them had turned a dark lead color, and several lost their hair. Hospital tests showed an alarming drop in their leucocyte count, and all of them became sterile. The vessel's radio operator, Aikichi Kuboyama, died six months later after a long and terrible illness that may well have been a direct result of radiological contamination.

The United States refused to reveal the precise composition of the radioactive ash that fell on the *Lucky Dragon,* which was in keeping with its policy of secrecy in the nuclear field, though some of its own officials were severely critical of this attitude. There was some feeling that a disclosure might have assisted in the treatment of the fishermen, and even possibly saved Kuboyama's life, without actually endangering United States security. Washington also stubbornly sought to play down the importance of the *Lucky Dragon* incident, in terms both of the fishermen's health and of the economic losses caused by radioactive contamination of fish. In the end, it gave a check to Kuboyama's widow and voluntarily paid $2 million in over-all compensation.

In many of these attitudes the United States was unknowingly setting the pattern for its reactions when the Palomares crisis, the first instance of exposure to plutonium contamination from a hydrogen bomb, came, nearly twelve years later.

Yet the United States had not been altogether unprepared for such a contingency. And, true to the whole pattern of the Palomares experience, luck was again with both the village and the United States.

In the first place, the Palomares drama was the type of nuclear-age accident the United States had anticipated for over ten years while hoping it would never happen. As a nuclear power engaged in the business of flying thermonuclear bombs around the world as part of its Cold War deterrent policy, the United States obviously had to be ready to react effectively in case of any foreseeable accident or combination of accidents.

Contingencies of accidental losses of nuclear weapons, of fires and TNT explosions in handling or in air accidents have been carefully studied and prepared. Additional safeguards against unauthorized or accidental nuclear bursts were provided in the electromechanical permissive-action links installed on weapons beginning in 1961. And, specifically, the type of situation that hit Palomares on January 17, 1966, had been anticipated—and feared—since 1955, when the first tests to simulate it were staged in Nevada.

Between 1955 and 1963 four separate sets of experiments with plutonium, simulating accidental spillings of the Pu-239, were conducted at the Nevada test site. A major test, known as Project 57, was held in 1957. Another realistic test, Operation Roller Coaster, was conducted in 1963 in a joint experiment with Britain in exploding four atomic devices. During Project 57 a kilogram of plutonium was detonated, though without a nuclear reaction, to provide proper test conditions.

The Nevada tests taught the United States a great deal about the behavior of plutonium and uranium in the wake of accidental TNT explosions. The experience gained in Nevada suggested the sophisticated containment and decontamination techniques that were to be put in effect immediately in Palomares. To study the effects of plutonium particles and alpha radiation on living organisms, animals were exposed to plutonium clouds in a series of biological experiments. Some of these animals were put to death at once, and scientists were able to determine the amounts of plutonium deposited in their lungs and other tissues. Other animals were allowed to live in the contaminated areas for six to twelve months without any attempt at decontaminating them. Only then was the plutonium in their tissues measured.

In the laboratories of the Atomic Energy Commission, rats, mice, rabbits, pigs, and beagle dogs were injected with citrates of plutonium. All these experiments provided vital information on the hazards of plutonium for animals, generally proving that cancer will develop through either inhalation or injection in large doses. For example, a dog injected with a plutonium compound at the radiobiology laboratory of the University of Utah developed osteogenic sarcoma—bone cancer—approximately four years later as a gourdlike growth formed on the bone of its right foreleg. In other instances, lung fibrosis and liver damage were observed in plutonium-injected Utah beagles.

While the studies on animals permitted projections on the effects of plutonium on human beings, the scientists supplemented them with experiments with people. Beginning as early as 1945, tests were made with sixteen terminal human patients to determine the rate of retention and excretion of plutonium. The hospital patients selected for these plutonium experiments were individuals over the age of forty-five whose illnesses made survival for more than ten years highly improbable. These tests contributed additional knowledge, but to this day there is no known satisfactory method of assessing plutonium body burden, particularly in the lung tissues. In short, then, a case of plutonium poisoning may be impossible to diagnose accurately. When Palomares finally did happen, the United States possessed a considerable, if incomplete, body of knowledge concerning the behavior and effects of plutonium. At the least, the experts knew with what they were dealing.

An accident that the United States had both feared and anticipated for a decade, Palomares became the first classic case of plutonium contamination. But in the way in which real life situations always differ from rehearsals, it presented deep differences from the simulated exercises in Nevada. Everything could not be anticipated or imagined and, as it turned out, improvisations were needed. As an important AEC scientist remarked on being apprised of conditions in Palomares, "Accidents seldom occur when and where it is the most convenient, and under the circumstances one can never anticipate all his needs."

The first difference was, of course, that the Palomares accident took place in a populated area and that human beings, not test animals, might have been exposed to the plutonium clouds. To compound matters, the populated area was in a foreign country. The second difference was that, while it is one thing to understand the effects of plutonium's alpha radiation, it is another thing to face the possibility that a number of innocent people, including children, may have been poisoned and condemned to a slow cancer death ten, twenty, or thirty years hence. The third difference was that, while the Nevada tests were conducted on level, sandy desert, the Palomares accident happened in unusually difficult hilly terrain grown over with tomato vines and other vegetation on which plutonium particles tended to accumulate at a higher rate.

And, finally, the over-all implications of the contamination of a Spanish village by the United States were obviously tremendous, particularly with the uncertainty over what had really occurred in the last twenty-four hours. Had any of the Palomares people been caught in the path of the two plutonium clouds? Had any of them inhaled dangerous quantities of plutonium? All these questions weighed heavily over General Wilson and the SAC specialists after their discovery that toxic plutonium from the two cracked hydrogen bombs was loose around Palomares.

The foresight of General Ryan, the boss of SAC, paid off on that tense morning. The immediate assignment from Offutt to Spain of Colonel Rhodes, the chief of SAC Ordnance Disposal, and of Colonel Norcross, the nuclear-safety specialist from the Air Force's Nuclear Medicine Division, provided General Wilson with top-level expert advice in the rapidly developing and immensely confusing situation. The two colonels, rushed to Spain aboard the first KC-135 emergency flight from Offutt, were on hand in Palomares just as the damaged bombs were found. They had gone more than twenty-four hours with virtually no sleep, flying from Nebraska to Torrejón and then to San Javier, and finally motoring the last three hours to Palomares.

The experts and General Wilson presently diagnosed the three factors in the situation that showed again how incredibly luck was on the side of the Americans and of the village of Palomares.

The first factor was the wind on the day of the accident, a blessing in disguise. While the actual scattering of plutonium and uranium particles after the TNT explosions occurred in a small area—perhaps 100 to 150 feet from the impact point of the two weapons—the strong wind instantly carried them a considerable distance, but in the right direction. The wind's chief blessing was that it was blowing to the southeast, thus carrying the plutonium cloud toward uninhabited areas and past only a few houses.

In any case, Weapon No. 2 had fallen in the empty hills of Cabezo Negro, and most of the brown-black cloud of plutonium particles lost itself in the rocky desert. It barely touched the houses along the Vera Highway, where the Ponces and their neighbors live, and it was highly diluted by the time its remains drifted to the outskirts of the village. Weapon No. 3, however, had dropped in the middle of a cluster of houses, and if it had not been for a combination of lucky breaks the contamination might have been exceedingly high there. As it was, the dark cloud seen by Pepé López after the TNT blast was quickly carried east over an uninhabited valley where only a few farmers were at work in the fields, and the dry bed of the Almanzora River, toward Sierra Almagrera. Inevitably, some contamination affected the *cortijos* (farm compounds) of Pepé López and Eduardo Navarro Portillo, which were directly in the line of travel of the scattering plutonium particles. But the bulk of them spared the populated areas. Had the wind been blowing to the northeast, as it often does in Palomares, the village would have received the full impact of radioactive alpha particles. Chaos, if not tragedy, would have struck with them. That the dispersal pattern of the plutonium clouds was toward unpopulated areas was rapidly established by General Wilson's specialists from the radiological decontamination teams as they inched on their knees around the bombs' craters with the gray PAC-1S alpha oscillator counters.

The second factor of luck was the nature of the TNT explosions. Weapon No. 2, which blew up in the desert hills of Cabezo Negro after landing without its parachute, suffered a detonation of its full 44-pound charge of TNT. The scattering of plutonium from the hydrogen bomb's warhead was thus complete. But in Weapon No. 3, which landed on Rabbit's Rise with a partially burned parachute, only one-half of the TNT exploded. Whether because the parachute somewhat slowed down the bomb's descent or for other reasons, the actual blast caused virtually no damage or harm to the neighborhood houses and their inhabitants. And, more important, the scattering of plutonium particles from the warhead was relatively reduced, even though the fallout from the cloud reached the mountains of Sierra Almagrera more than a mile away. Had the full 44 pounds of TNT blown up at Site No. 2, Pedro de la Torre Flores, the self-possessed octogenarian, might have received serious injury and the López and Navarro houses might have been damaged beyond a few broken window panes and a torn door lock. And it was a matter of conjecture how much worse the whole area would have fared in terms of radiological contamination.

The third lucky factor involving the nuclear weapons in Palomares was a seeming contradiction. This was the good fortune that the impact velocity of the two cracked bombs—the speed at which they were falling from the sky—was high, presumably because one of them had lost its parachute and the other came down with a burned silk. This high velocity may have been responsible for the TNT detonations in the first place, although they might have happened anyway when the bombs hit rocky ground. But as long as the bombs did blow up, it was lucky that the high velocity of the falling weapons delayed the detonations until the nose cones containing the plutonium and the TNT were buried in the ground. This way, a large amount of dirt was thrown up in the cloud along with the plutonium particles. The finest and therefore the most dangerous of the particles then mixed with the larger dust fragments and fell rapidly near the bombs' impact points.

Thus Palomares' combination of luck was that the two bombs fell at high velocity, that only one-half of the TNT charge blew up in the weapon near the López and Navarro houses, that plutonium particles and dirt blended in the toxic clouds, and that the wind was mercifully blowing in the right direction. Furthermore, because the wind on January 17 was strong, the time of the clouds' passage was short and the rate of atmospheric dilution of the plutonium was greater. All this was an immensely happy combination of circumstances because plutonium's biggest danger is to the people who may be immediately downwind at the time of cloud passage.

Dr. Wright H. Langham of the AEC, who may well be the world's leading authority on plutonium behavior and hazards, a man who was to play a crucial role in directing the Palomares decontamination operations, was to say later that "had the weapon that impacted on the very edge of the community [the bomb between the López and the Navarro farmhouses] impacted and detonated at low velocity with a gentle breeze blowing directly toward the village, the drama of Palomares might have been decidedly more grim." Dr. Langham did not question the subsequent conviction of Father Navarete, the village priest, that "the hand of God" had saved Palomares. But he whimsically remarked that "another way of looking at it is that the laws of probability occasionally, but not often, let a gambler fill an inside straight." So there it was: divine protection, science's laws of probability, and gambler's luck combining to save Palomares from an unpredictable fate.

That Palomares was spared a major disaster did not allay the fears of the American specialists over potential and extremely serious health hazards in the village. They knew that a number of villagers and civil guards had been near the two cracked bombs within a three-hour period following the TNT detonations and the scattering of plutonium. Realizing that the period between thirty minutes and three hours after the formation of a plutonium plume is the most dangerous, the American experts had to accept the grim possibility that some, if not all, of these Spaniards had been exposed to the particles and might have inhaled them. The second possibility was that some villagers might have been downwind of the two plutonium clouds drifting from the bomb sites. There had been people in the houses and the fields below Cabezo Negro at the time of the explosion, and the edge of the cloud could conceivably have reached them, even if it was already considerably diluted. A number of persons were also known to have been working in the fields in the valley extending between Rabbit's Rise, where Weapon No. 3 fell, and Sierra Almagrera.

The dangers involved in such a situation had been amply demonstrated during the AEC's Nevada tests in 1957 and 1963. Test measurements at the Nevada site showed that individuals remaining 500 feet from a non-critically detonated bomb during the first three hours would have received the maximum permissible lung burden of plutonium. At the same time, "significant" air concentrations of plutonium particles were recorded as far as 5000 feet downwind from the point of detonation. The published conclusions of the AEC scientists after these tests stressed that "the observed [radiological] levels definitely indicate a significant acute inhalation hazard to firefighters and rescue crews . . . respirators would be necessary during such operations."

The Nevada tests were primarily concerned with the effects of plutonium on firefighters and rescue crews in accidents during the handling of nuclear weapons. The assumption was that protective equipment would be available for containment operations and that no unauthorized persons would be in the vicinity of an explosion site. But in Palomares on January 17 there were no safety experts, no trained crews, and no protective equipment. Instead, there were well-meaning and courageous civilian and police volunteer rescuers totally unaware of the nature of the accident, numerous casual bystanders who simply wanted to see what had happened, and an unknown number of villagers in Palomares and the surrounding fields who might have breathed in the invisible plutonium particles. There also was Pepé López, the inquisitive shopkeeper who went to inspect the bomb and kick over the fire, but General Wilson and his advisers had not yet heard about him. Reminiscing later over the events of the first days in Palomares, one of the general's aides remarked that "at least we could preserve that much of our peace of mind."

In sum, the American group, keeping their disturbing knowledge to themselves, could conclude at this point that in terms of possible human contamination the worst in Palomares had obviously already happened in the first thirty minutes after the accident, or long before it was known that anything at all had happened. One of the most urgent tasks ahead, therefore, was to try to determine just what this worst might be.

The second task, and a formidable one, would be to determine the extent of plutonium contamination in and around Palomares and to proceed at once with the clean-up. If plutonium particles are left untouched in a contaminated area, a grave hazard remains indefinitely. Depending on the terrain and wind, the toxic particles may become in varying degrees resuspended in the air and again present a danger of inhalation and cancer-threatening poisoning. With Palomares' droughts and consequent dry soil and dust, and with its frequent winds, the chances of resuspension were high. And with plutonium's incredibly long biological and radiological half-lives, the particles would go on emitting their cancer-causing alpha emissions. There would be, to be sure, a considerable dilution, but nobody could be sure of its degree.

Palomares' tomato vines and other vegetation would also favor plutonium resuspension. While American specialists discounted the poisonous hazards of plutonium particles ingested with tomatoes or other crops, they were not prepared to take chances with them. And, finally, there was always the possibility that a farmer with a cut or an open wound would brush against contaminated soil or vegetation, with disastrous consequences for his health.

But even under the best scientific conditions, the United States simply could not leave behind a radiologically contaminated area. Political common sense and decency forbade it. Besides, the Spanish government would soon be apprised in detail of the extent and implications of the Palomares accident, and clearly it would insist that the Americans, having dropped hydrogen bombs over a Spanish village, restore the area to normal and fully safe conditions. As was to develop, the Spaniards had very strong notions about what constituted fully safe conditions.

A painstaking decontamination operation would have to be launched with the greatest dispatch. But first it was necessary to determine the limits of the contaminated ground. Before noon struck in Palomares, Colonel Norcross, the Air Force's nuclear-medicine specialist, told General Wilson that he must proceed immediately with the establishment of a "zero line," the outer boundary of contamination. He may not have realized what a tremendous task it was going to be.

The outside world, still remote from Palomares, went on ignoring the quiet drama that now was taking shape in the little Spanish village on the sunny Mediterranean coast. The speculation by the news agencies the day before that nuclear weapons might have been carried and lost by the huge B-52 bomber somehow failed to impress greatly a world that had long ago become accustomed to the nuclear age. And, of course, the United States government was doing nothing to advertise the accident. At Torrejón the Sixteenth Air Force limited itself on the day after the accident to issuing a communiqué giving only the names of the dead and the survivors in the aerial collision. In Washington, however, the Defense and State Departments closely and worriedly followed the Top Secret reports from Spain. The Defense Department granted a top priority to General Wilson's logistic and personnel requirements for Palomares. At the State Department the seventh-floor Operations Center, the special section handling hot situations, moved in on the Spanish problem. Only a handful of men in Washington, Madrid, and Palomares knew the full truth.

In the dusty village the instinct and imagination of the Andalusian peasants were making up for what they lacked in actual and specific knowledge. Excited talk of strange weapons and death rays was rife in the three Palomares bars where the men started gathering in midmorning. Unable to go to work in their fields, they whiled the time away at the taverns of Tomás Mula, Tomás Alarcón, and Antonio Saez, exchanging information, impressions, and gossip. And their concern was rising. Some of the January tomato crop was already in the warehouse in the lower part of the village, but most of it was still on the vines, and the farmers were afraid the tomatoes would spoil if they were left unpicked much longer. Several men told of trying to enter their fields to bring grass and alfalfa fodder for the cows they had in sheds near their houses and of being turned away by the *guardias*. In Palomares, milch cows, three or four to a family, are kept in barns and sheds because there are no proper pastures in the fields and because they must be kept away from the tomatoes and other cash crops. But if feed could not be brought to the cows, they would soon stop producing milk and starve gradually. Selling milk to Vera and Cuevas wholesalers was one of the sources of revenue for many Palomares families, and now this too was being threatened.

At the bar of Tomás Mula behind the village square, the talk was of yesterday's collision and the awesome things the planes might have been carrying, when José Manuel Gonzáles Fernandez walked in and asked for a San Miguel beer. Gonzáles had turned overnight into a truly important personage, the man who was dealing with the Americans. This new role vastly exceeded his limited prerogatives of *alcalde pedaño,* part-time mayor, of Palomares, and even the fact that he was wealthy. Since yesterday afternoon American officers, including the two generals, had been consulting with Gonzáles, deferentially asking his views on the situation in the village, and seeking his assistance in organizing their camp and their activities. It was already widely known in Palomares that Manuel Gonzáles had free access to the one-room office the Americans had set up above the general store in the square.

On entering Mula's bar, therefore, Gonzáles was at once surrounded by the worried men. Questions were fired at him anxiously, loudly, and chaotically. What was happening in Palomares? Why were the *guardias* closing the fields? Why were the Americans going into everybody's fields without asking permission, even where there were no pieces of the airplanes? Why were they wearing masks and gloves? Was it true about the terrible weapons lost in Palomares? When could the people of the *pueblo* go back to work?

José Manuel Gonzáles, a portly and somewhat officious man, held up his hands for silence. His own knowledge of the situation was not much greater than the villagers', but now his prestige and authority were at stake.

"Bueno," he said, taking a long swallow of beer. "The situation indeed is complicated. The Americans and the captain of the Guardia have told me certain things, but they were said in confidence because I am an official of the *comarca* government. Therefore, I must keep the confidence."

Gonzáles was sweating profusely and he paused to drink more of his beer. A murmur of voices rose in the bar. Gonzáles again held up his hands.

"But I can tell you this," he said. "The situation is completely under control and very soon everything will be back to normal. The Americans will find the things they lost yesterday and they will go away. They will pay us for all the damage. And all of us will be able to return to our fields. I'm telling you the truth. You people know that my fields too have been closed and my tomatoes too are rotting."

There was silence in Tomás Mula's bar. If Gonzáles was indeed telling the truth, this was good news. And the men in the crowded room desperately wanted to believe him and to be convinced that their suspicions and instincts were wrong.

But from a corner of the tavern an elderly man asked what Gonzáles could tell them of all these strange bombs that people were talking about. Since the evening before, old Pedro de la Torre Flores had been busily spreading the story of how a tremendous explosion had hurled him to the ground and nearly killed him. Pepé López had visited the bar earlier and told awed and hushed friends how he had put out the fire around a big bomb and kicked the bomb for good measure. The people who lived around Cabezo Negro had also heard a loud explosion and seen a bomb. And news traveled fast in the village, where most of the families were related to one another—Palomares was full of people named Flores, López, Navarro, or de la Torre—or knew one another well.

Like everybody else, Gonzáles had heard all these stories, but he did not know the truth behind them because the Americans refused to discuss the subject with him. Again that morning he had put questions to General Donovan when he saw him in the upstairs office, and again Donovan had quickly changed the subject. But Gonzáles, the Americans' trusted man, could not publicly admit his ignorance.

"*Hombre*," he said mysteriously, "this is one of the subjects of confidence and I am not permitted to talk about it."

He finished his beer quickly and picked up his hat from the counter. "I must go now," he said. "The general is waiting for me. *Adios*."

The men said *adios* and went back to their conversations. Tomás Mula was busily pouring beer and brandy. He and his fellow bar-owners in Palomares were already becoming the principal beneficiaries of the village drama. Idleness and need for swapping news and rumors were making the Palomares men flock into the three taverns. And the American airmen were beginning to drop in for quick beers to kill their thirst. Tomás Mula made a mental note to send a boy into Vera to order more beer for tomorrow. Someone turned on the big television set in the corner of the bar, but the lunchtime newscast dealt only with the inauguration of a new tourist hotel somewhere in the south, a blizzard in Paris, and the war in Vietnam. There was nothing about Palomares.

At María Badillo's house, near where the B-52 wing and landing gear had fallen, Father Navarete was paying a visit, as he had been doing all morning and the previous afternoon all over the village. Father Navarete felt his duty was to be in Palomares as much as possible, and he had obtained the permission of Don Enrique Arriaga, his Cuevas superior, to neglect for a while the other villages of the parish. At the Badillos' he was telling the family, as he had done in all the homes he visited, that the strong wind on the day of the accident was "the hand of God spreading over Palomares" and preventing the planes' debris from killing or injuring people or damaging houses. He had no way of knowing yet, of course, that God's hand had performed a second miracle in blowing most of the toxic plutonium clouds away from the village.

Father Navarete's metaphysical explanations were designed as much to calm the scared villagers as to score a useful theological point. Word had already gone around Palomares that the Americans and the Guardia Civil were temporarily evacuating eight families from their homes—the Spanish policemen were enforcing the recommendations of the American specialists—and some of the villagers were sending their children away to stay with relatives in other hamlets and towns. The two elementary schools, attended in two shifts by 125 Palomares children, did not open that morning because the Americans wanted the area around the aircraft debris to remain clear. Anyway, mothers kept their children at home and almost none were seen in the streets.

Father Navarete, therefore, took upon himself the mission of reassuring and calming the villagers when nobody else was available to do so. The Guardia Civil was too busy with its police work, and besides, policemen are seldom seen anywhere as a soothing influence in a crisis. Manuel Gonzáles was tied up with the Americans, and he too lacked the personal touch the priest could offer the worried Palomares mothers. In calming the population, Father Navarete used the argument that since God had shown His affection for Palomares by saving it from holocaust the day before, He would not now turn away from His flock in the village. It was an argument that would stand him in good stead a few days later.

In a nearby house someone turned on the radio. It blasted forth Barry McGuire's rendition of "Eve of Destruction," for some reason a top favorite of Spanish disk jockeys.

Aware since shortly before noon that a major problem of plutonium contamination existed in Palomares, General Wilson now had a three-ring circus in the making. A part of his force had to be instantly switched to intensive radiological monitoring with the PAC-1S instruments while another concentrated on a fingertip-to-fingertip search over the Palomares countryside for the missing fourth hydrogen bomb. Some men were assigned to the collection and classification of aircraft debris that was scattered all over the countryside. There were Top Secret components in the widely spread wreckage, and General Wilson was anxious to recover them too.

Wilson was woefully ill-equipped for this monumental triple task. He had to run his operations from a field tent in the riverbed camp with an orange crate serving as a desk and another as a chair. His communications facilities consisted of a deficient single-sideband radio link with Torrejón, but he could not use it for classified information because anyone with a good radio receiver could eavesdrop on him. And General Wilson was not prepared to tell the world that Palomares was radiologically contaminated and that a hydrogen bomb was lost somewhere ashore or in the Mediterranean. During the day it had been necessary for him to send couriers by road to San Javier and then by plane to Torrejón so that secret information could be safely radioed to SAC at Offutt and to the Pentagon.

Reinforcements were beginning to stream in from Morón and Torrejón—including the five wayward buses with the headquarters troops—but there still were severe limitations on how they could be used. Airmen, among whom were cooks and clerks, had to be taught the handling of the PAC-1S alpha oscillation counters. Thus far there were only three radiological decontamination teams on hand, and extra men were needed to work with the counters to mark the hot radioactivity spots and begin to trace the zero line.

There was still a shortage of vehicles to move the men around. And, worst of all, there were no adequate maps on which to plan a rational air and ground search for the lost bomb. When he first reached Palomares, General Wilson had had only road maps of Almería province. Captain Calín's *guardias* unsuccessfully looked for better maps until five o'clock in the morning. But when on the second day more detailed maps were finally procured, it turned out they were useless for General Wilson's purposes because Spain uses Madrid as a zero meridian instead of Greenwich. There would be complete confusion between the references on Spanish maps and those of the United States Air Force. General Wilson therefore had no choice but to ask the headquarters of United States Air Forces, Europe, in Wiesbaden, Germany for reconnaissance photo-mapping flights. The photo jets began sweeping over Palomares that same afternoon, but it was to be two more days before the charts could be assembled and reproduced, making it possible for General Wilson to launch a well-coordinated search.

Intelligence-gathering efforts were ordered simultaneously. Captain Joseph Ramirez, a Spanish-speaking officer of the Sixteenth Air Force, was sent on Tuesday morning to Aguilas to talk to the fishermen who had rescued the B-52 fliers the day before. General Wilson had the correct hunch that interviews with fishermen might yield useful information.

Captain Ramirez met Francisco Simó Orts at the Aguilas naval station and engaged in the delicate task of interrogating the fishing skipper about the day before, without indicating what he was trying to find out. Official instructions were that nuclear weapons, missing or not, were not to be discussed with outsiders, and thus Joe Ramirez was stuck with a major semantic problem. In any event, the combination of his skillful interrogation and Simó's garrulousness produced the information that the Spaniard had observed a "half-man" strapped to a parachute coming down into the sea. There also was a second parachute, he said. Simó recollected that the "half-man" had no legs. Anyway, he told Ramirez, "something was hanging down" from the parachute. Joe Ramirez pursued his questioning. What was the color of the parachute? Was it a solid panel or did it have colored ribbons that fliers use? What was the shape of the parachute? But Simó was vague on the points that could provide additional clues. It all happened so fast, he told Ramirez; though he thought the "half-man" was on a gray-white chute. However, he was able to show Ramirez on a map, using triangulation, the place where he thought the two parachutes had sunk. He insisted it was five miles offshore.

Around the village, General Wilson's officers worked through interpreters, gingerly interviewing farmers. Several villagers said they had seen parachutes over the sea, but the Americans realized these could have been the downed fliers. In a Cuevas bar a deaf-and-dumb shepherd conveyed through his brother to another officer the information that he had seen a parachute float down near the riverbed and that it had scared his sheep into a panic. But the interrogation with finger signs made it reasonably certain that the shepherd was referring to the already recovered first weapon.

At 5:30 p.m., as the day's search operations were drawing to a close with the oncoming dusk, a United States Navy ship appeared off Palomares and announced her presence by signal. She was the USS *Kiowa*, number ATF-72, a fleet ocean tug. The *Kiowa* was the vanguard of what was later to become a major naval task force, but for the moment General Wilson was uncertain what to do with her. He had his hands full ashore, and the Navy had not yet been formally assigned to the bomb search. A ship had been requested the day before by the Sixteenth Air Force as a precautionary measure, and the Sixth Fleet headquarters at Naples had sent the *Kiowa*, which happened to be in the general vicinity.

Darkness fell over Palomares, and General Wilson sadly concluded that the fourth hydrogen bomb was definitely missing and that it could conceivably be a long time before it was found. Both the nature of the topography of Palomares and the intelligence obtained from the fishermen in Aguilas made him fear that the United States was in for a lengthy search ashore and in the sea.

In his tent in the riverbed camp, Wilson drafted a report to this effect to his SAC superiors. Because the single-sideband radio link with Torrejón was unreliable, he dispatched an aide to Vera to call the base command from the public telephone station and relay the report in code.

It was a strange footnote to the nuclear age that it took forty minutes for the call reporting the loss of a hydrogen bomb to go through. And when the call finally came, the officer in Vera and the officer in Torrejón could not hear each other and in the end they were disconnected. At the Vera telephone station, where the living quarters of the operator are combined with his office, a radio was playing a current French favorite with the refrain warning that *"un jour, à Vietnam, Cuba où ailleurs, on poussera un bouton de trop"*—"one day, in Vietnam, in Cuba, or elsewhere, they will push one button too many." But the world remained oblivious of Palomares, its bombs, and its drama.

In the end, the world learned of the Palomares bombs and of the radioactivity in the village from an enterprising twenty-five-year-old United Press International reporter named Andró del Amo. It was inevitable that the "curtain of silence" over the Almería accident would be rent sooner or later, and the Pentagon's obsession with total secrecy served only to create confusion and alarm where they could have been avoided with an intelligent public-information policy. You simply cannot spill radioactivity over a populated area in a foreign country, misplace a hydrogen bomb, and hope that nobody will notice it when hundreds of troops are rushed in to undertake search and decontamination procedures with equipment that spells nuclear weapons even to the most ignorant layman. When a large naval task force later anchored off Palomares, the Pentagon fiction that there was nothing amiss in the area in terms of nuclear bombs became even more transparent and unavoidably exposed the United States to ridicule.

As it was, Andró del Amo happened to be the man who shattered the veil of secrecy over Palomares two days after the air accident. Del Amo, a bilingual native of Los Angeles, California, was the first Madrid-based foreign correspondent to go to Palomares. He left by car late in the evening of Tuesday, January 18, as speculation over a nuclear accident in Palomares grew increasingly intense in the UPI's Madrid office.

Del Amo, whose brother Tito owns a house in Mojácar, the

reconstructed Moorish town near Palomares, had volunteered for the assignment. Leo White, a veteran writer for the London *Daily Mirror,* who was in Madrid on vacation, told his friends at the UPI that evening that he would be driving to Palomares, even though most other reporters believed the story was over and it was not worth undertaking the punishing trip to Almería. Del Amo said on the spur of the moment that he too would like to go. Harry Stathos, the UPI Madrid Bureau chief, agreed at once that del Amo should go. The possibility of nuclear weapons in Palomares had been on his mind for two days, but he could only speculate on it so long as the Sixteenth Air Force at Torrejón and the American embassy stubbornly clung to their official "no comment" policy. But if his suspicion was well founded, Stathos reasoned, a reporter on the scene could not fail to come upon some indications to confirm it. Oddly enough, the thought of sending a reporter to Palomares had not yet occurred to any of the other wire-service bureau chiefs in Madrid. None of the numerous foreign correspondents representing United States and European newspapers, magazines, and radio and television networks in the Spanish capital had thought of going to the accident site either. Like everything else in reporting, it was a question of instinct, and on that evening Stathos and del Amo evidently had instinct in ample supply.

After driving all night, Andró del Amo and Leo White reached Palomares at 6:30 a.m. on Wednesday, January 19. Del Amo had been to the area three years earlier when he visited his brother in Mojácar and he was vaguely familiar with the local geography. Turning onto a dirt road from the Vera Highway, they came upon the KC-135 engines lying on a hillside. Nobody was there, and del Amo shot a few photographs of the twisted motors. About 7 a.m., as the winter sun was rising over the hills, a helicopter flew overhead. In the village, the two reporters examined the wreckage of the B-52's landing gear near the boys' school. Nobody disturbed them. There were Guardia Civil patrols at the main Palomares intersection, but they did not challenge the reporters' car. A villager told del Amo that the Americans' main camp was in the Almanzora riverbed and gave him directions.

The road from the village to the river crosses fields and skirts several *cortijos*—farmhouses—of neighborhood families. Driving up the road, del Amo suddenly slammed on his brakes. As he said later, he became "very excited" by what he saw. Long lines of American airmen in fatigues or bright yellow coveralls were moving through the fields, beating the bushes, tomato vines, and clumps of vegetation with long sticks and canes. They were doing it with extreme thoroughness, del Amo thought, as they slowly advanced almost shoulder to shoulder. Other airmen, closer to the road, were checking the ground with portable instruments del Amo and White assumed to be Geiger counters. Del Amo also noticed outsize badges on the uniforms of some of the airmen. He counted about 120 airmen working in this peculiar fashion in the fields between the school at the village intersection and the river.

"This place is obviously radioactive or something," del Amo said triumphantly to White. "Looks like we were right about nuclear weapons here."

The whole stretch of the sandy riverbed for one-half mile from the beach was taken up by a chaotic-looking military camp. There were tents spread here and there over the sand and remains of fires which the troops had lit the night before to fight the chill and heat up their rations. Eight or nine blue Air Force buses that had brought airmen from Torrejón and Morón the previous afternoon were parked helter-skelter in the riverbed. One bus was a hundred feet from the tall tail section of the B-52. There were United States and Spanish Air Force staff cars and station wagons. American officers and airmen walked around with Spanish officers and Guardia Civil troopers. After the unpleasant, chilly, and drizzly night, the camp was now bursting with activity. Although radioactive particles were believed to have accumulated on the vegetation, airmen were eating the big red tomatoes they picked from nearby vines.

Del Amo and White parked their car on the edge of the camp

and walked toward the center of all the activity. This center was General Wilson's blue station wagon, and the general himself stood there in his gray flight suit, issuing orders and consulting with aides. Just then a light blue single-engine spotter plane flew low over the camp and dropped a small red parachute to which a foot-long cylindrical container was attached. The parachute landed some 150 yards from the command vehicle, and an airman raced over to bring it to Wilson. The cardboard cylinder contained rolled maps, and Wilson spread them over the hood of his car. They were the first overlap aerial photographs of Palomares that had been shot the day before by the reconnaissance jets. The photographs had been developed overnight at San Javier and flown at first light by the spotter plane to Wilson's camp.

Del Amo, who had noticed the large badges on the uniforms of Air Force personnel in the camp, decided that they were adequate proof that a radioactivity problem existed in Palomares. They had windows of a light material, and del Amo was convinced they were radiation-detection badges. He tried to ask questions of officers at the camp, but the standard answer was "No comment." He was told to speak to Colonel Young, the Sixteenth Air Force's information director, but the colonel was not to be found. Del Amo drove back to Vera and telephoned to Madrid from the kitchen in the telephone station his first Palomares dateline story. It told of the airmen beating the bushes for what might be a missing atomic bomb and mentioned the radioactivity badges. Del Amo also shipped to Madrid the first photographs of the search operations.

After lunch he returned to the camp. This time Colonel Young was on hand. Normally an outspoken man, "Skip" Young now was a wall of silence. From the outset he told del Amo and White they were wasting their time in Palomares because there were no stories there, and they would do better to return to Madrid. Then del Amo noticed that on his left breast pocket Young was wearing a badge 1½ inches long and 1¼ inches wide. The badge was framed by metal, but instead of having the wearer's name or unit identification it had a blank window. It was a so-called film badge loaded with a sheet of X-ray film and designed to estimate the total amount of radiation to which an individual has been exposed.

"What's the badge you're wearing?" del Amo asked Young.

"Oh, its nothing. Just a different kind of identification badge," Young replied.

"It wouldn't be a radiation badge?" the reporter insisted.

"Now, why would you think *that?*" Young drawled.

The information director volunteered the news that the airmen were searching for pieces of the two planes' wreckage. When collected, he said, they would be dispatched to the United States for study to determine the cause of the collision.

But del Amo had one more question. "Are there any nuclear weapons involved?" he asked.

Young turned crimson and exploded with anger. "This is not a place for scandal stories or outrageous hypotheses," he shouted.

Colonel Young's parting warning to del Amo and White was to refrain from asking questions around the camp and Palomares, "if you don't want to get booted out of the area."

There was nothing else to be said, and the two reporters drove out of the camp. Colonel Young had set the pattern for the relationship with the newsmen who would soon be flocking to Palomares. To be sure, he was acting on orders, but this was one instance when orders left much to be desired if the United States was to deal intelligently with world public opinion on an extremely sensitive matter.

Along the road back to the village, some 500 yards from the camp, the reporters' car was stopped atop a hill by a young Air Police trooper. Del Amo quickly slid his cameras under the seat, but the airman had something else on his mind.

"Can anyone here speak English?" he asked.

Del Amo and White said they spoke English.

"Great," the air policeman said. "And maybe you guys can speak Spanish too? There's a fellow in that bean field, and I've got to get him out of there."

"Yeah, I speak Spanish," del Amo said, hiding his excitement. "I'll interpret for you."

He and White got out of the car and walked across the field

with the young airman. The air policeman was talking rapidly as they crossed the bean field and approached an old farmer. "You know, we've had a lot of trouble here," he said. "They're looking for some pretty important stuff. But I really shouldn't be telling you anything about it."

"Oh, that's okay," del Amo replied lightly. "We've been briefed."

"Take this old farmer, for instance," the air policeman went on. "He's in his own bean field, but I've got to get him out of there. Will you please tell him to get out? The field is contaminated."

The farmer was a short, wiry man with a wind-beaten, crinkled brown face. He was wearing a black beret, dirty patched trousers, and a stained white shirt. A donkey with a large basket strapped to its back stood patiently alongside the man. The farmer was cutting the beans, the big brown Almería *habas,* and putting them in the basket. Del Amo said, *"Buenas tardes,"* and told the farmer he should take his donkey and leave.

"You've been ordered by the Guardia Civil to get out of here and this American military policeman wants to advise you that you must obey and leave because all this area is contaminated by radiation," he said.

The old farmer squinted at del Amo through half-closed eyelids. "I don't know what this radiation is," he said slowly. "All I know is that this is my field, and I refuse to go. I've got *habas* to pick."

Del Amo translated the farmer's words, and the air policeman became nervous and upset. "But he doesn't understand," he said. "He must go away. This field is full of radioactivity. I was given orders to make him leave."

Del Amo suggested that the airman report to the camp that he had a problem with the old man. "The Air Force can ask the Spanish police to make this guy leave," he said. "They have more authority with their own people than we do."

They started back across the bean field, and del Amo decided to do some probing.

"You guys must be pretty worried about these damned bombs," he said casually. It was a shot in the dark.

"How do you know about the bombs?" the airman asked, suddenly suspicious.

"Hell," del Amo told him, "I've just come back from the camp."

The air policeman was reassured. "Well, they found three of them very shortly after the crash, but they're worried because they haven't found the other one," he said. They reached the car, and he pointed to the sites where the three bombs had been found. "One was in the riverbed where the camp now is," he explained. "The second bomb was near that white house over there, you see? And the third one way over in those hills in front of you. Now they're all worried about the fourth bomb."

Del Amo and White drove off toward the village. Del Amo said, "Can we go on this? I think so."

They arrived at the Vera telephone office, a two-story house on a narrow side street, at 5:30 p.m. It took del Amo one hour to get his call through to the UPI office in Madrid. The story told the world that the United States had, in effect, lost an "atomic device" in Spain and vaguely suggested the existence of a radioactivity problem in Palomares. Del Amo's dispatch also announced on "good authority" that "all but one" of the nuclear weapons carried by the B-52 had been recovered.

It was a major news beat, the UPI's chance to get even with the Associated Press for its original scoop on the aerial collision, but del Amo's story was inevitably full of gaps and inaccuracies. It placed the entire emphasis on the missing bomb, virtually ignoring the much more ominous fact that Palomares was in a state of radioactive contamination.

This approach to the story was to characterize the entire press coverage of the Palomares episode in the weeks to come, as the plutonium radioactivity question and its implications remained generally misunderstood by the reporters on the scene.

While del Amo did mention radiation-detection badges and Geiger counters—he had actually seen the PAC-1S oscillator counters for monitoring alpha radiation, since Geigers are used only for beta and gamma radiation measurements—the story gave the impression that all this equipment was related to the search for the missing bomb. As long as the basic story was out anyway, the United States was perfectly satisfied, of course, to let the bomb search overshadow the radioactivity aspects of Palomares. It was not a situation that Washington cared to advertise, particularly in the initial days of the decontamination operation and when it was still uncertain what harm might have been caused.

But at the time the fact that UPI had broken the story at all caused deep unhappiness among the United States military services. Del Amo was given a taste of this unhappiness the next morning when he visited General Wilson's new camp on the Quitapellejos beach, directly south of the village. The installation, now known informally as Camp Wilson, had been moved on the morning of Thursday, January 20, partly because it was discovered that the riverbed camp was in the area contaminated by the plutonium particles from Weapon No. 3 that had fallen on Rabbit's Rise. The new site also provided better road connection with Vera and Garrucha, had a better beach for landing craft, and could be better guarded. The camp was set up next to the ruins of the old Fábrica del Hambre foundry, so that it had an oddly bombed-out aspect. In fact, an Italian magazine subsequently published photographs of the foundry's ruins, describing them as the results of the explosion of the American bomb in Palomares, in what was one of the most irresponsible of the many irresponsible stories to come out of Palomares during the search.

It was there that del Amo ran into Colonel Young. And, according to del Amo, the director of information gave him "unadulterated hell." Del Amo's notes on their conversation attribute these words to Young: "Generals Wilson and Donovan are furious with you. You really goofed this time. Generals Wilson and Donovan saw a part of your story last night, and I think this is no way to make a name for yourself as a foreign correspondent. You better go back where you came from and learn a little more about newswriting."

To del Amo's vast surprise, however, Colonel Young proceeded to take him on a tour of the area where airmen were searching for the bomb and to encourage him and Mike Gore, a British free-lance television cameraman, to take photographs. But he was still angry at del Amo.

"You're *persona non grata*," he said. "Even the Guardia Civil was angry with you. They want to throw you in the clink. You better get out of here. But first let's go to the new camp so that you can shoot some pictures. You can shoot from one hundred yards."

At the new camp the atmosphere was almost picnic-like. A number of young girls in bright dresses, with their *novios*—boy friends or fiancés—stood watching as the airmen busily put up their tents. Farmers and laborers stood to one side, exchanging comments on the scene before them. A yellow motor grader driven by a Spaniard was enlarging the parking lot and the helicopter landing pad. Then Guardia Civil troopers gently went over to the girls and their *novios* and the peasants and asked them to leave.

Del Amo did not know it at the time, but just as Colonel Young was upbraiding him for his story of the day before, the headquarters of the Sixteenth Air Force at Torrejón issued an official communiqué that went far to confirm his report.

The statement, which was made available in Madrid and Washington "in response to inquiries," said:

> The SAC bomber which was engaged in a refueling operation off the coast of Spain and suffered an accident with a KC-135 tanker was carrying unarmed nuclear armament. Radiological surveys have established that there is no danger to public health or safety as a result of this accident.

The communiqué, of course, raised more questions than it answered. It told of "unarmed nuclear armament" but failed to say what had happened to it. And, to put it mildly, it was quite premature in its claim that no danger to public health or safety existed. The radiological surveys had barely started when the communiqué was issued, and there still was to be quite a scare before anyone could talk with assurance of total safety.

Palomares raised again the fundamental problem of United States public-information policies in major emergencies. In the case of nuclear accidents such as those of the *Lucky Dragon* and Palomares these policies were of virtual total secrecy. Yet, as many American officials in Madrid stressed privately, the United States, and the world, had to face the reality of the nuclear age and its implications. As a major nuclear power, the United States seemed to gain nothing from a policy of secrecy for secrecy's sake. In fact, as events were to demonstrate, it would have stood to win more understanding and respect if it had told more of the truth. And in Palomares the truth, and the American performance, turned out to be infinitely better than the fiction that the Pentagon long insisted on offering to the world.

The principle that secrecy in nuclear matters can be overdone was enunciated at the time of the 1954 *Lucky Dragon* accident by Dr. James G. Beckerley, then director of the AEC's Office of Classification. Said Dr. Beckerley: "Atom bombs and hydrogen bombs are not matters that can be stolen and transmitted in the form of information. . . . The Swiss watchmaker does not export all his secrets when he exports a watch."

But under the official policy of denial and "no comment," the field was being left to what frequently was wild speculation, and to enemies of the United States.

Thus, at one o'clock on Thursday afternoon, January 20, Communist propaganda guns began firing away. The first salvo came from Radio España Independiente (Radio Independent Spain), a station purporting to be broadcasting clandestinely from somewhere near Spain, but widely known to be located in Prague. In its lunchtime program beamed to Spain, Prague asked pointedly: "Was there an atom bomb in the American plane which crashed in Almería?" Then it told of the United States search efforts and quoted press rumors on the possibility that nuclear weapons had been lost in Spain.

To be sure, the Spanish Communist broadcasters in Prague

knew precious little at that moment about the Palomares situation
—they did not even seem to know that Palomares existed—but
they enjoyed one special advantage. This was the fact that they
had an audience in Almería and were telling that audience more
than anyone else had at that stage. Spanish newspapers, radio,
and television—all of them controlled by the Franco regime—
were deliberately ignoring the whole situation on orders from the
Ministry of Information. The Madrid government's policy in the
first days after the accident was to impose complete silence over
everything that pertained to nuclear weapons. Foreign newspapers
carrying the original UPI dispatch from Palomares and subsequent
news were prevented all that week by the official censorship from
reaching the newsstands in Spain. As far as both the United States
and Spanish governments were concerned, nothing of importance
had happened in Palomares.

Prague radio, however, has its listeners in Palomares as it does
elsewhere in Spain. In general, Spaniards listen to Prague not
because they are pro-Communist—very few people in Spain are—
but because it offers a relief from the immensely dull news diet
provided by the National Radio of Spain, and fairly often it broadcasts nuggets of information about Spanish events that are not
otherwise known.

In Palomares, where nearly every family owns a radio receiver,
an additional reason for the habit of listening to Prague is the
Republican tradition of the region. In the Spanish Civil War the
area encompassing Vera and Palomares was a Republican hold-
out against the Franco forces until the bitter end, and the memories are not quite dead.

It was routine, therefore, for the people of Palomares to tune
in their receivers to Radio Independent Spain as well as to the
BBC in London, to Paris, and to Algeria. All of them were broadcasting on Thursday hints of a nuclear accident in Almería,
though Prague was doing it most pointedly. Conspicuously absent from the air waves in southern Spain was the Voice of
America. Spanish-language broadcasts for Europe had long ago

been abandoned by the Voice because of Congress-imposed economies, and obviously few Spaniards bothered to listen to the newscasts in English.

The first news the people of Palomares had about what was happening in their own village thus came in part from a Communist source. That the Communists ultimately failed to derive much advantage from the Almería situation was primarily due to the fact that they can be even worse than the West at producing credible propaganda.

iv

The Spanish government was advised on the afternoon of Wednesday, January 19, that a radiation hazard existed in Palomares. This was more than twenty-four hours after the scattering of plutonium particles from the two cracked hydrogen bombs was discovered by the SAC specialists on the scene and about the same time as UPI's Andró del Amo was filing his story reporting that United States airmen were combing the Palomares countryside with radiological detection instruments. It was never made clear why the United States waited so long to tell the Spaniards that one of their villages was radioactively contaminated.

But, on the other hand, the American embassy in Madrid, which had to handle the political consequences of the Palomares accident, was not told about it either until sometime on Wednesday. The information was given the embassy by an Air Force major, wearing a missileman's badge, who had flown in from Palomares. The major brought the news that two hydrogen bombs had cracked and scattered plutonium. The remains of the bombs, he said, had been taken by truck to San Javier and flown to Torrejón to be shipped to the United States.

Dr. José Maria Otero Navascués, president of Spain's Junta Energia Nuclear (Nuclear Energy Board), was at his office in the JEN building on the outskirts of the sprawling Madrid University campus when his telephone rang at 5 p.m. on Wednesday. His caller was Industry Minister Gregório Lopez Bravo, to whom

JEN is responsible, and he wanted to advise Dr. Otero Navascués that the government had just been informed that "some hazard of radiation" existed in Almería in the wake of the accident two days earlier involving two United States aircraft. The Minister told him he thought JEN had better look into it. He suggested a scientific team be dispatched to Palomares at once.

Although Spain is not even potentially a nuclear power, she possesses some of the world's most important uranium ore deposits. Two nuclear power stations are under construction in central and northern Spain, and a third one is planned on the Mediterranean coast not far from Barcelona. For all these reasons, JEN was created in 1951, and over the years it has developed a staff of first-rate scientists, many of whom were trained in United States universities and AEC laboratories. The Health and Safety Division was one of JEN's strong points, a fact that was to become important in the ensuing hours and days.

Dr. Otero Navascués was told by the Minister that an aircraft was being made ready for an immediate flight to San Javier, whence the JEN team would drive to Palomares. He called Dr. Eduardo Ramos, the chief of the Health and Safety Division and a Ph.D. from the University of Rochester, and directed him to be ready for departure within ninety minutes. Dr. Ramos summoned Dr. Emilio Iranzo, a biochemist in charge of JEN's Industrial Hygiene and Toxicology Section, and Rafael Nuche, the Junta's director of transportation, to accompany him. Simultaneously Dr. Otero Navascués made arrangements for five additional JEN specialists to go to Palomares by car that night.

Ramos, Iranzo, and Nuche spent the night in San Javier and left for Palomares about five o'clock in the morning. The three Spanish scientists had no clear idea of what had happened in Palomares except that a nuclear situation was involved. But as soon as they reached Camp Wilson at 7:30 a.m. on Thursday, January 20, they were briefed by General Wilson and Colonel Norcross, the Air Force's nuclear-medicine expert.

Dr. Iranzo recalled later that the Americans were "very worried" by the plutonium contamination. Visiting the village to assess the situation there, he found fear. The villagers had now been kept out of their fields for three days without any explanation. They had been watching hundreds of American troops, many in strange protective gear, comb the countryside with their instruments, uproot tomato vines, and bulldoze over the fields and hedges. Red flags on tall bamboo poles marked the limits of restricted areas. Big red fire trucks of the Air Force incessantly watered down the roads and the fields. It was not surprising, Dr. Iranzo said, that there should be fear in Palomares: "In a place where nothing happens, something had suddenly happened."

Foreign radio stations—and not only Prague—were now broadcasting wholesale news of lost atomic bombs and of radioactivity. Dr. Iranzo noted that "the people knew about atom bombs because they had heard about Hiroshima and Nagasaki." They did not understand the new word *radioactividad* that had invaded their vocabulary, but suddenly, as Dr. Iranzo put it, "to them it was the worst thing in the world."

Conchita Fernandez de Arellano, the teacher at the girls' school, was among those who worried most. "Although the Americans say there is no dangerous radioactivity here," she told a Spanish visitor, "I know of the Hiroshima and Nagasaki cases. I hope the Americans will not forget that—and us."

"It was very difficult to convince them that this was not the same as Hiroshima," Dr. Iranzo recounted later. "Most of them thought they were going to die; many of them wanted to leave right away."

And, along with the fears of *radioactividad,* there was the fear of a collapsing economy. Nobody had been able to work for four days; the tomatoes went unpicked and the fields untended. Animals could not be adequately fed.

What the Spanish scientists found in Palomares was not only a problem of plutonium contamination, its dimensions still unknown, but, perhaps even more important, a human and psychological problem. The United States Air Force had begun from the first moment to deal efficiently with the contamination and the bomb-search problems, but the human aspects of the Palo-

mares drama were virtually ignored for four days. Because of
the language barrier, official secrecy, and the fact that the Americans on the scene were, as foreigners, not competent to deal with
the population—and had no time for it—Palomares was left to
fend for itself as well as it could until the arrival of the JEN team.
Despite the Spanish peasants' instinctive distrust of all authority,
the quiet persuasion of the Madrid scientists began to have some
effect.

The first task before the JEN men was to determine if any
villagers or Guardia Civil troopers had actually been contaminated
on January 17. The other was to work with the American monitors on establishing the zero line of contamination. This was
necessary because the two governments would then have to work
out an agreement on maximal and minimal levels of radiation for
decontamination purposes. Starting Friday, January 21, each Air
Force monitor was accompanied by a JEN worker, identifiable
by his white coveralls.

Also on Friday, Dr. Ramos and Dr. Iranzo launched their
radiological survey of the Palomares population. At first they set
up shop with an alpha oscillator counter at Tomás Mula's bar.
Word was circulated to the inhabitants that all those who had been
near the two exploded bombs or any major pieces of aircraft
wreckage should come to be examined. The Guardia Civil commanders were told to send for examination the troopers involved
in the first day's rescue operations.

But, as it immediately turned out, everybody in Palomares
wanted to be checked for radiation to make sure he had none of
the dreaded *radioactividad*. All day long men and women streamed
into the bar, with their children, to have the JEN men run the
alpha counter over their bodies and clothes. This was the so-called
external examination, designed to establish who might have been
exposed to radiation in the first place. If the invisible plutonium
particles had collected on a person or his or her garments, the
sensitive PAC-1S instruments immediately registered them in terms
of the count per minute of alpha emissions. Not unexpectedly, radi-

ation was detected on most of the villagers and Guardia Civil who had been in the vicinity of the hot spots on January 17. This form of contamination, however, was completely harmless. Inasmuch as alpha particles cannot pierce skin or clothing—and not even a thin piece of paper—the JEN scientists simply told the persons who had undergone exposure to go home, take a shower, and carefully wash the clothes they had worn on the day of the accident. The same procedure was being used by the Air Force and the JEN field workers. At the end of each day's work the men shed their uniforms, took showers at the camp, and put on clean clothing. The clothes worn during the day were washed overnight. After a few days, in fact, the American airmen became so casual about the whole thing that they stopped using protective clothing, gloves, and masks even around the hot spots.

The people of Palomares were less casual. In the dusty village, where water is precious and expensive, a veritable shower-taking obsession swept the population. Miguel Castro Navarro, a farmer who was not even near the explosion sites, told a newsman that "we've never taken so many showers in all our lives as we have this week." The people who had been around the accident sites burned their clothes instead of just washing them.

As more equipment arrived from Madrid and more people demanded examinations, the JEN team moved its headquarters from the bar to the Capri Cinema in the village square. The scientists patiently told everyone that there was no real danger in the contamination, even if an alpha count was registered, and that there was nothing to worry about. But there was a sharp limitation on the explanations they could offer the anxious villagers. The secrecy rules imposed by the United States and Spanish governments allowed the scientists to tell people they should not worry, but not to go into any detail as to what had happened and *why,* indeed, they had no cause for concern. So in the end it was the word of the JEN technicians that had to count. It had to go against the vaguely understood myth of radiation which was quickly spreading through the village and the surrounding region.

Men were concerned that exposure to radioactivity might render them sterile or impotent. Someone remembered reading that all the men in Hiroshima and Nagasaki had lost their manhood after the atom bomb attacks. But it was impossible to explain the difference between beta and gamma rays from nuclear explosions, which did cause sterility in some cases, and the alpha rays emitted by plutonium particles without a nuclear reaction, which did not. A man told of being thrown out of a bar in Cuevas because he was thought to be radioactive. All this was the awesome mystery of the nuclear age for the average citizen, and twenty years later Hiroshima and Nagasaki came back to haunt the United States in a remote Spanish village.

The external examinations proceeded to divide the population and the Guardia Civil officers into two main groups: those who registered an alpha count and obviously had suffered exposure, and those who did not. Out of 1800 persons checked for external contamination—many of them were from faraway villages but insisted on examination because fear of radioactivity was spreading far and wide in the Almería countryside—the JEN scientists selected about 200 for separate internal surveys. These were people who either had plutonium particles on them or were known to have been in the vicinity of the detonated bombs.

Starting Friday night, the JEN office began requesting urine samples from the two hundred persons who remained under suspicion of serious contamination. The reasoning was that if they had been exposed to the plutonium cloud on the day of the accident, they might have inhaled the particles. If so, they might be in danger of plutonium poisoning and, twenty or thirty years later, in danger of cancer. This was a gruesome thought, and naturally the JEN scientists did not share it with the men and women who trooped to the Capri Cinema office with white plastic bottles containing urine samples. Urine-testing is the only known way—and not completely satisfactory—of establishing whether a person has received more than the permissible body burden of plutonium. The first shipment of urine samples was flown by helicopter to San Javier and then by plane to Madrid for analysis.

By late Friday, January 21, the Palomares operations were well under way.

Working with JEN, the Air Force had checked the air in the area of the accident, particularly around the Rabbit Rise site of Weapon No. 3, and both groups agreed there was no need to evacuate the population en masse. The possibility of having to do so did exist at the outset. An analysis of air samples carried out in JEN's mobile laboratory inside a Volkswagen car showed that radiation within a radius of 2.5 miles of the worrisome Site Three was well below the maximum permissible amount of 0.04 microcuries. A curie is a unit of radioactivity indicating the quantity of any radioactive material disintegrating at a certain rate per second, and a microcurie is its millionth part. Most of the recorded radiation apparently came from the natural background, mainly from potassium and strontium in the soil. The negative readings suggested that no plutonium particles had remained suspended in the air where they could be inhaled.

The immediate safety measures were the temporary evacuation of twelve persons from the vicinity of Site No. 3 and the treatment by the Air Force of houses known to have been in the path of the two plutonium clouds. Three houses around Rabbit's Rise and three below Cabezo Negro, where the Ponces and their relatives lived, were washed down with water and, as an extra precaution, given a new coat of whitewash. Some of the families protested at first that treating their houses disturbed them as well as gave them a bad name, but finally the JEN scientists convinced them it was for their own good. A continuing safety measure was the wetting down of roads and the areas around the hot spots, to prevent the resuspension in the air of the plutonium particles. Using sixteen 1500-gallon fire trucks flown to San Javier from as far as Germany, the Air Force poured 125,000 gallons of deep-well water across Palomares—more water than has ever been seen there. But for days many villagers still walked with handkerchiefs held to their noses in a too literal interpretation of JEN's warning against dust inhalation.

Meanwhile, the twenty-eight monitors from SAC's radiological teams pursued their backbreaking effort to establish the zero line of soil contamination. Working on their knees with the PAC-1S alpha counters—every square inch of topsoil had to be checked—the men each averaged 1 acre in a 12-hour day under the hot Palomares sun. When they returned to camp in the evening, they had just enough strength left to shower down, change clothes, eat, and collapse into bed in their tents. A hard-eyed SAC sergeant named Benedict was the direct boss of the monitors and the man responsible for the maintenance of the delicate PAC-1S instruments. To ensure that they were working properly, each of the fifty counters that General Wilson finally succeeded in assembling for his operation was flown to Torrejón every other day to be checked. At this point Wilson did not want any radioactive surprises.

With his force close to five hundred men by the end of the week, General Wilson had them split up in several basic work groups, aside from the radiological monitors. Some flights (the Air Force name for platoons) were cutting down vegetation, including the tough cacti and the *Macrochloa tenacissima,* to clear the field for the searchers. Occasionally bulldozers and motor graders had to be used to chew away the cacti and the esparto grass. Because of the possibility that small fragments of aircraft wreckage—conceivably including secret parts of the mission bomb, such as the fuse, the armer, or the fire-control mechanism—might have fallen in the vegetation, Wilson had no choice but to order the clearing of nearly seven hundred acres of land.

One hundred men were detailed to the clearing task and to the cutting down of crops. Even before the zero line was fully established, the decision was made to destroy all the crops in what was believed to be the contaminated area. Since plutonium particles could theoretically be harmful if ingested, hundreds of thousands of pounds of tomatoes, beans, wheat, and oranges had to be sacrificed. With them, bushes and vines had to go too.

In charge of the cutters was Captain Finkel, the young officer who had brought the first busload of troops from Torrejón to

Palomares the day after the accident. A good-natured, blue-eyed, partly bald man, Finkel asked for volunteers from his headquarters squadron, and immediately his outfit became known as Finkel's Farmers. He equipped them with straw hats and divided them into competing squads to see who cut more vegetation in a day. The competitive spirit was an important morale-builder—or morale-preserver—in the immensely demanding physical work of the cutters.

When they started cutting down the Palomares vegetation on Wednesday, January 19, Finkel's Farmers had nothing but hand sickles and pocket knives. This bordered on the ridiculous, Bob Finkel realized, and the next day he received permission to buy large Spanish sickles and machetes in Vera stores. Later, machetes, axes, and what the men called "idiot sticks" arrived from the United States. The idiot sticks were weed-choppers. This new equipment helped somewhat, although Finkel's troops had to get back on their knees to cut down fifteen acres of wheat with little hand sickles. But the tomatoes were the worst. They were staked and tied to bamboo poles, which meant the men first had to slash the bamboo and then cut the tomatoes. At the end of each day the cut vegetation and crops were loaded on trucks and taken to a collection site in the riverbed to be burned.

The cutters' day in the fields ended at 4:30 p.m. Before returning to camp, they went through decontamination, scrubbing themselves down with water and chemicals. Then they showered in portable showers, changed clothes, and were driven in buses to camp. When they were working at some distance from camp, helicopters brought them hot lunch. The morale remained good, but there were some casualties. A middle-aged airman first class suffered a heart attack and had to be evacuated to Torrejón. A warrant officer informed Bob Finkel one day that he wanted to resign from the cutters' team. "I didn't join the Air Force for *that*," he explained.

A third group was assigned to the actual search for the missing bomb. At the end of the first week, some two hundred airmen, led by officers equipped with walkie-talkies, crisscrossed the countryside in long lines, walking fingertip-to-fingertip. They un-coiled miles of twine to mark their progress, and later the flight officers transposed to charts the areas covered each day. The searchers wore black berets for morale purposes.

But there was no bomb. Actually, General Wilson was "95 per cent" sure from the outset that the fourth hydrogen bomb had gone into the sea. Colonel Hirsch went to Aguilas on Saturday, January 22, for a second interview with Francisco Simó and heard essentially the same story Captain Ramirez had been given earlier. He talked to thirteen other fishermen, the crews of the rescue vessels, and they all supported Simó's story of the "half-man" floating into the sea on a parachute. Looking at Simó's map, Hirsch figured out the precise coordinates by triangulation, with his dividers. Only later it developed that the Spanish soundings charts were incorrect and had to be revised. Simó volunteered to recover the bomb with his nets and remarked laughingly that he would charge the United States $1 million for the job. Colonel Hirsch laughed with him, not suspecting that Simó was quite seri-ous about collecting a large number of dollars from Uncle Sam.

As matters stood, however, the search had to be pressed both on land and in the sea. Ashore, General Wilson's men were literally checking every inch of the countryside. On the sea, the first naval units began arriving off Palomares early Friday after-noon, even though the Navy had not yet officially joined the search. They were Sixth Fleet's minesweepers USS *Sagacity* and USS *Pinnacle,* and their first task was to launch underwater reconnaissance, using AN/UQS-1 mine-detecting sonars. Four Navy frogmen from an explosives ordnance team started searching the shallow waters off the Palomares beach, where aircraft debris had fallen.

The decision to launch a full-scale naval search in the Mediterranean was taken in Washington on Saturday, January 22. This was five days after the accident, and General Wilson had become convinced not only that the missing hydrogen bomb would not be easily retrieved, but that the probability was high that it was lost somewhere in the Mediterranean in the vicinity of Palomares. His recommendation, therefore, was that an intensive sea search be carried on concurrently with the land operation already under way.

On Saturday morning W. J. Howard, who is the assistant to the Secretary of Defense for atomic matters, called on Dr. Robert W. Morse, the Assistant Secretary of the Navy for Research and Development. He briefed Dr. Morse on the Palomares situation, telling him that "we spent a good part of the week in establishing how bad things were, that we really were missing a fourth bomb." Then he said to Dr. Morse, "The sea search must be undertaken in an aggressive way."

Dr. Morse agreed and immediately went to see Admiral David L. McDonald, Chief of Naval Operations. Admiral McDonald and Dr. Morse then conferred with Secretary of the Navy Paul H. Nitze. As the Navy was to put it later in Congressional testimony, McDonald and Nitze "that morning ordered an all-out Navy effort and utilization of whatever resources were required to conduct this operation."

In a sense, their decision was a simple one. The reality of the

situation was that the United States could not rest until the misplaced hydrogen bomb was recovered and returned home. From
the day of the accident, General Wilson in Palomares was granted
top priority for all his requirements, and now that it appeared
that the bomb might be in the sea there was no choice but to
launch the "all-out" effort by the Navy.

In numerous previous accidents certain components of nuclear
weapons had been lost by the United States. In two instances—
near Savannah, Georgia, in June 1958, and near Eureka, North
Carolina, in June 1961—the search for what was described as
"non-explosive, non-hazardous components" was finally abandoned after fruitless efforts. When the United States nuclear submarine USS *Thresher* sank in 8400 feet of water off the New
England coast in April 1963, hydrogen-warhead Polaris missiles
were believed to have gone down with her. Although attempts to
raise the submarine were ultimately suspended, her location—
and that of the Polaris missiles—was known with utter precision.

But never before had a Western power actually *lost* an entire
nuclear weapon as far as anyone outside the Pentagon knew. And
furthermore, the American hydrogen bomb had vanished either on
the territory of a foreign nation or in the waters adjacent to it.

It could conceivably be argued that if the Palomares incident
had received none of its worldwide publicity and if the fact of the
missing bomb had remained a secret, the United States might not
have embarked on the costly and suspenseful search that was now
in progress in and around the little Almería village. But this would
be a purely academic argument. While the risk of a nuclear explosion was more than negligible, the United States could take no
chances with an accidental detonation of the TNT charge and the
subsequent scattering of another plutonium cloud, as long as the
possibility remained that the fourth bomb was on land. Similarly,
it could take no chances that someone would come across the
highly secret weapon.

In the water, the bomb was believed to present no hazards
whatsoever. From the outset the administration and its civilian
scientists and military specialists firmly took the view that an

accidental nuclear explosion in a hydrogen weapon in the sea or
on land was completely out of the question. Regardless of whether
or not the missing bomb's TNT charge had been detonated at the
time of the accident, they said, no nuclear reaction could occur
because the weapon was not armed in the first place. And in order
to arm a thermonuclear weapon a whole series of human, electronic, and electromechanical procedures are required.

These steps start with the complex command control system,
under which not only must the directive to arm and drop a bomb
come personally from the President of the United States, but two
or more men aboard the aircraft carrying the weapon must decide
independently that a Presidential order has really been given. An
elaborate system of procedural and mechanical checks and counter-
checks is further built around this method to prevent unauthorized
nuclear bursts. In any case, obviously no such Presidential order
was given in the Palomares situation.

The bomb itself carries a mechanism of permissive-action links.
These links are electromechanical locks which must be opened by
secret combination before the start of a nuclear reaction is possible. The permissive-action links were installed on nuclear weapons
following the June 1961 accident in North Carolina, when four
out of five arming interlock switches of the old type had been
thrown open in a bomb that spilled from a crashing B-52 and
suffered a TNT detonation. Only one switch was left on hold to
prevent a nuclear explosion.

The United States government is now convinced it has a fool-
proof system in the permissive-action links. But of course there is
always a tiny margin of human error in all of man's works. Dr.
Ralph E. Lapp, a veteran nuclear scientist and onetime head of
the Nuclear Physics Branch of the Office of Naval Research, remarked shortly after the Palomares accident that while the probability of detonation in the missing bomb had been much reduced
since 1961, "the whole history of science is replete with examples
of where the unexpected has happened."

Once it became known that an American hydrogen bomb was
lost, it was inevitable for people everywhere to speculate on the

chances of an accidental nuclear burst, despite repeated United States reassurances that it was not really possible. All the fictionalized stories of nuclear accidents—*Fail Safe* and the like—were remembered, along with the fragments of half-understood information about real accidents with nuclear weapons in the United States. And for the Spaniards, who, so to speak, were sitting on the missing bomb, the speculation was particularly disturbing.

To be sure, the power of the lost weapon was never disclosed by the United States, and therefore the actual extent of potential destruction could not be imagined. The best informed guess was that the Palomares bomb packed 20 megatons—the equivalent of 20 million tons of TNT—but subsequently Senator John O. Pastore, chairman of the Joint Congressional Atomic Energy Committee, suggested that the lost weapon's power was "only" 1.5 megatons. Senator Pastore's estimate, however, was not much of a consolation for the worried Spaniards.

Even assuming that the lost bomb had a 1.5-megaton yield, the air-blast effects alone of a surface burst would have caused severe damage to brick structures within a radius of 4 miles. Combined with incendiary heat effects, it would have meant the virtual leveling of Vera, Cuevas, and Garrucha. Palomares, of course, would have been totally obliterated. A surface burst would also have sucked into the fireball 600,000 tons of soil and rock, turning them into radioactive gamma and beta particles.

Radioactive fallout from such a fireball could have contaminated an area easily exceeding 1000 square miles. Death or severe radiation and blast injury would have afflicted the population of the entire southeast of Spain—between 1 and 2 million people—unless they could be speedily evacuated in less than 96 hours after the explosion. The 15-megaton hydrogen blast in the Pacific in 1954, which poisoned the *Lucky Dragon* fishermen, led to a virtually lethal contamination of an area of 7000 square miles, even though the bomb was detonated on a coral reef and a minimum of debris was sucked into the fireball. In Palomares, the mass of sucked debris would almost have compensated for the difference in the yields of the two bombs. A seaward wind would have lessened the radiation threat, but one of the frequent Palomares winds blowing strongly from the sea would have pushed the radioactive cloud even farther over Spain.

An underwater blast of 1.5-megaton power, if the missing bomb were submerged, would have caused considerably less damage on land and less radioactive fallout. But, on the other hand, it would have poisoned the Mediterranean and its fish life for uncounted hundreds of square miles.

If the lost weapon actually packed 20-megaton power, of course, all these estimates of damage, death, and injury would have to be multiplied by the appropriate factor. Havoc wrought in much of Spain and North Africa would be incalculable. It was unthinkable, at least for psychological reasons, to tolerate a situation with even such theoretical possibilities.

If the bomb were left in the sea after having suffered only a TNT explosion in the air—a long-held Air Force theory was that it had actually undergone a conventional detonation before hitting the water—its radioactive alpha particles would have contaminated a small area of the Mediterranean and possibly some of the fish. The hazards would have been fairly negligible because of the particles' dilution in the water. The danger of plutonium poisoning of the population through the fish cycle—eating fish and shrimp that *might* have ingested alpha particles—was considered virtually nil. But, again, the problem would have been psychological and probably impossible to overcome. It might have easily killed all tourism in southern Spain—and tourism is Spain's main source of revenue—along with the fishing industry. This was one reason one of the Navy's first steps off Palomares was to establish a constant watch over the radioactive content of the sea water.

The final possibility was that the bomb had plunged undamaged into the Mediterranean and remained so. In such a case, it would have slowly disintegrated under the ravages of the sea, without offering any hazards whatsoever. But there was the remote chance, which the United States could not altogether disregard, that in time the bomb would be found by a fisherman, if not by an unfriendly vessel or submarine. And of course Washington did not want even a hypothetical *Thunderball* situation under the Mediterranean. And, just as hypothetically, a Spanish fisherman might some day have caught a fish that had tasted disintegrating plutonium and have tested it with a sensitive alpha counter.

For all these plausible and implausible reasons, the United States would have had to go on looking for the missing hydrogen weapon even if the world had not been apprised of the loss. And the reality was that the whole world was aware of the missing hydrogen bomb and was breathing hard down the necks of the American searchers. Despite the apparent absence of hazards, the bomb had to be found. As a top United States scientist remarked, "The knowledge of the bomb being there could have had a considerable psychological and economic impact on the people and the area, and it would have remained a source of ulcers for the people who worry about our nation's defenses, our national image, and our weapons' secrets for an indefinite period."

The political fallout from the missing bomb began within three days of the Palomares accident, when the Spanish government let it be known that it would no longer authorize SAC's overflights with nuclear weapons and therefore the refueling operations over Spanish territory. Even though the 1953 and 1963 military agreements with Spain gave the United States the rights of overflights and refueling, after the Palomares collision Washington was politically in no position to argue with the Spaniards.

The suspension of overflights and refueling operations was confirmed in an exchange of secret messages on Thursday, January 20, between General Earl Wheeler, the Chairman of the Joint Chiefs of Staff, and Captain General Muñoz Grandes, the head of the Spanish High Staff. The official announcement that the SAC operations over Spain were being suspended was made the following evening by Information Minister Manuel Fraga Iribarne at the end of a regular cabinet meeting presided over by Generalissimo Franco. While the official version suggested that the overflights and the refueling operations were being discontinued by mutual consent, the truth was that Spain had no desire to expose herself to further risks of this type in her alliance with the United States. Yet, for the United States, a silver lining in this otherwise gloomy situation was that the bombs had dropped on Spain rather than elsewhere in Europe. "Can you imagine the bloody hell that would have broken out if these damned bombs had fallen on France or Italy?" a State Department official asked.

Even so, grave political problems loomed ahead. All the military accords with Spain, including specifically the operation by the United States of the Polaris submarine base at Rota, were up for renewal in 1968, and it immediately occurred to officials in Washington that the outcome of the Palomares search might have an important bearing on these approaching negotiations. They could not foresee, however, that the political fallout from the Palomares bomb would continue in Spain long after the bomb was finally retrieved.

The immediate effect of the Almería accident was to complicate grievously SAC's airborne alert operations. Unable to fly and refuel over Spain, the SAC bombers had to concentrate on the northern route toward the Soviet borders, with resulting losses in flexibility and efficiency and increases in cost and difficulties. Refueling over the Mediterranean by tankers operating from Torrejón and Morón was also ruled out at that time for political reasons, but there was no answer to the fundamental question of why these operations had not been carried out over the sea in the first place. One possible answer was that refueling over fixed land points, such as Saddle Rock near Palomares, was easier navigationally and that the tankers used less fuel when remaining over the Spanish land mass.

There were hopes in the Pentagon in these first days that the overflights and refueling could be resumed after a decent interval following the recovery of the missing bomb. These hopes were to be proved vain, but at the time the strategic need to go back to normal procedures over Spain was among the reasons the Pentagon pressed for a quick and successful search.

In short, then, the United States had every imaginable reason for finding Weapon No. 4 as expeditiously as possible and, after five days of fruitless land search, the Pentagon was amply justified in ordering the all-out Navy effort.

The Navy swung into action as instantly as the Air Force had done on January 17 when the first word of the collision was received in Torrejón, Offutt, and Washington.

As soon as the decision for an "aggressive" naval search was made, Admiral Horacio Rivero, Jr., the Vice Chief of Naval Operations, took two initial steps. The first step was to name Rear Admiral Leroy V. Swanson to head and coordinate all the operations in Washington. The second step was simultaneously to order Vice Admiral W. E. Ellis, Commander-in-Chief of the United States Sixth Fleet in the Mediterranean, to dispatch to Palomares all the immediately available ships that could aid in the search and recovery efforts. Throughout the day signals were radioed to the ships of Mine Division 84, directing them to steam for the Almería coast. With the minesweepers USS *Sagacity* and USS *Pinnacle* already on the scene since the previous afternoon, the USS *Skill* and USS *Nimble* were now proceeding at full speed toward Palomares. USS *Nespelen,* a fleet gasoline tanker, likewise set course for the Spanish coast to act as a floating refueling station.

As naval reinforcements were thus being deployed, the *Pinnacle* used her time on Saturday to take Francisco Simó from Aguilas to the area in front of Villaricos where he claimed to have seen the "half-man" plunge into the sea on a parachute the morning of the air collision. With total assurance, Simó pointed to a spot 5.5 miles offshore.

Meanwhile Admiral Swanson moved during Saturday to set up a technical advisory group, as had been done during the *Thresher* search in 1963, to oversee the naval operations and support them logistically. His group was also to coordinate the whole activity with the Air Force and the AEC. Ideally, the Navy's Deep Submergence Group in San Diego, California, which was created after the *Thresher* recovery attempts were abandoned in 1964, would have been the organization best suited to take on the Palomares sea hunt. But because budgetary and other problems continued to hold back the whole deep-submergence program, which is designed to concentrate on the recovery of small objects, including weapons, from the sea floor, the San Diego group was still in an infant stage of organization. Admiral Swanson's technical advisory group was thus established in Washington to operate in its place.

The Swanson committee's immediate task was to set in motion an effective search operation off the Spanish coast, and within hours urgent telephone calls started going out to private industrial firms specializing in underwater work to obtain equipment and expert personnel. One of the first calls went to Ocean Systems, Inc., a subsidiary of Union Carbide Corporation, which had wide experience in industrial underwater work and equipment. Ocean Systems, in fact, was forthwith asked to act as the chief civilian contractor for the Navy, coordinating the activities of other civilian concerns and specialists. Other calls went to firms specializing in underwater and precision navigational instruments, the Reynolds Submarine Service Corporation, the General Precision Decca Company, the Honeywell Corporation, the Westinghouse Corporation, the General Instrument Corporation, and the Straza Corporation.

Despite the fact that this was a weekend, the response was instantaneous. By nightfall the first pieces of equipment and the first experts began moving toward commercial airfields and Air Force and Navy bases to be transported to Spain. The very first item of equipment to be flown to Torrejón and then on to the assembling bomb-hunt fleet near Palomares was an underwater television camera that can operate at depths down to 2000 feet. Admiral Swanson's advisers had realized at once that the Navy would need underwater eyes if it was to find anything at all in the murky depths of the Mediterranean. And besides finding the lost bomb, the Navy had the parallel mission of locating and recovering the wreckage of the B-52 and the KC-135, including the tiniest pieces, that had fallen into the water. The job ahead was indeed formidable.

Although the Navy had never before faced the problem of

finding and retrieving a hydrogen bomb, its initial moves on January 22 were not pure improvisation or guesswork. The whole experience of the submarine service and oceanography was thrown into the planning. And the lessons learned in the two summers of hunting for the *Thresher* were a crucial starting point for the Palomares operation. As was to be the case off the Spanish coast, the *Thresher* search called for charting the bottom of the sea and the use of special devices ranging from deep-diving research vessels to underwater television, high-resolution sonar, and scanners. The growing importance of "inner space," as the Navy now called the depths of the oceans, following the introduction of nuclear submarines in the 1950s, had also resulted in much newly acquired expertise.

The Navy's outstanding underwater and salvage specialists were immediately assigned to Aircraft Salvops Med (Aircraft Salvage Operations, Mediterranean), which was the Navy's freshly coined designation for its Palomares project. Lieutenant Commander J. B. Mooney, who had been the pilot of the research bathyscaph *Trieste* during the dives for the *Thresher* in August 1964, was sent to the Palomares task force as principal adviser in the use of the special submersible vehicles that were presently to be added to the bomb hunt. The *Trieste* held the world deep-diving record of 35,800 feet (6.78 miles), and Mooney was as qualified as anyone in the Navy to run "inner space" submersible operations. He was rushed to Spain from San Diego, where his current assignment was the command of deep-submergence activities at Ballast Point. Lieutenant Commander Malcolm I. MacKinnon, who was project officer on the design and construction of *Sealab II*—the underwater diver's station—was dispatched from San Francisco to Palomares to advise in recovery operations. Commander William F. Searle, the Navy's Supervisor of Salvage, was put on the technical advisory group in Washington to handle outside procurement and modification of purchased, borrowed, and leased equipment. Captain H. C. Page, the Sixth Fleet's maintenance and salvage chief, was named chief of staff for the Palomares operation. And countless other submarine and salvage officers throughout the Navy found themselves being summoned for duty in Spain.

On Sunday, Admiral McDonald, the Chief of Naval Operations, worked out the minimal ship requirements for Palomares. Task Force 65, the naval group organized for the bomb search, was to start out with the four ocean minesweepers and the gasoline tanker already on the scene or en route to it. In addition, Admiral McDonald ordered to Spain the guided missiles frigate USS *MacDonough*, the landing ship docks USS *Fort Snelling*, the hydrographic survey ship USS *Dutton*, the fleet ocean tug USS *Kiowa* (which had already visited the Palomares coast four days earlier), and an unnamed submarine rescue ship. Ten ships thus constituted the initial strength of Task Force 65. The four explosives ordnance disposal team frogmen who reached the Palomares beach on Friday were to be reinforced by a full-fledged underwater demolition team arriving aboard the *Fort Snelling*. Within twenty-four hours of the decision in Washington to launch the "aggressive" naval hunt, a major fleet operation was already in the making in the blue Mediterranean waters where the Phoenicians once sailed and where until five days before only shrimp fishermen had plied the sea.

The man chosen to head Task Force 65 and the whole unprecedented sea hunt was Rear Admiral William Selman Guest, a fifty-two-year-old Georgian who has had one of the most extraordinary careers in the United States Navy. If there was a logical choice for commander of the immensely complex, unpredictable, and frustrating job of finding a hydrogen bomb lost in the sea near the shores of a foreign country, "Little Bulldog" Guest was unquestionably it. In his thirty years in the Navy, he has been successively an outstanding war hero, massively decorated for his impressive personal courage, an imaginative combat leader, a naval planner, a White House aide, a military diplomat, a high-level administrator, and a top operational and strike forces commander. An Annapolis graduate and a superb aircraft-carrier pilot, Guest has served in every war and war theater in which the United States has been involved in the past quarter of a century. He flew in the Pacific and the Atlantic in World War II and personally sank the first Japanese ship of the war. He was in the Korean war. And in 1964 he was the on-scene naval commander off Vietnam during the Tonkin Gulf incident which led to the United States bombings of North Vietnam. Six months before the United States lost its hydrogen bomb over Palomares, Guest arrived in Naples to take over his latest assignment as Deputy Commander, Naval Striking and Support Forces, Southern Europe. When the Spanish emergency came, therefore, the Navy did not have to look very far for the man to do the job.

Guest was as much at home flying a dive-bomber or running an aircraft-carrier division as he was dealing with Washington bureaucrats, European politicians and generals, or elegant hostesses from Hong Kong to Rome. As this kind of man, completely self-assured and immensely adaptable, he had managed to pack into one career what might have been several careers for many other admirals. Rather short and stocky, he was a tough, demanding, no-nonsense commander with a widespread Navy reputation as a stickler for detail and a bit of a martinet. Hence his nickname of Little Bulldog. But he also was a great improviser under pressure and fire, a man with an infinite capacity for hard work, no hobbies except the Navy, and something of a character. As commander of Carrier Division Nine off Vietnam, he insisted that the mess stewards on the carrier USS *Constellation* place little Japanese-style hot towels in wicker baskets on his table. Off Palomares, he was to contribute some interesting sartorial innovations to naval attire.

Famous for a terrible temper and total impatience with anything even remotely smacking of inefficiency, Admiral Guest may not have been exactly a beloved-leader figure to his subordinates, but he commanded respect aboard his ships as well as in the Pentagon. He was intense, a chain smoker, but he could be completely cool and imperturbable when the circumstances demanded it. His light blue eyes turned hard when problems or men stood in his way.

Facing an audience, he was a highly articulate and engaging speaker, drawing on an easy turn of phrase and total recall.

In dealing with Guest, it was sometimes difficult not to think of George Patton, or, better still, of a streamlined and intellectualized version of the picturesque general who breathlessly led his tanks across Europe after D-Day. Both men were military commanders who defied the stereotype, both were tough, quick-tempered, and imaginative, and both of them had a talent for doing things in their own way, often quite regardless of form and protocol. But this is how the most exacting assignments are best carried out, especially if luck runs one's way.

For Rear Admiral Guest, this particular assignment in Spain began at 9:30 a.m. on Sunday, January 23, when a radio-telephone call from Vice Admiral William E. Ellis, Commander of the Sixth Fleet, reached him at his apartment in Naples. Speaking from his flagship, the *Springfield*, then anchored in Villefranche, France, Admiral Ellis simply told Guest to proceed to the Torrejón Air Force base, then to Camp Wilson in Palomares, where General Wilson would brief him on the search and recovery situation. Guest was then to go aboard a minesweeper to become the on-scene commander for the naval part of the search. Nothing was said about missing nuclear bombs, and all Guest knew at that point was the speculation he had read in newspapers.

Equipped with five or six shirts and few other personal items, Guest left Naples three hours later aboard a Navy C-54, not even taking his aide along. After an eight-hour flight he arrived at Torrejón, where Colonel Jenkins gave him the preliminary briefing. One hour before dawn on Monday, January 24, he took off for San Javier, then transferred to a helicopter for the flight to Palomares. For two and a half months, Admiral Guest was to remain in the waters off the little Spanish village.

Because the over-all responsibility for recovering the bomb— and bringing the whole situation in Palomares back to normal— was vested in the Air Force, which owned and had lost the hydrogen weapons, Admiral Guest reported on arrival to General Wilson. In theory, the Navy's role off Palomares was to support the

Air Force's operation. Although the two men at once set up a system of consultations—not yet realizing the awesome communication problems that would face them—Admiral Guest was evidently going to run his own show on the sea while General Wilson ran his operation ashore and in the air.

After the briefing in Wilson's tent on Quitapellejos beach, Guest went up in a helicopter for an aerial survey of the area, flying at altitudes ranging from 100 to 1000 feet. Then he boarded a rubber boat with several Navy divers for the trip to the minesweeper USS *Skill*, his first flagship. A few hours later, the USS *MacDonough*, a guided missiles frigate, arrived on the scene and Guest transferred there to break out his two-star command flag. Task Force 65 had become formally constituted.

Armed with General Wilson's information on the details of the aerial collision, the debris pattern ashore, the location of the first three weapons, and the reports of the Aguilas fishermen on the spot where the "half-man" had sunk, Guest closeted himself in his stateroom to work out the outlines of his operation. Before night fell on his assembling task force, he had decided that his primary search area would be roughly 10 by 12 miles, a rectangle of 120 square miles. It was quite a bit of sea in which to look for a 10-foot object in virtually uncharted depths going down 4000 feet or more.

This prospect, however, did not faze Admiral Guest, even though his only major salvage operation prior to Palomares had been the removal of a Navy bomber from a snake-infested swamp near Norfolk, Virginia, in 1940. As he was to tell a visitor later, he believed that "the background of almost any aviator would qualify him" for search and recovery. And, he remarked, "I have volunteered for anything that will give me additional experience," suggesting that he would gladly have asked for the job if the Navy had not selected him in the first place. "I am open to this sort of thing happening to me at any time," he said.

vi

January became February, and a routine of sorts settled over Palomares, Camp Wilson, and the Navy's task force offshore.

For Palomares this routine signified that the village was still caught in the skein of the nuclear age. General Wilson's troops— now there were some eight hundred men bivouacked in the beach camp—came and went daily across the rutted streets and the dry fields on their chores of radiological decontamination and bomb searching. The tomato and bean and wheat fields remained closed to their owners and the farmhands. Red pennants fluttering in the wind on tall poles guarded the contaminated areas. Guardia Civil troopers, now bored with the whole thing, stood or sat at crossroads and intersections to enforce the quarantine. In the main square of Palomares the men gathered to watch the comings and goings of the Americans' trucks and motor graders and the JEN's jeeps, and to worry about the future. For days now the buyers in Vera, Cuevas, Almería, and elsewhere had refused to touch the produce, the milk, the eggs, the shrimp, and the fish not only from Palomares but from the whole area between Aguilas and Garrucha. "You people have *radioactividad,*" the buyers said apologetically to the farmers. "Your products are getting a bad name."

At Camp Wilson the routine meant seven days a week of tough physical work for the airmen. From sunup to sundown the men labored in the fields without respite, except for the brief lunchtime break, but with maddening monotony. They cut and burned vegetation, and they scraped the topsoil from the eroded hills and from fields made naked by the decontaminators. They trudged slowly across the countryside, forward and back over the same terrain, and they scaled rocks and mountainsides, poking into old mine shafts, tunnels, and galleries, looking, looking for the bomb. They grumbled and complained, as GIs always will, but their morale remained surprisingly good, despite the many restrictions and minimal recreation facilities.

From the very beginning General Wilson had decided on a policy of no contact after hours between his troops and the village. The camp was closed every evening at 6:30 p.m., and air policemen saw to it that no airmen sneaked out for a sociable bottle of beer or other possible forms of entertainment in the village. Wilson felt he had enough nuclear problems in Spain without adding human problems. An open-air movie theater was set up in the ruins of Fábrica de Hambre, and the men could assuage their hunger for contacts with the outside world by watching *What's New, Pussycat?* and other pictures supplied from the Navy ships offshore, but there was nothing more. In the daytime there were badminton, volleyball, and football scrimmage on the brown sand before lunch and dinner. Some officers and civilian scientists were free to live in the hotels and boarding houses in Vera and Garrucha, but a quiet after-dinner drink or a hand of poker was the total of their entertainment. "But don't kid yourself," an experienced Air Force captain said one evening. "This beats Vietnam any time."

For Task Force 65 life also settled to a busy pattern. Frogmen from the underwater demolition teams, a colorful elite group whom the Navy treated with tenderness not normally associated with naval discipline, busied themselves in the water, looking for aircraft debris and for clues to the bomb's whereabouts. They worked initially in shallow waters near the beach in depths up to 6 fathoms—36 feet—and came up with more and more pieces of the aircraft. The debris fall pattern was scattered from the shore into the sea along a mile-long front, and in the first days this was considered a highly promising search area. But the frogmen, swimming under water fingertip-to-fingertip, just as the airmen ashore marched through the Palomares fields, came up with everything except the bomb or its components.

The Mediterranean and Camp Wilson now resembled a wartime invasion beachhead. Ships stood offshore or moved in various directions. Helicopters hovered overhead between the camp and the fleet. Landing craft, launches, and the frogmen's rubber boats crisscrossed the blue waters. On Tuesday, January 24, Admiral Guest sent the USS *Pinnacle,* one of his ocean minesweepers, to the Spanish port of Cartagena to have an ocean-bottom-scanning sonar system installed. Cartagena had become the Navy's principal support base, just as San Javier, eighteen miles away, served as the gateway for the Air Force's growing airlift. Equipment for Admiral Guest was flown to San Javier, taken by road to Cartagena, and then picked up by the ships that transported it in a few hours to the fleet off Palomares.

On Saturday, January 29, Admiral Guest thus acquired the first of his Jules Vernesque underwater vehicles. It was the Deep Jeep, a two-man self-propelled submersible craft equipped with motors on either side of its hull and capable of vertical and horizontal movement. It was the only deep-diving research vehicle the Navy had available at the moment, and it was flown to San Javier from the Naval Ordnance test station at China Lake in California. The fleet ocean tug *Kiowa* brought it from Cartagena, and Admiral Guest ordered it prepared for work at once. On another trip from Cartagena the *Kiowa* transported a complete Decca Hi-Fix navigation system, the Honeywell Sea Scanner and Precision Profiler, and underwater television cameras.

The navigational equipment was absolutely vital to Guest. He had discovered on arrival that there simply were no adequate sounding charts of the area and nothing to give him an idea of the sea bottom's configuration. As he remarked to a visitor, he felt at first like Vasco da Gama, the fifteenth-century Portuguese navigator, who plied the seas of the New World without any charts. Before he could launch a rational underwater search, he had to know what perils and problems lurked in the deep. Essentially, he was facing on the sea the same mapping problem General Wilson had initially encountered ashore.

With the permission of the Spanish government, a shore control point for the Decca navigation system was set up in tents on a hill near Villaricos. A Navy geodetic team and sixteen men from a LORAC support team were flown in to start the Decca operation in cooperation with civilian specialists.

The *Pinnacle* returned from Cartagena and proceeded to survey the bottom with the ocean-bottom-scanning sonar. The OBSS is an acoustic fish towed by its mother ship over the sea floor. In two days the *Pinnacle* made twenty-eight underwater contacts—it spotted twenty-eight objects—and Admiral Guest thought at least three of them were promising. But the admiral and his officers would soon learn not to give themselves easily to optimism. The OBSS received signals bounced off underwater rocks as it did from fragments of aircraft and from objects that, conceivably, could have been the missing hydrogen bomb. Later the underwater hunters discovered that naval battles had been fought off Palomares in the dim past and that what seemed to the sonar scanners a twentieth-century nuclear bomb was really a sixteenth-century iron cannonball.

While the Decca system was being set up on the wind-swept Villaricos hill, hydrographic ship USS *Dutton* went to work charting the bottom. In Washington, Admiral Swanson thought that Guest's task force would need even more assistance in underwater work and on January 22 he had ordered the USS *Mizar,* a hydrographic research vessel that had seen extensive service in the Antarctic, rushed to Palomares from the Philadelphia shipyard where she was being refitted.

The task force grew in ships, men, and sophisticated equipment. On Sunday, January 30, Admiral Guest received aboard the *Mac-Donough* the visit of Admiral King, the Sixth Fleet Commander, who arrived aboard his flagship, the cruiser *Springfield*. Later that day Admiral Guest shifted his own flag and headquarters to the USS *Boston,* a 18,240-ton guided missiles cruiser. Now the sea hunt was launched in a big way.

vii

While the world's attention was riveted on the bomb search, radiological decontamination was proceeding painstakingly but satisfactorily in and around Palomares. Because it was not yet generally known that two of the hydrogen weapons had cracked and scattered plutonium, the real nature of the contamination problem was not fully understood by newsmen and other outsiders —and certainly not by the villagers.

Radioactividad was known to exist—it was now the most popular word in this corner of Almería—but few people knew why it existed and what had caused it. The virtually unquestioning acceptance of the fact of radioactivity in Palomares by the press and public opinion in these first weeks, without any determined effort to look into the causes behind it, was a strange commentary on mental processes in the nuclear age. There was a vague assumption that in some mysterious manner the three bombs that fell on land had produced radioactivity in the area, but most people were prepared to let it go at that. Twenty years of the nuclear age may, indeed, have dulled the senses as to the meaning and implications of radiological contamination. And to the people of Palomares, of course, the whole subject was an unfathomable mystery.

The problem of decontaminating Palomares rested, however, in the hands of two Texans who, despite their totally dissimilar backgrounds, shared not only high technological expertise but, more important, humaneness and an understanding of farm land

and its people. Set against the efficient but cold professionalism of most of the nuclear-age experts on the scene, these two men emerged, quietly and unobtrusively, as the true human heroes of the Palomares experience. Both also had a sense of humor.

The men were Dr. Wright H. Langham, the great authority on plutonium from the AEC's Los Alamos Scientific Laboratory, and Colonel Alton E. White, the director of civil engineering of the Sixteenth Air Force. As a scientist, Dr. Langham was responsible for providing the guidelines for the decontamination operation. As a military executive, Colonel White was responsible for putting these guidelines into effect. In their very different ways, the scientist and the colonel had prepared themselves all their lives for the task that now brought them to Palomares.

At the age of fifty-five, Dr. Langham was the division leader of biomedical research at Los Alamos. A slim man with a small mustache, he had lived with nuclear problems, and particularly plutonium, from the day in the spring of 1943 when, as a young Ph.D. in biochemistry, he joined the atom bomb's Manhattan Project in Chicago. Working desperately against time and in deepest secrecy, the men at the metallurgical laboratory of the University of Chicago, across the street from Enrico Fermi's first nuclear reactor, raced to produce enough plutonium to construct the first atom bomb. Dr. Langham's assignment was to analyze the plutonium separated from pile-irradiated uranium for impurities that would prevent its use as a fuel for the atomic bomb. A year later, as the bomb approached its birth, Dr. Langham was sent to Los Alamos to work at Site Y in the assembly of either a plutonium or a uranium A-bomb. When the decision was made to test the plutonium bomb at Site Trinity near Alamogordo, New Mexico, Dr. Langham was given the job of worrying about nuclear fallout —though the word had not yet been invented. The problem was that if the bomb either fizzled out or produced only a low nuclear yield, its unburned plutonium could spread over the New Mexico countryside.

On July 16, 1945, Dr. Langham witnessed from a fourteen-mile distance the first atomic explosion; as he put it later, he was a "bridesmaid" at one of the biggest "scientific weddings in history." Beta radiation from the bomb burned the backs of New Mexico cattle, the first victims of the nuclear age, but plutonium was spread so thin that Dr. Langham could not detect any alpha radiation with his primitive 70-pound counter. He did use the alpha counter's methane tank, however, to fill the flat tire on Dr. Fermi's car when he came upon it on a back road in the test area. Dr. Langham, who has a highly developed sense of whimsy and of the improbable, still likes to think of his emergency road service to the father of nuclear fission as one of the offbeat highlights of his career.

After the war Dr. Langham remained a bridesmaid in nuclear history. When the Bikini tests against naval vessels were ordered in 1946, Dr. Langham found himself with the twin tasks of checking on plutonium's toxic effects and, immensely improbably, of hand-carrying the nuclear components of an atomic bomb in a canvas bag from Los Alamos to Oakland, California, where they were to be placed aboard a destroyer. With a military escort, Dr. Langham traveled in a bedroom compartment of Santa Fe Railroad's California Limited, wondering what would happen if the weapon's nuclear components exceeded the temperature of 110 degrees Fahrenheit. He had been told to watch out for rising temperatures, but someone forgot to tell him what would occur in such an event. The entire Bikini project then nearly suffered a critical delay when an old night watchman on the Oakland pier, who had not been told about atomic bombs, obstinately refused to admit Dr. Langham and his bomb. To Dr. Langham, who admires guts, the old watchman with the droopy tobacco-stained mustache remains one of the great contemporary heroes.

At Kwajalein, Dr. Langham became engaged in the vast test operation of which General Wilson was also a member. The two men did not meet until nearly twenty years later, when, ironically, Palomares and plutonium brought them together. But it was at Kwajalein that Dr. Langham first came face to face with plutonium's lethal effects. Dr. Lewis Slotin, a fellow Los Alamos scientist, was testing the criticality of plutonium when he let his screwdriver slip and the plutonium became critical. Nine days later Dr. Slotin was dead from acute radiation exposure. Dr. Langham, who analyzed some of his dead colleague's tissues to obtain more data on radiation effects on man, was to remember this tragedy keenly when the Palomares accident came. In the years that followed Bikini, Dr. Langham continued his studies of plutonium's toxicity, becoming the recognized world authority on the subject. As he was to say later, "Plutonium has stuck with me like my shadow."

But if his plutonium experience eminently qualified Dr. Langham for the scientific aspects of the Palomares operation, his childhood and youth qualified him in another way. An orphan at the age of seven, he lived in little towns in northeastern Texas, then was taken by an aunt to Texhoma in the Oklahoma Panhandle. He graduated from Panhandle A & M, a fact of which he is intensely proud, and did postgraduate work at Oklahoma State University. Back at Panhandle, Dr. Langham became a chemist at an experimental station, specializing in the problems of the Dust Bowl. His first scientific paper, in fact, was on the "Effect of Wind Erosion on Soil Fertility," a subject that would serve him in good stead thirty-one years later in a Spanish dust bowl. He worked on the production of emergency livestock feed "from anything remotely green in color," grass reseeding, and feasibility of deep-well irrigation—all of them problems later to be crucial in Palomares. As he was to say in 1966, "The problems of the man who makes his living from the land, be it in Palomares or in the Panhandle, are something I have a little feeling for."

Colonel White was another man who had "a little feeling" for the land and its people. A forty-five-year-old native of Pearsall, Texas, he went to Texas A & M and graduated in agriculture. He worked as a county agricultural agent with the Texas Extension Service. Like Dr. Langham, he worried about wind and dust and erosion. After four wartime years with the Army Air Corps' Fourteenth Fighter Group in North Africa, Italy, and Britain, Colonel White returned to Texas and agriculture. But in 1951, with the intensification of the Korean war, the Air Force claimed him again and he became a civil-engineering specialist in Labrador, at the Omaha SAC headquarters, and finally at Torrejón. He had been in Spain since 1963.

Because Pearsall is only a hundred miles from the Mexican border, Colonel White had spoken Spanish from childhood—the border brand. His three years in Spain improved his Spanish, and when he arrived in Palomares on Saturday, January 22, he was one of the few Air Force officers able to communicate fluently—and, in his case, enthusiastically—with the people of the village. Reporting to General Wilson, he was put in charge of detection of contamination—the tracing of the zero line—as well as of actual decontamination, collection and removal of aircraft debris, and whatever civil engineering was required in the different phases of the whole operation. All this made Colonel White the Air Force's most important technical man in Palomares.

It also made him one of the best-known Americans in Palomares. A rugged, somewhat bald blue-eyed man given to mild but explosively delivered swearing, he seemed to be everywhere in and around the village. Driving his blue Air Force station wagon, he supervised operations and dropped in on farmers all over the area to discuss not only the problems created by the nuclear accident, but wheat-planting, irrigation, and cattle-raising. In the end, chances are that the Palomares farmers learned a lot about farming from Colonel White, who has never quite ceased to be a country agricultural agent.

In Dr. Langham's and Colonel White's hands, then, the Palomares situation acquired some humanity.

To decontaminate an area of plutonium particles, the standard procedure calls for the removal to atomic cemeteries of soil with the highest count of alpha emissions, and the plowing under of land showing a lower degree of contamination. The plowing of plutonium into the soil or its mixing into the surface does not produce a health hazard because the alpha-emitting particles are dangerous only if they are resuspended in the air, where they might be inhaled. Plowed into the land ten inches below the surface, plutonium is not more dangerous than arsenic, another deadly

poison, which exists in all soil. When it is diluted through mixing
with soil, plutonium cannot be absorbed into the ecological cycle
in toxic amounts. Besides, the plutonium oxide is about as soluble
as sand, which means that it can be taken into plants in extremely
minute amounts. In other words, the danger of plutonium absorp-
tion by persons eating fruit or vegetables grown in once-contami-
nated soil is virtually nil. Anyway, there is no reason to think that
even the direct ingesting of plutonium particles can produce poisoning. Plutonium is a health hazard when it is inhaled and becomes
deposited in the lungs and the skeleton, raising the threat of
cancer.

As soon as it became obvious that Palomares had been contaminated by the scattering of plutonium particles from the two
cracked bombs, United States experts advised their JEN counterparts that very "hot" soil would be scraped away and removed
and the rest of it would be plowed under. This would be done,
they said, as the zero line, outlining the contaminated zone, was
being traced. The idea was that decontamination should start as
rapidly as possible, with the teams of scrapers and plowers moving
in the footsteps of the radiation monitors. In the very hot spots
around the craters at the Cabezo Negro and at Rabbit's Rise decontamination began at once. But for the over-all operation an
agreement had to be reached with JEN on the radioactivity levels
that should determine whether soil should be removed or just
plowed and irrigated. Decisions had to be made as to acceptable
levels on cultivated land, on one hand, and arid wastelands, on the
other.

It turned out immediately that the Spaniards insisted on higher
standards of safety than the United States considered necessary.
The radiation-count levels varied wildly from place to place. They
ranged from the maximum of 2 million alpha emissions per
minute around the two craters to 300 counts per minute on the
flanks of Sierra Almagrera on the other side of Villaricos, nearly
three miles from the impact point of Weapon No. 2. The Spaniards
insisted at the outset that all soil with more than 7000 counts be
scraped and removed and that in the cultivated areas land register-

ing more than 700 counts be plowed over. The Americans thought this was excessive, but the JEN experts were motivated as much by psychological and economic considerations as by purely health-hazard factors. As Dr. Iranzo pointed out, the Palomares situation was essentially psychological and the Spanish government would be remiss in its duties if it failed to impose the most reassuring safety standards. After all, he said, Palomares and its farm production were acquiring the awesome reputation of being *in-fectados,* and everything should be done to counteract it.

So that the Air Force could start decontaminating without any waste of time, a tentative agreement, roughly on Spanish terms, was reached on Friday, January 21, between Colonel Rhodes, the SAC chief of ordnance disposal, and Dr. Ramos, the senior official in Palomares of the JEN. Because at that moment nobody knew the limits of contamination, the Americans and the JEN arbitrarily decided that all farm activities must cease, even in the most remotely suspected areas. Fields, therefore, could not be irrigated and the tomatoes could not be picked.

This was the situation in Palomares when the AEC resolved that a scientist of Dr. Langham's caliber and reputation should be dispatched to the scene of the accident to supervise the decontamination operations and, if need be, persuade his Spanish colleagues that the area could be cleaned up more rapidly and efficiently if criteria of lower levels were accepted.

On Saturday, January 22, Dr. Langham, who lives in Los Alamos, was in Washington, presiding over a meeting at the National Aeronautics and Space Administration on radiation hazards of manned space flights—his latest interest—when he received orders from the AEC to proceed at once to New York to catch an airline plane to Madrid that same evening. He instantly turned his back on space flight to rush to New York, where he was joined by Dr. John Lawrence and Dr. Dean Meyer of the health-physics staff at the Los Alamos Laboratory. The two men had just arrived from New Mexico.

Dr. Langham and his colleagues were not, however, the first

AEC scientists to be dispatched to Palomares. Already on the scene two days after the collision were William H. Chambers of the Los Alamos Laboratory's weapons division and Douglas F. Evans from the high-explosives division. Chambers, who is familiar with every single feature and part of a nuclear warhead, had the mission of identifying and retrieving the nuclear components of the two cracked bombs for diagnostic and security purposes. Evans, who specialized in the handling, deactivation, and disposal of chemical high explosives, had the responsibility for the TNT components of the detonated weapons and for disposing of any bits of them that might not have blown up on January 17—as in the bomb that fell on Rabbit's Rise and exploded only one-half of its TNT charge. Both men examined and secured the two bombs before they were shipped out of Palomares on January 20. As it happened, Palomares was Evans' last job before retirement. As a friend of his remarked afterward, he had made it to retirement age despite the fact that he had worked with bizarre high explosives for most of his life. The presence in Palomares of the two weapons experts and later of Dr. Langham and his medical colleagues was Top Secret at the time.

Traveling by commercial airliner, Dr. Langham, Dr. Lawrence, and Dr. Meyer arrived at Madrid's Barajas International Airport at 7:30 a.m. on Sunday, January 23. A waiting Air Force car took them to Torrejón for an hour's briefing on the situation. Then Dr. Langham and Dr. Lawrence were flown aboard a Sixteenth Air Force jet to San Javier and from there by helicopter to Palomares. They reached Camp Wilson at noon. Dr. Meyer had remained in Madrid.

Recollecting later the impressions of that first day in Palomares, Dr. Langham admitted that he was "apprehensive" during the trip from New York. "I could visualize not one but two of the maximum credible accidents we had anticipated for over ten years having occurred in a populated area and involving several hundred people," he said. "But within thirty minutes, after seeing the radioactivity levels and trajectories of the contamination patterns with respect to the village, I was no longer apprehensive. Even though the plutonium from the warheads had been dispersed, the maximum credible hazard situation had not occurred."

Dr. Langham reached other conclusions on the situation he found in Palomares. He felt that "it was fortunate indeed that one of the weapons was missing for a time" because "the spectacular thought of a hydrogen bomb that could wipe out an entire city lurking just offshore diverted attention from the real drama enacted on the edge of the village of Palomares. Except for the combination of a number of fortunate circumstances, bordering almost on miraculous, a number of people could have been killed or had their health jeopardized," he said.

Dr. Langham remained in Palomares for four days. During that time he achieved two important things. One was to work out what he considered to be the proper decontamination levels, based on the years of AEC study and experimentation in Nevada. JEN's Dr. Ramos and Dr. Iranzo rejected them, however, holding out for the very stringent criteria they had set up originally. Their stand was strengthened by the fact that the wind, which had helped to save Palomares on January 17, continued to blow strongly during Dr. Langham's negotiations and provided JEN with the additional argument that plutonium particles might still be spread around. As the negotiations on the decontamination criteria became deadlocked for the time being, Dr. Langham came up with his second major contribution to the lessening of Palomares' fears.

Just before he arrived in Spain, a highly alarming situation had quietly developed in the village. The first urine samples from the inhabitants and the Guardia Civil troopers exposed to radiation on the day of the accident showed a high degree of plutonium contamination. This indicated that scores of people had inhaled the alpha particles, that the particles had become lodged in their bodies, and that therefore they had received plutonium poisoning. Since the urine count apparently far exceeded the maximum permissible body burden, the terrible spectre of radiation sickness, cancer, and death for countless people arose immediately. Despite efforts to keep these awesome findings a secret, the word quickly leaked out that a number of villagers and Guardia Civil members had suffered radioactive contamination. Overnight the story appeared in foreign newspapers and over foreign radio stations. Although newsmen confused this radiation with harmless alpha emission from particles still clinging to the skin, clothes, and shoes of the examined inhabitants and policemen—the urine-sample count was never mentioned—the mere mention of radioactive contamination of people in Palomares had a powerful impact.

To Dr. Langham, the discovery of plutonium contamination in the urine after he had found the village radioactivity levels to be so reassuring was surprising and downright unbelievable. The samples were analyzed again, and the results were still the same. Suddenly Dr. Langham had an inspiration. It occurred to him that the urine samples might be contaminated because plutonium particles had dropped into the test bottles from the clothing of the villagers and the *guardias*. He ordered new samples to be collected, making sure that this time the clothing of the people involved was free from plutonium particles. As if by magic, the new samples were absolutely devoid of any contamination.

Presently Dr. Langham left Palomares and flew to Washington to brief officials of the AEC, the State Department, and the Defense Department. He also testified in secret before the Joint Congressional Committee on Atomic Energy. It happened that he had caught a common cold in Spain and arrived in Washington slightly ill. This fact immediately became a highly classified bit of secret information. Fearing that news of his trip to Palomares might have leaked out, officials thought his illness might be construed as a form of radioactive contamination. Dr. Langham flew home to Los Alamos to recover from his cold and to allay the nervousness of Washington officials.

A week later, no longer sneezing, he was back in Spain in the company of Dr. John Hall, the AEC's assistant director for international relations. Now high-level negotiations secretly opened in Madrid between the American team—made up of Dr. Langham, Dr. Hall, Ambassador Duke, and General Donovan—and high Spanish officials, to seek to reduce the Palomares decontamination criteria. An agreement was finally reached when Spain accepted new levels only slightly above those Dr. Langham had originally proposed. Soil showing radiation exceeding 50,000 alpha counts per minute was to be removed and shipped away. Cultivated areas with a count between 7000 and 50,000 emissions were to be plowed under and irrigated. Where the count stood below 7000 emissions, the soil would simply be irrigated to dilute whatever plutonium particles might have remained. Dr. Langham, who was as concerned as the JEN over possible health hazards, felt the agreement was reasonable and generally fair to all concerned. Once it was reached, he was secretly installed in an office in the political section of the American embassy to maintain liaison with JEN and supervise technical problems. Newsmen learned of his presence in Madrid, but the embassy flatly refused to produce him, in accordance with the official secrecy policy on most aspects of Palomares.

While United States and Spanish officials were negotiating in Madrid, Colonel White's radiological monitoring teams in Palomares completed the establishment of the zero line. The contaminated area turned out to be a 640-acre rectangle stretching roughly north of the village between Cabezo Negro and the farm land east of Rabbit's Rise in the direction of the Almanzora River. Its maximum width was three-quarters of a mile, around Site No. 3 and the houses of Eduardo Navarro and Pepé López. According to the agreement on decontamination levels reached in Madrid, 385.68 acres of land had to be plowed 10 inches deep. Because this area was split up into 854 individual plots, and care had to be taken not to erase the barely visible property limits, the decontamination became one of the trickiest high-speed plowing undertakings in farm history. In addition, 1.5 acres of hot soil around Rabbit's Rise and 4 acres on Cabezo Negro had to be scraped 2 inches deep and replaced with new topsoil from elsewhere.

With 185 airmen engaged 7 days a week in monitoring, decontamination, and related tasks, aided by motor graders, tractors, soil mulchers, and front-loaders, Colonel White set the deadline

of April 1 for restoring Palomares to its physical condition prior
to the accident. This was the publicly announced objective of the
United States. But Colonel White, the farmer, was to outdo
himself on this assignment.

viii

On a sunny Tuesday early in February a group of Palomares men stood in front of the general store on the village's main square, chatting with an American civilian. They had been watching families walking to the whitewashed house with green shutters up the hill where JEN technicians were still examining people for alpha radiation. The men also idly watched passing United States Air Force trucks and a station wagon loaded with television equipment. When a helicopter swept low over the village, they hardly bothered to look up. Their initial bewilderment had now given place to boredom, restlessness, and passive resentment against whatever powers had conjured up their ill fortune. It had been over three weeks since the accident, three weeks since most men in Palomares had worked and three weeks since their lives had been utterly disrupted. With no money coming in from crops or wages, and the American compensation payments barely beginning to trickle to Palomares families, the men of the village no longer whiled their time away in the taverns. They just stood in the sunlit square, wondering and waiting.

Miguel Castro Navarro pensively chewed on a straw when the American asked him what his plans were. "If I didn't have this farm I inherited from my father and if I didn't have my tractor and my six cows, I'd just leave and go to work abroad. People from here have always emigrated, so why not?" he said.

"That's right," Antonio Saviote, his friend, chimed in. "Nobody has worked here for three weeks, and the tomatoes are rotting, and we have to keep the tractors idle, and we can't sell what we produce."

The other men nodded gravely in the solemn manner of Andalusians. One of them told how he had not been able to sell his chickens or the milk from his cows. "They're all afraid of *radioactividad*," he said. "It's supposed to be something strange, the people say, like the plague. You can't see it or hear it, but it could make you sick.

"But I'll tell you something else," he went on. "The truth is that I don't eat my own chickens either. Now I go to Vera, to the store, and I buy food in cans."

The men laughed sheepishly, and all of them said that they too were afraid to eat their chickens or their eggs or give their children the milk from their cows.

"And the women at home are beginning to worry," a tall serious man in a black beret said. "My wife says that this can't go on, that I should go some place and make some money."

A very old man with crinkly laughter lines around his pale blue eyes joined the group, and the other men said, *"Olá, Pablo. . . . Buenos días, Pablo."* Pablo, whose last name was de la Torre, and who was a cousin of Pedro, the octogenarian thrown to the ground by the TNT explosion, replied, *"Olá, Olá,"* and stared at the American.

"Americano?" he asked, pointing his finger. "Very good. They tell me you Americans are going to pay us for all the damage here. Is it true? I don't know. But I can do this: I can tell you the 'Cuento del Compadre.' "

The men laughed appreciatively and Miguel Castro patted him on the back. Pablo was somewhat of a village philosopher, and the men liked listening to his *cuentos*. The "cuento del Compadre" was the tale of the two friends.

"It goes like this," old Pablo said. "There was this man near Córdoba who owed a thousand pesetas to his best friend. But years went by and he did not pay his debt. So the friend went to complain to the judge. The judge called the man and asked him in a friendly way when he would pay his debt. The man answered, 'I will pay. But first I must wait for my father-in-law to die so that I can inherit his *finca*. When I inherit the *finca,* I will plant a whole grove of olive trees. After five years, or maybe seven years, the trees will mature. Then I shall pick the olives and I will have them ground for olive oil. When I sell the olive oil, I will pay my friend his thousand pesetas.' So what I'm telling you is that I think the Americans will pay in the way of that *compadre* in Córdoba."

Everybody laughed loudly, but there had been no bitterness in old Pablo's manner when he told his *cuento,* and now there was no bitterness in the men's laughter.

"That's a good *cuento,* Pablo," Miguel Castro said. "But I hope you are wrong and that the Americans will pay well and quickly."

The question of losses to the Palomares villagers had for days been one of the favorite themes of Communist radio stations, along with warnings that the lost hydrogen bomb was contaminating large areas of the Mediterranean. The broadcasts from Prague, Moscow, and Peking were being heavily jammed by the Spanish authorities, but the Spanish Communists were broadcasting from Czechoslovakia over four frequencies, and the programs could be heard in Palomares. The American asked the men if they ever listened to Prague. They looked at one another; then one of them said yes, most people in Palomares listened to Prague.

"But we are not Communists," he added quickly, glancing at two Guardia Civil troopers who were crossing the square.

Not surprisingly, the Soviet radio was continuing to broadcast on the Palomares accident. In its 11 p.m. Spanish-language broadcast on January 26, for example, Moscow announced that Almería peasants were forbidden to sell their crops and slaughter their cattle for meat. It added, "Apparently the atomic bomb or bombs that have fallen in the sea have lethal radiation." On January 29 Moscow curiously raised the question of whether the bomb lost in Palomares was a uranium or a plutonium weapon, as if the Soviet Union itself were keen to know the answer. It added the remark that "scientific circles fear that the bomb may contaminate a large area of the Mediterranean." The following evening Moscow insisted on the problem of the lost bomb's characteristics, offering the comment that "the possibility has not been yet discarded that the bombs may be plutonium bombs, which are extremely dangerous." On February 3 Moscow told its listeners, "In addition to radiation, the rocket fuses have plutonium and, if not dismantled, produce *en masse* poisoning." On February 4 Moscow produced the highly reputed Soviet biologist Nikolai Dvni with the information that the Almería population "has been exposed to intense radiation." The Soviet biologist added that this radiation could "cause cancer, as occurred in Hiroshima with the bomb dropped by the Americans in the Second World War."

Actually, all this propaganda proved, in the end, to be rather self-defeating. People listened to it in the beginning because very little other information was available. But the Communist stations were essentially broadcasting scientific nonsense, though Soviet nuclear and biological specialists, including Mr. Dvni, obviously knew that even a plutonium bomb in the water, damaged or not, does not produce "lethal radiation." When the stubbornly advertised "lethal" consequences of exposure to "intense radiation" failed to materialize, Communist credibility suffered accordingly. And, finally, the Eastern radio output had an immediate antidote in Father Navarete, the village priest. Apprised of these broadcasts, the young prelate tirelessly toured the village, telling his flock and anybody else who cared to listen that if the "hand of God" had not abandoned Palomares on January 17, it would not do so three weeks later.

But not only political propaganda was making scientifically invalid claims. Roberto Puig Alvarez, the architect who had gone to inspect the cracked Weapon No. 3, insisted publicly that he had suffered a radiation burn the size of a dime on his leg after kneeling over the bomb. What Puig evidently did not know was that alpha radiation does not produce burns in the absence of a nuclear reaction. If he did acquire a burn, it was from the TNT-caused fire, and therefore he could not be suffering from radiation on his leg. Because of the possibility that he might have undergone exposure

to plutonium particles—and because he made such a public production of it all—Puig was carefully tested by Spanish and United
States specialists in Madrid. At one stage Ambassador Duke,
highly concerned about Spanish public opinion, received Puig for
a long interview, but it was never made clear whether the architect's real interest lay in his alleged injury or in the hopes of
collecting compensation payments for supposed economic losses in
connection with his apartment buildings in Mojácar.

But evidently not only Communist propagandists were concerned with the Palomares bombs. While the villagers themselves
now had every reason to be disturbed by the radioactivity and its
implications, the very notion of lost bombs brought malaise among
people far and wide.

In a world hardened by twenty years of the Cold War, talk of
the nuclear age had become so common as to lose its real meaning
to political leaders, journalists, and even the people who some
day might become victims of the atom. Thus the events of Palomares inevitably injected a sudden sense of reality into the words
and concepts of the nuclear era. "Overkill," a French professor
in Madrid remarked one day during the search, "may be a
strategic doctrine or even the title of a novel. But in that little
Spanish village the implements of 'overkill' are laid bare and
menacing and, at last, significant. My God, I keep telling myself,
they really exist."

In Bonn and London there were questions in parliament. American editorial-writers tended to stress the safety features of the
bombs, as the Johnson administration did, but in Mexico and
Nigeria and Japan the newspapers saw Palomares as a frightening
reminder of what the world seemed to be all about. A dichotomy
therefore developed between the United States view—the matter-
of-fact view of a nuclear power—and that of the "Third World,"
the world that may be caught between the nuclear powers.

As the Palomares drama lengthened, the discrepancy between
the United States' military and scientific effectiveness in dealing

with the crisis and its inability to cope with the related political and psychological issues became increasingly more pronounced. The overriding fact was that the needs of both the Palomares population and Spanish public opinion were being largely ignored. Because of the exaggerated policy of secrecy imposed by the Pentagon, and partly because the American military men and scientists on the scene had no time or inclination to deal with the villagers —except for some exceptions on a personal level—the people of Palomares were paradoxically left out of their own drama.

To a large extent the United States military contingent around the village acted as if the population did not exist, except as potential radiation victims to be checked, potential authors of compensation claims, potential day laborers, or potential trespassers into their own fields. The mission of the Air Force's public-information officers, such as Colonel Young, was to deal with newsmen, mainly American and foreign, and, in the initial period, to discourage their reporting. Such individuals as Dr. Langham, Colonel White, and Captain Ramirez had an interest in the human aspects of the Palomares situation, but their time and effectiveness were limited. Dr. Langham worried about the villagers' farm problems. Colonel White lectured them on agriculture and sometimes found the time to drop in on citizens such as old Eduardo Navarro Portillo—a steelworker in Gary, Indiana, forty years ago and now the prosperous owner of the land where all three hydrogen bombs had fallen—for a quick chat and a quick glass of cognac. Captain Ramirez, because he spoke Spanish fluently, inevitably had contact with some of the people on behalf of his command when it was required. A corporal from New Mexico, who spoke border Spanish, befriended the Ponce family down by the Cabezo Negro hills. An airman first class from Georgia, who spoke no Spanish at all, got to know scores of villagers because he liked people.

The only contact General Wilson had with the Palomares people in the first month of Broken Arrow was on January 31, when he went with Air Force Brigadier General Arturo Montel Touzet, the Spanish commander of the operation, to address the heads of families at a meeting at the Capri Cinema. The initiative for the meeting came from General Montel, who was worried about the developing "psychosis" in Palomares and proposed to Wilson that they "take the bull by the horns" and tell the two hundred village elders that there was nothing to be concerned about and that compensation would be paid. The two generals and Colonel Young personally prohibited the presence of newsmen at the meeting—Alvin Rosenfeld of the National Broadcasting Company was physically barred at the door—and the proceedings got under way. General Wilson spoke to thank the villagers for their help. When General Montel opened the meeting to questions, a Cuevas lawyer and landowner named Emilio Mulero got up to announce that nobody had any questions and that the two generals could depend on the villagers. The villagers never had a chance to speak for themselves, but they were flattered that an American general had come to speak to them.

Aside from the Capri meeting, which was somewhat less than revealing, the Palomares people had as little information or help from their own authorities as they had from the Americans. Almería Province Governor Luiz Gutiérrez, who had never visited Palomares before, paid a visit of a few hours to the village at the end of the first week after the accident. As a matter of fact, the American military had just as little time for him. When he completed his tour, no helicopter or Air Force car was available to take him back to his capital. In the end he was driven home by two young American diplomats who had been sent to Palomares to try to find out for the embassy in Madrid just what was happening at the accident site.

Up to that point, the embassy had been less than well informed on a situation that was being entirely handled by the military. From the outset, however, Ambassador Duke realized the broader political implications of the Palomares incident and the fact that ultimately he would be responsible for them in terms of United States–Spanish relations. To inform himself more adequately, on January 21 he dispatched to Palomares Joe Smith and Tim Towell, the two young officials who had so anxiously searched for him in Madrid on the morning of the accident.

Smith and Towell, like many other civilian embassy officials who were to follow them on subsequent Palomares pilgrimages, promptly discovered that the military viewed their presence with extremely limited enthusiasm. They were made to feel that they were rather in the way of the hush-hush operations. Nobody seemed anxious to tell them anything. In fact, the two embassy emissaries were treated by the military in virtually the same way as were the inquisitive newsmen, even though they were functionaries of the United States government on a mission for their Ambassador, who is supposed to be the senior American official in the country. The attitude of the military was that Palomares was *their* problem and that civilians, even if they represented the same government, had little business poking their noses into the operation. That Palomares was also a problem affecting the people in the area and the whole political relationship between Spain and the United States appeared to have occurred at that time to only very few of the men in uniform.

After a most cursory meeting with General Wilson, Joe Smith and Tim Towell were left pretty much on their own. Because they had their own car, they were able to move about. Because they spoke Spanish, they were able to establish the first meaningful— and sympathetic—contacts with the Palomares population. They chatted with the men in the bars and visited several homes. The little that the embassy in Madrid did learn of the Palomares situation in the first week after the accident came, therefore, from Smith's and Towell's conversations in the village. But when the pair asked questions of the Air Force's public-information officers at Camp Wilson, they were given the same standard "No comment" or "I don't know" answers that the reporters received.

Back in Madrid, Smith and Towell briefed their superiors on what they had found in Palomares. Immediately a confidential telegram was sent, informing the State Department of the political problems posed by the military information policy and of the general shortcomings in the handling of the Palomares situation. The telegram, over Ambassador Duke's signature, suggested, in effect, that there was not enough feeling at Camp Wilson for the

Spanish mentality and that the men in charge of the Palomares operation were too concerned with the military aspects and not enough with those concerning Spain and the rest of the world. The feeling at the embassy was that, having accidentally contaminated a Spanish village with radioactivity and lost a powerful hydrogen bomb, the United States could not act as if only military considerations were involved. But everybody's hands had been tied by a directive from Arthur Sylvester, the Assistant Secretary of Defense for Public Affairs, determining that nothing should be said about anything concerning Palomares. SAC had detailed contingency papers on how to deal technically with a nuclear accident, but not a word on how to handle public opinion in a foreign country where such an accident might occur.

It was at this juncture that Ambassador Duke decided the time had come for him to enter the picture. At the age of fifty, Angier Biddle Duke was that peculiar and interesting combination of diplomat, politician, and wealthy socialite which the Eastern Seaboard establishment of the United States occasionally produces. On a more limited scale and at a younger age, Duke was somewhat reminiscent of Averell Harriman. Working hard to live down an earlier reputation as a playboy, he approached with utter seriousness, and a lot of imaginative improvisation, the delicate business of being United States Ambassador to Spain at a time of deep changes in Spanish society and politics.

Duke had arrived in Madrid in March 1965, ten months before the Palomares accident, after serving as the State Department's Chief of Protocol under both President Kennedy and President Johnson. When he was named to the Spanish post, the assumption in Washington and Madrid alike was that he would be an elegant political appointee concentrating on good entertainment at the embassy and close contacts with the Spanish aristocracy and the international jet set, while resisting any temptation to upset political applecarts in either capital. That, as a matter of fact, was exactly what Duke, then thirty-six years old, had done in Madrid during his year there in 1951 as special assistant to Ambassador Stanton Griffis. He played and partied, befriended the grandees of Spain, and acquired a Spanish wife. A year later President Truman suddenly raised him from his low Foreign Service rank to the position of Ambassador to the Central American republic of El Salvador, a move that may have been related to the unflagging Democratic party loyalties of the millionaire Biddle and Duke families. Duke's career in El Salvador lasted a year, until Dwight D. Eisenhower's entry into the White House sent out a new set of political appointees to the world. During the eight ensuing years Duke whiled his time away dabbling in New York State Democratic politics, and concerned himself with refugees, immigrants, and Puerto Ricans. In 1961 he returned to the limelight as President Kennedy's Chief of Protocol and immediately became a familiar face in the new entourage. He dealt with the world's emperors, kings, presidents, and prime ministers with an easy social grace, while others worried about the political aspects of the foreign dignitaries' visits to Washington and the President's own trips abroad.

In Madrid, therefore, Duke was instantly typed as a middle-aged playboy who could be depended upon to give everybody a good time and stay away from such awkward problems as, for example, the United States attitude toward the approaching end of Franco's thirty-year rule and the succession. Then, surprisingly, it turned out that Duke would not play the role that had been expected of him. He took the matter of Spanish succession with immense gravity. He became a tireless brain-picker on every conceivable subject in Spain, lengthily interrogating Spanish officials, labor leaders, and students along with American businessmen, professors, and news correspondents. It also developed that the smiling, glad-handing Duke could be quite tough in pushing his viewpoints both in Madrid and with the Washington bureaucracy and that there was nothing sacred to him about applecarts. This was something that the military in Palomares and aboard the flagship of Task Force 65 were to discover.

To be sure, Duke was not opposed to the notion of having a good time while being dead serious about the political side of his ambassadorship. The embassy residence, a large white mansion behind the chancery building, became one of Madrid's active social centers, and the Dukes—Angier and his new wife, Robin (his Spanish wife had died some years earlier in a plane accident) —crisscrossed Spain in search of political and economic knowledge and lively relaxation. When the Palomares accident came in January, and with it Duke's first crisis in Spain, he handled calmly and competently the diplomatic aspects of what might well have turned into a major calamity. At first he took the view that his role was to remain in the background and let the military run the whole Palomares operation by themselves. He spent the second weekend following the accident high in the Sierra Nevada, demonstrating his athletic prowess as he skied with his wife down steep hills covered with sheer ice. But four days later, as it was becoming increasingly obvious that neither the embassy in Madrid nor the State Department in Washington—to say nothing of newsmen and world public opinion—understood what was happening in Palomares, Duke decided to take matters into his own hands. On February 2 he flew from Madrid to San Javier and on to Palomares by helicopter to inspect the operations there. First General Wilson and Admiral Guest briefed him on the progress of the search for the missing bomb and the decontamination work. Then Duke went to the village to meet as many people as he could in order to question them closely about the problems born of the nuclear accident.

He returned to Madrid with several clear notions. One of them was that maximum attention must be given to the material and psychological welfare of the villagers. He felt that, among other things, just compensation must be quickly paid to the people of Palomares who had lost revenue from their quarantined fields or their wages, or whose property had been damaged in some way. Otherwise, he believed, the United States would never live down, in the minds of the Spaniards, the contamination of the village. Another notion that Duke brought back from Palomares was that something had to be done about the problem of public information.

In fact, he wasted no time in doing something about it. He summoned the American correspondents in Madrid to his residence within hours of his return from Palomares and provided them with the first coherent explanation of what was happening on the scene. While he was not allowed to admit for the record that a hydrogen bomb had been lost—Washington still insisted on maintaining the fiction that no such thing had happened—Duke drew a detailed picture of the sea search, telling the newsmen about the hard-hat divers, the Deep Jeep, and some seventy underwater contacts made by sonar devices. It was a rather artful description of the hunt by the steadily growing naval task force, without any mention of what was being hunted. The official explanation still was that the Navy was searching for aircraft debris. Duke's briefing threw much-needed light on the mysteries of Palomares, but the next day it also brought sharp expressions of unhappiness from the Pentagon, which felt that the Ambassador had willfully ignored its "no comment" directives. Duke, who had been daily urging a liberalization in the information policy, took in stride the Pentagon reaction.

That a public-opinion problem over the lost bomb did exist in Spain, and had better be handled with as much truth as possible, was proved twenty-four hours after Duke's meeting with the newsmen. A small but lively demonstration by about one thousand persons took place in front of the embassy's chancery on Calle Serrano on February 4. The demonstration was well advertised ahead of time by leaflets circulated throughout Madrid, summoning people to a protest meeting at the American embassy against nuclear overflights. Consequently hundreds of gray-clad riot policemen gathered around the embassy at sundown, giving it an embattled and besieged appearance. One hour before the time appointed for the manifestation, the iron gates leading to the embassy's garden and parking lot were shut. Duke watched the scene from behind closed shutters in his fifth-floor office.

The demonstrators, moving in small groups, arrived about a half-hour late, and at first the policemen allowed them to parade up and down Serrano, shouting anti-American slogans. Most of the demonstrators were students, but there were many adults in their ranks. Then suddenly the police decided that enough was enough.

Their wooden clubs raised, they charged the demonstrators, pushing them into a side street and methodically beating them until the crowd broke up and fled. Small groups of youths burning newspapers and chanting, *"Cuba sí, Yanqui no!"* and, *"Libertad, libertad"* ("Freedom, freedom"), re-formed a few blocks from the embassy without being bothered by the police. By 10 p.m. the whole thing was over.

As anti-American demonstrations go, the one in Madrid that evening was extremely modest. Chances are that even without the massive police presence it would never have reached major proportions. But it made the point that the Palomares episode was a good propaganda issue against the United States not only for the shouting youths, but also for others who saw potential political capital in the nuclear accident. If nothing else, it again drove home the need to complete the Palomares operation as rapidly as possible and, in the meantime, to defuse the hostile propaganda potential. The longer the mysteries of contamination and the lost bomb persisted, many embassy officials reasoned, the more disturbed public opinion would become and the greater in the long run would be the political problems. Moscow and Prague were keeping up their barrage of dire warnings about the bombs of Palomares without any contradiction from Washington.

But the Pentagon was not alone in bearing the blame for the "no comment" policies. The Spanish government too was reluctant to agree to the release of too much information about Palomares. With tourism responsible for the biggest share of Spain's foreign revenues—some 14 million tourists had brought over $1 billion in 1965—the government was concerned that excessive talk about radioactivity and missing bombs might scare the precious visitors away. Spain was lucky, of course, that the accident occurred over Almería, which is one of the least developed tourist areas, instead of the resort belt of the Costa del Sol, for example, where hundreds of thousands of foreigners spend their dollars, pounds, and marks the year round. But, even so, there already were reports of cancellations of reservations in Costa del Sol hotels, three hundred miles from Palomares, and the Spanish government was unwilling to take chances. Thus Washington's excessive concern over military security and Madrid's fear of losing the tourist trade combined to keep an unnecessary curtain of secrecy over the continuing Palomares drama.

ix

Along the remote wind-swept coast of Almería, the month of February was a time of frustration for the bomb hunters, both ashore and on the sea. The bomb's obstinacy in remaining lost defied men and their ships, submarines, helicopters, and computers. The elements, too, turned on the searchers as if to discourage them from their task. High winds, sometimes real gales, blew from the north or from the Strait of Gibraltar to churn up the Mediterranean waters and paralyze the fleet's operations. They tore at the tents in Camp Wilson, smashed the antennae at the communications and navigation-aid installations, and chilled with their dagger-like gusts the airmen in the Palomares hills and aboard Admiral Guest's ships.

For the people of Palomares also, February was a month of frustration and mounting concern. Their winter crops were irretrievably lost, their fields remained closed to them by the radiological decontamination teams, and the assessments of damage claims were bogging down in controversies involving the American and Spanish authorities and the villagers themselves. Although some of the men were given jobs by the Air Force driving tractors in the plowing operations, most families were running out of money for their immediate needs. In Villaricos, a community of fishermen and laborers infinitely poorer than the Palomares people, the situation was even worse. The Villaricos fishing boats could not go out to sea because the whole area was declared out of bounds by the Navy. Admiral Guest could not have fishermen wandering with their nets in the midst of his complex search activities. So the dark-skinned men of Villaricos—next-door neighbors of the Palomares inhabitants but racially different from them through some quirk of history and early settling patterns—sat silently in their miserable houses or sullenly watched the Navy ships offshore.

And for eight American fliers February was the time of death.

They were the crew of an Air Force C-124 Globemaster that left the Morón base near Seville for San Javier in the late afternoon of Saturday, February 12, with a cargo of two buses, intended for ferrying troops around Palomares, and other equipment for Camp Wilson. The plane and the crew, normally stationed at the Hunter Air Force Base in Georgia, were on temporary duty in West Germany when they were mobilized for the Palomares operation. They had flown several support missions between Morón and San Javier before taking off at 6:26 p.m. on February 12 for what was to be another routine one-hour flight.

The Globemaster was never heard from again, but late at night word was received in Granada from villagers living high in the Sierra Nevada that they had heard an explosion near the 11,418-foot-high Mulhacén peak during a raging snowstorm. The next day two H-43B helicopters from Morón spotted the Globemaster's wreckage on the southern flank of the Mulhacén. They landed on six feet of snow to find the smashed bodies of the fliers strewn all over the mountainside. These were the remains of Captain William T. Cornwell, Captain James P. Cisco, First Lieutenant John S. Arceheaux, Staff Sergeant Donald G. Gallitzin, Staff Sergeant Ronald W. Hickman, Staff Sergeant Charles R. Henderson, Technical Sergeant James W. Thompson, and Airman Second Class Kenneth C. Young.

With the seven fliers killed in the January 17 collision, the death toll for the Palomares episode now stood at fifteen men.

BOOK FOUR *The Find*

i

Off Palomares, Admiral Guest finally succeeded on February 17, exactly one month after the loss of the bomb, in narrowing his high-probability search area from the initial 120 square miles to 27.33 square miles. It was a major step forward in the search effort, since the bigger section had offered rather limited chances of success in the foreseeable future. But even in the narrowed area the hunt in the dark depths, with underwater visibility averaging 8 feet and often much less, sometimes seemed an impossible undertaking. As Admiral Guest put it, "It was like going up in the hills behind Palomares at midnight on a moonless night and taking a hollow can and putting it over one eye, covering the other eye, and taking a pencil flashlight and starting to look through 120 square miles of area."

The new high-probability area was calculated by Admiral Guest on the basis of tracing the aircraft debris pattern from the beach to somewhere between five and a half and six miles out to sea, roughly where Francisco Simó, the Aguilas fisherman, had seen the parachute with the "half-man" sink in the Mediterranean. The debris pattern was established after more than two weeks of diving by frogmen and hard-hat divers and the use of high-resolution sonar and other acoustical devices. Pieces of the aircraft were recovered in the area and sonar contacts were made with numerous other objects. Simultaneously, scientists at Sandia Corporation in Albuquerque, New Mexico, worked out with computers the probable spots where the bomb might have fallen, taking into consideration all possible variables ranging from wind speeds at different altitudes on the day of the accident (it was a near-hurricane 80.5 miles per hour at 30,500 feet when the planes collided, and progressively less at lower altitudes) to a series of hypotheses and ballistic trajectory theories as to where the missing weapon was separated from the bomb bay and the disintegrating B-52. The factors which both Admiral Guest and the Sandia scientists had to consider included the altitude at which the bomb's parachute might have deployed and the possibility that the weapon had come apart in the air because of a TNT explosion or for some other reason. The terrific gravity forces—8 Gs—at the moment of the collision were another factor in this maddening equation.

Speculative as these calculations perforce had to be, the narrowed high-probability search area was as logical a site to start the actual bomb hunt as could be devised. To mark the new area, known as Alpha One, Admiral Guest drew a circle one mile in radius roughly around the point where Francisco Simó had reported seeing the plummeting gray parachute. Then he added two trapezoids south of the circle, naming them Area Bravo and Area Charlie. A secondary section nearby was designated as Delta. Bravo and Charlie were the areas where Admiral Guest thought the weapon might have fallen if it had broken up during or after the collision. The circle and the trapezoids added up to the 27.33 square miles of Alpha One. Its farthest point was 12 miles from shore. The lower-probability area, Alpha Two, stretched for 10 miles along the beach, covering the shallow waters where some debris had been found earlier.

The shrinking of the primary search area—naturally, assuming that the bomb actually *was* there—made the subsequent hunt reasonable if not a sure-fire proposition. Before establishing Alpha One, the Navy had produced an estimate of at least 300 working days to comb the sea floor, literally inch by inch, if it had to go over the original 120-square-mile area. Allowing for bad weather, this would have meant one full year of searching for the bomb, a highly disturbing prospect from every point of view. Nonetheless, the United States was prepared to keep up the hunt for a year to satisfy itself that the bomb was not in the 120-square-mile area or in the still larger area ashore where General Wilson's troops were inching their way up and down the Palomares hills. At the end of the year, other plans would have been devised and the search would have gone on indefinitely until the weapon was retrieved, even if it had taken a lifetime. For both military and political reasons, Washington simply could not abandon the bomb hunt, and both General Wilson and Admiral Guest knew it. A young Navy lieutenant, watching the movements of the task force's vessels from the bridge of the flagship, turned to a friend and said, "You know, I have visions of Palomares becoming a permanent Navy station, like San Diego or Norfolk."

On February 17, the day Admiral Guest radioed his calculations of the sea search priority areas to the Chief of Naval Operations in Washington, the Palomares military commanders still had to operate on the assumption that the hydrogen bomb was either ashore or in the water, although scientific opinion was increasingly inclining to the view that the Mediterranean was the most likely place. But because the three other weapons had come down on land and because the helter-skelter pattern of the aircraft debris both ashore and in the water provided no really logical basis for reaching definitive conclusions, some Air Force ballistic experts held fast to the theory that the elusive bomb was wedged in a mine shaft in Sierra Almagrera or buried in the sand somewhere around Palomares. In the end, the searchers had to accept the fact that they were facing a complete mystery, that they had to keep looking in the water and on the ground, and that they needed luck as much as their sophisticated devices to be able to solve the puzzle of the lost weapon. A SAC colonel summed it all up one evening as he relaxed over a drink at the Maricielo hotel bar after another hard day of searching.

"It has occurred to me," he said pensively, "that this must be the devil's own work. If someone had sat down to figure out the hardest way to lose a hydrogen bomb, he could not have come up with anything more devilish than what we've got to cope with."

In Madrid, Mingote, the cartoonist for the newspaper ABC, put it another way. He drew a picture of a little old Spanish lady praying in church "that I may find my pen, that Rosita may find a fiancé, and that the Americans may find their bomb."

To find this bomb, Admiral Guest had at his disposal by mid-February the best that the United States could offer in the way of underwater vehicles and equipment, navigational aids, and human resources and talent.

His task force off Palomares averaged 15 ships—there were always vessels joining and leaving it or running errands to Cartagena—and the manpower aboard exceeded 2200 sailors. At the height of the search in the shallow coastal waters during the first month he had 130 frogmen from underwater demolition teams and explosives ordnance teams. Under Commander DeWitt Moody, a man who knew a lot both about diving and nuclear weapons, was a staff of 20 naval officers specialized in underwater work and 75 civilian scientists and specialists attached to 7 industrial corporations and 8 Navy organizations ranging from the Pasadena Naval Ordnance test station to the Naval Civilian Engineering department. These specialists were assigned to different ships of the task force and to shore installations.

To perfect navigational capabilities on the surface and under the sea, Decca installed a complex system consisting of a master station near Villaricos and two slave stations aboard ships receiving electronic signals from the shore. These finally permitted the correction of errors on the existing charts—some of these errors were up to 250 yards—and, as operations developed, pinpointing of specific locations for miles off the coast. Without the Decca system, Admiral Guest would have been playing blind man's buff under the sea. To complement this navigation system, the oceanographic ship USS *Dutton* surveyed the contours of the sea bottom and produced detailed charts, on the basis of which a plaster cast was fashioned to give Guest a visual idea of what he was up against. Later the admiral described to visitors how awesomely rugged the underwater terrain was.

"You can see that it has deep canyons," he said, "but off these canyons there are many smaller canyons and gullies, and what it doesn't show is that within these are many ditches which vary in depth from 3 feet to over 100 feet. Another thing that it doesn't show is that within a small area such as this there are cliffs that are 100 to 150 feet high, sheer cliffs, that drop off at 90 degrees."

In this kind of nightmarish terrain, where the depths reached 9000 feet at some points, Guest had to look for the 10-foot-long bomb as well as for hundreds of pieces of the two aircraft. His mission included recovering from the sea floor everything that could be of possible value or interest to the Air Force, which meant just about everything from the B-52 and the KC-135 that had collided over Palomares. Both planes, but especially the bomber, carried highly secret equipment that the Air Force felt it simply could not leave in the Mediterranean.

After studying his underwater maps and the plaster cast, Admiral Guest devised his concept of operations, assigning his men and specialized equipment to depths where they could be the most effective. Up to depths of 130 feet, Guest used frogmen working visually, Honeywell electronic Sea Scanners, and minesweepers equipped with high-resolution sonar. Between 130 and 200 feet, aqualung MK-6 swimmers searched the waters from *Sealab II,* a 57-foot-long cylindrical underwater laboratory with bunks to rest on and galleys. The sonar minesweepers, Honeywell Sea Scanners, and the ocean-bottom sea scanners dragged by ships along the sea floor operated at the same depth. Between 200 and 400 feet, Guest assigned hard-hat divers, men in diving bells, minesweepers, the ocean-bottom sea scanners, and the Perry Cubmarine, a tiny submersible, which was flown from the United States to San Javier and then delivered to the fleet through Cartagena. Four hundred feet was the safety limit for the divers, and below that level men could go down only in submarines. In depths greater than 400 feet not even the Cubmarine could operate. Two research submersibles, the Alvin and the Aluminaut, were given the responsibility for the "inner space" search below 400 feet, along with underwater television cameras and the ocean-bottom sea scanners. From the surface of the Mediterranean down to thousands of feet below it Admiral Guest thus populated the waters with his fishlike men and an array of specialized equipment never before gathered together in one spot. As defined by him, the undersea mission was to search and locate, verify and mark, and finally recover everything of interest from fragments of the two planes' airframes to the hydrogen bomb.

The frogmen, spending long hours in the chilly waters, swam for days at arm's length from each other, holding knotted ropes that recorded their progress and served to mark their findings. On February 1 they recovered a 30-foot-long and 8-foot-wide section of one of the B-52 wings. On February 6 they brought up another wing panel and a wing fuel tank. But the frogmen were just as proficient in finding objects as small as three by four inches and weighing only a few ounces. On February 9 they came up with what the Navy tersely described as "one piece of classified material." Somehow word of this find leaked out and the legend of the Black Box sprang to life, never to be dissipated as far as many newsmen and Palomares villagers were concerned. This legend had it that the Black Box was Top Secret equipment for targeting the SAC bomber on a hydrogen-bomb drop. A better guess was that it was an electronic computer designed to decipher coded radioed instructions of "war" to the B-52 crew if the President of the United States decided to order a nuclear attack. In any event, the more the Air Force spokesmen denied the existence, or the finding, of a Black Box, the more Spanish reporters regaled their readers with tales of it.

Many American and British newsmen, on the other hand, saw in the frogmen's operation an irresistible, if facile, parallel with *Thunderball*. The spectacle of the frogmen and science-fiction submersibles searching the bottom for a lost hydrogen bomb recalled the James Bond story, and the parallel became unpleasantly striking even to the Navy when a Soviet trawler appeared on February 18 on the scene of the search. The trawler, acting as a fishing vessel but chock full of electronic gear, was normally stationed in international waters in the vicinity of the Polaris submarine base at Rota on Spain's Atlantic coast, presumably to peek and eavesdrop. Behaving as obviously as she did, she was under permanent watch by the United States Navy. When she finally chose to move across the Strait of Gibraltar to the Almería coast, United States planes and ships tracked her all the way and set up a full-time watch when the Soviet master decided to take up station less than a mile from the Alpha One high-probability search area. Naval Intelligence, which wondered in the first place why it had taken the Russians nearly a month to dispatch the trawler to the scene, assumed the vessel wanted to see and hear as much as she could of the operation. However, most of the task force's radio communications were coded and there was not very much to learn visually from observing Admiral Guest's ships coming and going and the submersibles diving. Sonar eavesdropping was not likely to produce a great deal of vital information either, and after nearly two weeks of loitering around Alpha One the Soviet trawler departed on March 2 under the Americans' gratefully watchful eyes. There was no real concern about her, but Admiral Guest had enough problems of his own without having to worry about inquisitive foreign ships.

His principal operational problem was to keep functioning efficiently his three research submersibles, the Alvin, the Aluminaut and the Cubmarine, in the face of mechanical difficulties developing in untested conditions, frequently adverse weather, and inevitable crew fatigue. But the submersibles were vital. It was clear from the beginning that, if the bomb were to be found at all, the job would have to be accomplished by the little submarines.

The three craft were the last word in underwater science. They were the inner-space equivalent of the first exploratory outer-space vehicles. Deep-submergence specialists had for some time been talking of the unfathomable ocean depths as the "inner space" of man's terrestrial environment. Just as the astronauts were intent on conquering interstellar space, the new divers were determined to conquer and explore the deep waters and ocean bottoms of the earth. Their trips were perhaps less spectacular than the space flights, but inner space has its own fascination, romance, and drama.

The star of the Palomares underwater drama was the white-painted Alvin, a highly maneuverable little deep-diving research submersible capable of operating down to depths of 6000 feet. On a test dive she once actually reached 7500 feet. The bathyscaphe *Trieste* could go down deeper—she had dived 8400 feet in the *Thresher* search—but lacked the mobility required in the hunt for the bomb that, relatively speaking, was the needle in the underwater haystack. The 13-ton Alvin, named after her inventor, Dr. Allyn Vine, was 22 feet long and 8 feet wide. She had room for a pilot and two observers and could cruise at 2 knots. Her top submerged speed was 4 knots. Working under water, the Alvin has a range of 15 to 20 miles, which meant that she could cover quite a bit of territory in one dive. She could stay submerged for more than 24 hours at a time. While the Alvin carried scanning sonar, a ground detector, and closed-circuit television for search purposes, she was also equipped with a grappling arm that, Admiral Guest hoped, would ultimately serve to snag and retrieve the hydrogen weapon. For communications with her control ship or other submersibles she had a sonar telephone system.

The Alvin had been built for the Office of Naval Research by the Applied Sciences Division of Litton Industries and was operated by the Woods Hole Oceanographic Institution in Massachusetts. It was to there that an urgent telephone call had gone out on the evening of January 22, from Admiral Swanson's technical advisory group in Washington, requesting Dr. Paul Fye, the institution's director, to make the Alvin available for the Palomares operation. As it happened, the Alvin was just then being overhauled in a borrowed hangar at nearby Otis Air Force Base, to correct mechanical and electrical problems that had cropped up during the deep-diving test program the summer before. But Dr. Fye and William O. Rainnie, Jr., the forty-one-year-old oceanographic engineer who was the Alvin's chief pilot, decided that their craft could be made ready for Palomares in a week's time.

The first plan was for the Alvin to be shipped to Spain aboard a large catamaran, a special ship designed to launch and retrieve the submersible. But the Navy, anxious to start underwater search operations for the bomb, felt that would take too long. Consequently, the Alvin and its support equipment—battery-charging vans, the machine shop, and the electronics shop—were loaded aboard two United States Air Force cargo planes on February 1 for the flight from Otis to the Rota naval base on Spain's Atlantic coast. The Alvin's conning tower had to be removed for the loading. Rainnie and the submersible's two other civilian pilots, Valentine P. Wilson and Marvin J. McCamis, prepared to fly over with their craft.

But bad weather, which seemed to plague the Palomares operation in its every phase, forced a delay in the Alvin's departure. Finally, after flying the long route through Labrador and Britain, the Alvin reached Rota on February 5. It took four more days to reassemble the submersible and take care of mechanical problems created by aircraft vibrations before she could make a test dive in the Rota harbor and then proceed to Palomares.

On February 9 the Alvin was loaded aboard USS *Plymouth Rock,* a 10,500-ton landing ship dock (LSD), which had just arrived in Rota from Florida with the Aluminaut. This was the research submersible that was to be the Alvin's partner in the Palomares undersea adventures.

The Aluminaut, painted a bright red, was a big ship compared to the tiny Alvin. She was 51 feet long and 8 feet wide and displaced 81 tons when submerged. Carrying a crew of 6 men, the Aluminaut could dive as deep as 15,000 feet—almost 3 miles—but for operational purposes her depth limit was 6000 feet. Inside her hull she carried a fantastic array of instrumentation. It included underwater telephones, an electronic fathometer for depth measurements, continuous-transmission frequency-modulated scanning sonar, bottom-scanning sonar, underwater illumination equipment, two trainable underwater television cameras, and a gyrocompass. Built by Reynolds and the Electric Boat Division of General Dynamics, the Aluminaut was owned and operated by Reynolds International, Incorporated, as a purely civilian craft. She was accompanied by her own tracking ship, the 250-ton *Privateer,* a converted Navy submarine-chaser. Among the *Priva-*

teer's specialized equipment were a precision depth recorder capable of measuring down to 24,000 feet of water and an underwater telephone with a 12,000-foot range.

The *Plymouth,* normally used by the Navy for amphibious assaults, was equipped with an aft floodable deck, 394 feet by 48 feet, from which the two submersibles could be launched and recovered. With the Alvin and the Aluminaut in the floodable deck, the *Plymouth* sailed all night from Rota and arrived off Palomares on the morning of February 10.

Immediately the Mediterranean weather, as if conspiring with the lost bomb to help it elude the searchers, hit the task force. As Admiral Guest ordered the two submersibles transferred from the *Plymouth* to USS *Fort Snelling*, another LSD that was to serve as their mother-ship, a seventy-knot gale swept over the sea. Both the Alvin and the Aluminaut had already been launched from the *Plymouth*, but now the wind and the high seas would not allow the transfer to be completed. The two submersibles had to be moored to buoys and left there with their crews, bobbing wildly on the waves for nearly twenty hours. In the process the Alvin suffered some damage, which again forced the postponement of the undersea hunt.

Ashore, the gale also bore down on the Broken Arrow searchers. The antennae of the Decca navigation system atop the hill near Villaricos were blown down in midafternoon, and it went off the air. At Camp Wilson the wind tore off the plywood roof over the improvised cafeteria in the ruins of the old foundry, slightly injuring a man. The officers and airmen huddled in their tents, unable to go out to work.

Two days earlier Admiral Guest had had the first major casualty of his operation. The electrical system in the Deep Jeep broke down, and it was beyond the capabilities of the task force to repair it. Regretfully Guest ordered it shipped back home. Other unscheduled diversions complicated his activities that week. On February 7 Francisco Simó was taken out again aboard a minesweeper to the area where he had seen the "half-man" sink with its parachute on January 17. But this time the Spanish fisherman pointed to a spot 500 yards west of the position he had originally reported. Visibly annoyed, Guest turned to an aide. "Does he really know what he's talking about, or what?" he asked. On February 8 operations again slowed down when the task force intercepted an SOS from a merchant vessel near Palomares reporting that she was sinking. A warship was dispatched to help the freighter, but it turned out she was not sinking and needed no assistance.

On February 11 the Mediterranean *mistral* went on blowing, but it was possible for the Alvin to be taken back aboard the *Plymouth Rock* late in the day. The next morning, as the winds abated somewhat, the little white submersible was finally shifted to the *Fort Snelling*. The Decca navigational system returned to the air after twenty hours out of commission. Admiral Guest was ready to order the resumption of search operations when the winds roared out again in full force. Again the Decca antennae were blown down on the Villaricos shore, depriving the task force of its navigation guidance. In despair, Guest radioed for permanent antennae to replace the portable field equipment that could not withstand the Mediterranean wind gusts. On Sunday, February 13, the task force had no choice but to take the day off because of high winds and seas. It was then that Admiral Guest and General Wilson learned of the C-124 crash on the Mulhacén. Everything seemed to be working against the bomb hunters.

The next day, however, the weather cleared. The Decca system was back on the air and Guest could finally order the Alvin and the Aluminaut to attempt their first dives. The floodgate of the *Fort Snelling*'s aft deck was thrown open and first the Alvin and then the Aluminaut floated out onto the sea. Navy frogmen in rubber boats escorted them to their assigned diving spots, paying out the taut lines attached to each of the two submersibles until the "submerge" order was given from the *Fort Snelling*. The Alvin, which went down 1800 feet on the first dive, had been assigned the area south of the spot marked by Francisco Simó. This was the extremely difficult high-probability area where the sea floor broke off into an underwater canyon. She explored the rough canyon walls to give her pilots a taste of the terrain where they would be working and returned to the surface a few hours later without anything notable to report. The Aluminaut was at first given the flatter bottom, north of the high-probability area, where she could operate better. Unlike the smaller and more agile Alvin, the Aluminaut could not wedge herself in the narrow submarine canyons. On their first dives the crews of both submersibles became aware of the formidable visibility problems under the sea off Palomares. Aside from the darkness, which limited the view through the portholes to less than ten feet, surface winds churned the waters down to considerable depths, often sending swirling sandstorms around the submersibles. Though both of them were equipped with underwater lights, the pilots had to go easy on them in order to save their batteries.

On February 14, the day the Alvin and the Aluminaut dived for the first time, Admiral Guest received the Perry Cubmarine, the third of his science-fiction underwater vehicles. The yellow Cubmarine, oddly suggesting the imagined shape of a Martian spaceship with its 14 round portholes, was a research craft capable of taking 2 men down to 600 feet. She was 22 feet long, exactly the length of the Alvin, but less than one-half her width, and she was strictly a visual-search craft. She arrived with her three pilots and Jon Lindbergh, the son of Colonel Charles A. Lindbergh, who is a deep-submergence expert and an executive of Ocean Systems, Incorporated, the firm which acted as the prime civilian contractor for the Navy in the Palomares hunt. Jon Lindbergh, thirty-three, a friendly man who lives near Seattle, Washington, was drafted for the Palomares operation as he stopped in New York on February 3, on his way home from the coast of West Africa, where he had been engaged in offshore oil explorations.

Using the cruiser *Boston*, Guest's flagship, as her mother-ship, the Cubmarine began diving within a day of arriving on the scene of the Salvops. Lindbergh, who took the submersible down a few times himself and indulged in quite a bit of scuba-diving with the frogmen, made another contribution to the search. Together with

Ray Pitts, the boss of the ocean systems team, he fashioned a full-size mock-up of the missing hydrogen bomb, using the same metals for the casing as went into a real weapon. The purpose of this experiment was to determine how much of an acoustical or magnetic signature the bomb was likely to emit. As it turned out, high-resolution sonar could track the mock-up at 250 feet, but without telling the hunters whether they had located a bomb or an old anchor. And, as the undersea operations were demonstrating, there was quite a long way between making a sonar contact and actually locating an object in the dark, turgid waters—particularly if the object was stuck in some inaccessible canyon or gully.

And both Admiral Guest and the Ocean Systems specialists kept reminding themselves that, for all they knew, the bomb might have broken up into many fragments and might lie wildly scattered over a sizable area of the Mediterranean bottom. It was because of this disturbing possibility, and the related possibility that the bomb's plutonium core had spilled out into the water, that one of the task force's ships was assigned the daily mission of sampling the sea off Palomares for traces of radioactivity. Although the invariably negative results of the sampling were doubtless encouraging, it still could not be assumed that the bomb had not broken up into a multitude of fragments, which would have made the hunt a nearly hopeless task. Thus, when Admiral Guest established his priority search areas on February 17, the truth was that he knew as little about the probable location of the lost weapon as he had on the day he landed in Palomares.

The new week opened on February 19, with the arrival on the scene from Philadelphia of the oceanographic research ship USNS *Mizar*, which, at least scientifically, was to become perhaps the most important single vessel of Task Force 65. This strange-looking 3300-ton ship was a floating laboratory with 18 scientists aboard and a search-control center. She was equipped with sonar, underwater television, and still cameras which could be towed on sleds along flat areas of the sea floor, listening and looking for interesting objects. Both sonar findings and television pictures could be relayed to the *Mizar* over three miles of armored signal cable to produce a record and navigational plot of all the contacts. Operating as a search ship, the *Mizar* could survey one-quarter square mile daily, which, given the underwater conditions, is much more impressive than it sounds. Her underwater tracking equipment provided accurate readings as deep as 2000 feet. But the *Mizar*'s other function—and in the end the most important one—was to vector, or direct, the Alvin and the Aluminaut toward any object with which contact had been established and which was to be recovered. Guided by the *Mizar*, the submersibles could then attempt to attach a lifting line to such an object and let the oceanographic ship hoist it to the surface on her main winch, capable of handling up to 5 tons in weight.

As of February 19, however, Admiral Guest's hunters had not located anything promising that the *Mizar* could lift out of the water. Instead, they had one problem and frustration after another. On February 16 the minesweeper *Pinnacle* lost the sled on which she towed her ocean-bottom-scanning sonar. On her third dive, the Aluminaut had to resurface after a few minutes when it suddenly developed that her battery voltage was too low. On February 19, just as the *Mizar* appeared off Palomares, the Aluminaut's left-hand-side motor was damaged when it was struck during a dive by an 8-foot-long fish. On February 21 winds again churned up the Mediterranean, preventing the two submersibles from diving. On February 22 the accident-prone Aluminaut ran into serious trouble. As she was searching the depths at 1818 feet, she slid down an underwater slope, momentarily out of control. In hitting the slope, the Aluminaut provoked something of a slide, and 4000 pounds of mud oozed into her keel compartment through the limber holes. With considerable difficulty Robert Serfass and Robert Canary, the two pilots, succeeded in bringing her back to the surface.

And the problems and contretemps continued as the week wore on, trying the patience and mettle of the searchers. On February 23 the task force was again battered by high winds and seas, accomplishing very little in the course of the day. On February 24 it was the *Mizar*'s turn to give Admiral Guest headaches. Attempting to vector the Alvin toward an undersea contact, the oceanographic ship discovered that her guidance computers were not working properly. On February 25 a signal from the salvage ship *Hoist* reported that three Navy scuba divers had developed mild cases of bends after working at 160 feet under the water for several hours. The *Hoist*'s skipper thought the accident was due to faulty gauges in the ship's decompression chamber. Guest, tense by nature, was becoming increasingly touchy and irritable as day after day reports of mishaps and difficulties were brought to him at the *Boston*'s flag command. He snapped at his aides and cursed the foul weather and the inanimate obstinacy of the Air Force's hydrogen bomb that refused to let itself be found. But his bulldog-like tenacity hardened as the problems mounted.

The week of Sunday, February 27, opened with a sense of promise. The task force's three ocean tugs completed the job of dumping at sea, far away from the search areas, the 200,000 pounds of wreckage from the B-52 and the KC-135 that General Wilson's debris-collection teams had assembled on the beach in a huge junkpile of green- and yellow-painted twisted metal and wiring. Classified equipment was removed before the wreckage was loaded onto the barges that the tugs towed out into the Mediterranean. Simultaneously, scuba divers from the submarine rescue ship USS *Tringa* pulled out of the sea another large wing section of the B-52, this one 10 feet by 32 feet. It was examined by experts before being dumped back into the water. The Aluminaut, taking advantage of reasonably good morning weather, spotted two pieces of aircraft wreckage in the south portion of the Alpha One area, where no debris had been found before or had been expected to be found. This discovery pleasantly startled the task force's plot specialists. It suggested that other objects, too, might lie there. But before the Aluminaut could continue her survey, a 50-knot wind hit the Palomares waters. The wind further gained in strength during the night, and at 10 p.m. it once more knocked the Decca Hi-Fix navigation system off the air. The Decca station was repaired in the middle of the next afternoon, but gales again churned up the waters and no real work was done all day. "This is where we came in," a civilian scientist said dispiritedly to a Navy captain at dinner in the *Boston*'s officers' mess that evening. "Looks like we'll be here for years."

On Tuesday, March 1, the Alvin went down on her ninth dive off Palomares. Valentine Wilson was at the controls that morning as the white submersible descended to 2400 feet in the Alpha One circle, not far from where the Aluminaut had located the two pieces of aircraft debris two days earlier. The Alvin was assigned to cover on this particular dive a 1000-square-yard section of the grid worked out by Admiral Guest as the highest-probability area. Because of powerful bottom currents, Guest accepted the theory that the 5000-pound bomb and its parachute might have moved quite a distance from the spot where Francisco Simó thought he had seen them sink six weeks earlier. The Alvin's operating technique, therefore, was to carry on a contour search of the mountainous bottom, sliding in and out of the underwater ravines at a constant depth. It was, as a Navy submariner put it, "like walking down an old farmer's cowpath."

Moving slowly over a steep mountain slope that dipped into a deep sea valley, Wilson spotted in the mud a semi-cylindrical furrow that resembled a torpedo track. Since the hydrogen bomb's shape was nearly the same as that of a torpedo, Wilson concluded that the track might well have been left by the heavy weapon as it was dragged by the current.

"I have a mark," Wilson yelled into his sonar telephone. Aboard the *Mizar*, the control officers excitedly looked at each other. Could it be?

Wilson swung the Alvin to follow the track, hoping that the bomb lay somewhere at the end of it. But visibility was atrocious and strong currents were pulling the submersible away. Presently Wilson lost the track. He and Marvin McCamis, the copilot, tried for hours to find it again, but the Alvin's batteries were running low and she had to surface.

The immediate problem facing Admiral Guest now was to make

up his mind whether the furrow briefly seen by the Alvin had indeed been made by the bomb and whether he should concentrate all his equipment on that particular area. His own inclination was to remain skeptical, even though Wilson's report was the most promising—and exciting—development since the task force had assembled off Palomares. In fact, skepticism was Guest's attitude through the whole suspenseful period that was to follow. The tough little admiral would believe only what he could see, and the report of the furrow was too sketchy to satisfy him. To complicate matters, Francisco Simó decided that same day, after going to sea again aboard a warship, that the spot where he had rescued Major Messinger, the B-52's staff pilot, was eight and not twelve miles from shore. This could change some of the basic calculations used to determine the possible trajectory of the bomb—if it had indeed gone into the Mediterranean.

In any event, the Alvin made six more dives during the week without any luck in spotting the torpedo-like furrow again. In these dives the Alvin was vectored by a surface ship using the coordinates provided by Wilson when he had found the mark on March 1. Looking back at these long frustrating hours of daytime and nocturnal dives, the Alvin pilots felt that surface tracking errors by the Navy ships that week were responsible for their inability to relocate the furrow. The crude tracking procedures, they claimed, gave the Alvin positions somewhere in a circle of 900 to 1200 feet—completely off the mark—instead of shooting her straight down on the target.

The wisp of hope provided by the Alvin's find was vanishing quickly. The outlook again was for an indefinite stay off Palomares.

On land, General Wilson's bomb-search teams went on criss-crossing the four-square-mile high-probability area between Palomares and Sierra Almagrera with dogged obstinacy but absolutely no success. By late February the hunt ashore had become both highly scientific and immensely tough on the airmen and their boots. Sandia Corporation scientists and Air Force ballistic experts had defined the land high-probability area on February 13, and now this square as well as the surrounding rough mountain terrain were being explored painstakingly by eight search flights, each made up of twenty-five airmen, advancing in a sweeping line across each grid. In some instances the individual grids were covered nine times by the men moving slowly at six feet from each other. No grid was covered less than twice, as the orders were to check and double-check, and to check nine times if it seemed advisable.

Acting as the "field marshal" of the land search, Colonel "Shep" Shepard assigned a junior officer and a sergeant to lead each flight, while he hopped from team to team by jeep or helicopter. Flight leaders had compasses and radios to assure navigational accuracy, and to communicate with each other and with Colonel Shepard, and the men carried bags of numbered wooden stakes, orange cloth squares, and reels of nylon line. As they advanced, the airmen played out nylon line to mark their progress —each reel had two miles of line on it—and drove the stakes into the ground for reference points. The orange cloths served to help air coordination of the search. After the first few weeks the tan-and-green Palomares countryside was dotted with 150 stakes and scores of orange squares and strung with miles of nylon line. The nylon line, however, had a way of vanishing once in a while. Returning to their assigned areas in the morning, the searchers sometimes discovered that as much as a half-mile of line had disappeared during the night. To replace it was one of the many petty nuisances attached to the operation.

Boots were another nuisance. They kept tearing as the men climbed the sharp rocks and slag heaps of the Almagrera flanks, lowered themselves into old mine shafts, galleries, and passageways, and crawled through tomato patches. Ordering new boots flown in for the searchers became a somewhat irritating logistics problem, as the Air Force had to make sure the footwear fitted each individual. Fatigues too tore, and Washington had to worry as much about keeping the airmen shod and clothed as about supplying them with all the sophisticated scientific equipment for the hunt.

In some cases helicopters dropped men atop mountain peaks so that they could work their way down looking for signs of the hydrogen weapon. At other times men just climbed up goat paths and even sheer rock faces. After coming down a particularly difficult stretch of mountainside late one morning, Colonel Shepard came upon a small boy who had been sent by the mayor of a tiny village in the high hills with a lunch invitation for the American group. Shepard looked the boy in the eye and said, "My friend, I wouldn't go up that mountain again even to have lunch with Brigitte Bardot."

There were no limits to the searchers' inventiveness and improvisation. In New Mexico the Sandia Corporation constructed mock-ups of the hydrogen weapon, and Air Force planes dropped them from different altitudes, with and without parachutes, to determine trajectory and fall patterns. These experiments also suggested how a bomb could disintegrate on impact with rock or sand. The conclusions were sent on to the search headquarters in Palomares to refine even further the on-scene techniques. One of these techniques called for the use of Navy frogmen to survey the bottoms of water-filled wells, reservoirs, and holes which pocked the Palomares area. The frogmen, equipped with powerful lights, were lowered on bosuns' chairs into some of the reservoirs. In other cases they just crawled into the waterholes. All these holes were also a danger to the searchers, and it became necessary for the Air Force to mark over 150 of them to avoid accidents. Between Vera and Garrucha, for example, the airmen one day suddenly came upon an 800-foot-deep well in the middle of a grassy plot.

Scientists too were mobilized to assist in the land search. William Barton, an aerodynamicist from the Sandia Corporation, played an important role in defining the high-probability area ashore. His initial slide-rule calculations were subsequently confirmed by computers at Sandia's New Mexico headquarters. Because of the possibility that the bomb had fallen into a mineshaft, the United States Bureau of Mines dispatched to Palomares a specialist from its Pittsburgh office. Robert Kingery, the specialist, did not find the bomb, but he and Colonel Shepard became fascinated with Almagrera's ancient Phoenician mines, and the two men used whatever spare time they had to study them. If nothing else, the land search produced a great deal of new research on the lead-and-silver history of old Palomares.

A short-lived experiment was the use around Palomares of a United States Army mine detection team flown from Germany in the first week of the hunt. While it had reasonably occurred to someone in the military chain of command that mine detectors might locate the lost hydrogen bomb, it turned out immediately that the magnetic pull of the iron and lead deposits in the Palomares area sent the instruments' needles flying wildly. So the search had to go on the hard way, using men's muscles and men's eyes to comb the tough terrain in the monotonous, exhausting sweeps up and down the eroded hills, staring, always staring at the ground for the most minute clue to the bomb's whereabouts.

One afternoon late in February a clue finally did appear, sending a wave of excitement through the search forces ashore and aboard the ships. This clue was a small metal tail plate from the missing bomb, and it was found by airmen in the sand on the beach at the dry mouth of the Almanzora River, not far from the spot where Weapon No. 1 had landed intact. The finding of the tail plate proved one vital thing almost beyond the shadow of a doubt: that the bomb's parachute had deployed at some point after the midair collision. This was certain because the plate covered the aperture through which the bomb could eject and deploy its parachute. That the plate belonged to the lost weapon was also easily established through its serial number. Each component of a hydrogen bomb carries its own Top Secret serial number so that both the Atomic Energy Commission and the Air Force can at all times keep track of all the parts of each bomb in the United States arsenal, and of its spare parts. In fact, one of the first steps taken in Washington after the Palomares collision was to prepare a list of the serial numbers of the four bombs aboard the B-52, to facilitate the hunt and help determine which pieces belonged to which weapon. The serial numbers are highly classified because they relate to the specific types of equipment—such as arming and guidance devices—used in different bombs according to their strategic functions. In the immensely complex puzzle of international nuclear espionage, the knowledge by Soviet scientists of the serial number of an American bomb's component could become a crucial lead for determining United States weapons designs. And weapons designs are nowadays the most jealously guarded nuclear secrets.

But while the finding of the tail plate seemed to confirm the belief that the missing weapon had descended under a parachute, it still left unanswered many basic questions. For aerodynamicists on the scene, such as Sandia Corporation's Bill Barton, it opened a new field of conjecture and slide-rule and computer calculations. Since the possibility could now be virtually eliminated that the bomb had fallen without a parachute and in nearly direct trajectory governed mainly by its own weight and the collision's centrifugal forces, the altitude at which the silk had actually deployed and the corresponding wind speeds became urgent questions. The ballistic experts' equation was now more complete, but they still lacked the most important factor, the deployment altitude. Their calculations, therefore, were at best highly educated conjecture. One of the conjectures that the Air Force could not quite disregard, particularly in the light of the finding on land of the bomb's tail plate, was that the weapon might have landed ashore, as did the three others. The parachute might have caught fire from a piece of flaming debris, and then the bomb would have plummeted almost straight down, at variance with all the ballistic calculations. Some Air Force experts nearly convinced themselves that the bomb was on land, and the search by General Wilson's teams gained new momentum. When, a few days later, the Alvin spotted the underwater torpedo track, majority opinion again swung to the theory that, after all, the bomb had to be in the sea. But Shep Shepard's searchers, oblivious of scientific theories, kept up their quest through Palomares' tomato patches and mineshafts.

Though the work was backbreaking and seemingly hopeless, the troopers' morale remained fairly high as the men competed in searching for interesting pieces of aircraft debris and producing distinctive designations and insignia for their individual teams. Mock awards were given for significant finds. A Broken Arrow insigne was designed by someone and reproduced on beret shields and shoulder patches. It had a background of the Palomares mountains, the two stars of General Wilson, a tepee representing the search camp, and an elongated broken arrow to signify the nuclear accident. Later General Wilson had the emblem reproduced and mounted on wood to be sent as a souvenir to United States and Spanish officials involved in the operation. The search flights acquired special names inscribed on campaign pennants and colors for the men's scarves. Just as Captain Finkel's vegetable-cutters were known as Finkel's Farmers, the bomb hunters were Wesson's Warriors and Meredith's Marauders, after the names of the flight commanders. An energetic flight commander from the

Morón base became known as Robin Hood after he grew a full black beard. It did not last very long, though: The Air Force felt that beards were going a little too far even in morale-building, and the young captain was ordered to report to Camp Wilson's Spanish barber for a tonsorial treatment. The same captain wrote his name seven times on a mountain marker to record the back-and-forth sweeps by his search team. The troops were encouraged to sing as they marched to and from the hunt areas, and an anonymous author contributed this Palomares marching song:

> If you've got a low IQ,
> You can be a searcher too.
> Hup, two, three . . .

In the village of Palomares, life was not quite so cheerful. Although the decontamination operations were nearing their end as the month of March began, most Palomares men had now been out of work for close to six weeks, and uncertainty over their futures weighed heavily on the village families. They still were told precious little by the Spanish and American authorities. The processing of their damage claims was excruciatingly slow, partly because of United States laws and partly because of the policy adopted by Spanish officials to prevent what they considered excessive demands.

Actually, the United States began paying the first claims at the end of January—less than two weeks after the accident—when the Air Force's "bagman" arrived on the scene. The bagman was Lieutenant Colonel Joseph Stulb, a slight white-haired, bespectacled lawyer who served as the Sixteenth Air Force's deputy judge advocate at Torrejón. A native of New Orleans, Colonel Stulb spoke Spanish, mainly because his mother was Spanish, and from the outset he developed a certain rapport with the people of the village. Sitting in a small tent behind a folding table, he listened to the villagers' damage claims, took copious notes, and made small individual payments with crisp brand-new peseta bills from his blue satchel. But he could meet only simple and incontrovertible claims—for damaged fences or broken water pipes—and could not solve Palomares' basic problems.

In the first place, the United States Foreign Claims Act limited individual payments to $15,000. Special Congressional appropriations were needed for larger claims, and inevitably most of them ran high. The second complication was that there were no readily available criteria for assessing damages for the unsold January crop or, in the face of many claims, for future crops that might go begging for buyers because of Palomares' *radioactividad* fame. Many of the farm-owners sought to collect such "advance" damages, but Colonel Stulb could not commit the United States to such future obligations without creating impossible precedents. And finally, there was the problem of the Spanish policy on claims.

Early in February the whole system became increasingly bureaucratic, but not necessarily more efficient. Colonel Stulb and his staff moved into permanent headquarters at a green-shuttered house at the foot of the village. A wooden sign in Spanish identifying the house as the Air Force Claims Office was hung outside. A survey of the Palomares crops—production, acreage, and prices —was undertaken. Then a Spanish military judge, whose surname was Palomares, arrived to direct the processing of the villagers' claims. Two agricultural experts from Almería were assigned to advise him on the crops. To many Americans—notably to Ambassador Duke and General Donovan—the claims problem was largely psychological and political, but the Spaniards inclined to see it as a purely actuarial one. On numerous occasions the Spanish judge pared down the claims even though the Americans were willing to consider them. The result was that hostility developed between the villagers and their own authorities. Charges were loudly made that Almería's Governor Gutiérrez and Palomares' Mayor Gonzáles were conspiring for vague political reasons to deprive the villagers of just compensation. Someone inevitably pointed out that this section of Almería had been in socialist and anarchist hands during the Civil War and that Franco officials had long memories. Then other accusations were voiced that

Gutiérrez and Gonzáles were in cahoots with the Americans to keep the payments down. In the end resentment began to build against the United States, and old Pablo's *cuento* about the man from Córdoba who refused to pay his debts was being increasingly repeated in the Palomares bars.

Finally it became necessary for the Americans to step into the claims picture on the highest possible level. In the first week of March, General Donovan flew back from Madrid for a meeting with General Montel, the Spanish military commander in Palomares, and twenty-one Palomares family heads. After a long discussion, a formula devised by Donovan and calling for a 27-percent across-the-board increase over previously offered levels was accepted. The main deadlock over the claims was broken, but a great deal of paper work still lay ahead before payments could catch up with the needs of the village.

In the meantime steps were taken by both the Americans and the Spaniards to bring some relief to the area. Colonel White hired twenty-eight men from Palomares and Villaricos to drive the tractors and plows in his decontamination operation. Men providing their own equipment and gas were paid the equivalent of $2.50 an hour, and those with tillers received $5.00. The village's farm machinery was being used again, and some money trickled down to such men as Miguel Castro Navarro and Antonio Saviote. Forty-two laborers—Palomares field hands and Villaricos fishermen—found temporary housekeeping jobs at Camp Wilson. Some of them had gone unemployed for months even before the bombs fell on Palomares, and now the sudden inflow of cash led to results that surprised at least one American colonel. Driving back from Villaricos one afternoon, he came upon a laborer sprawled under his bicycle. He stopped the jeep to discover that the man was drunk and sleeping it off on the road. Later the colonel asked General Montel why people who were so poor wasted all their money on drink. The Spanish general, who knew his people well, replied, "I understand him. He's a man who never before could afford more than a glass of wine a month."

But making money available to the village through temporary

jobs and even claims payments was not the whole answer. General Montel, fifty-seven, a Cuban-born career aviator and nuclear specialist, feared mostly the radioactivity "psychosis" that could do Palomares long-lasting if not irreparable economic harm. Shortly after arriving on the beachhead, Montel became aware that the boycott against Palomares crops and Villaricos and Garrucha fish and shrimp was mounting. Buyers refused to touch tomatoes and beans even from areas a mile or more removed from the Palomares radioactive zero zone. Garrucha shrimp found no takers, either, and their market price dropped by mid-February from 200 pesetas to 40 pesetas a kilogram—from $3.33 to 66 cents. In West Germany, which normally imported Almería tomatoes, a deputy rose in the Bundestag to inquire whether it was safe to continue this practice. In Madrid a grocer indignantly replied, "Certainly not," when a customer asked whether his tomatoes were from Palomares. A Spanish movie director proposed a fantasy concerning a man radioactively contaminated by a Bloody Mary. All of this was cause for alarm, and General Montel knew that so long as the lost bomb remained in the sea and radioactivity still contaminated the Palomares fields, the deadly cloud of economic ruin would hover over the whole region.

Psychological efforts to reverse the tide of fear had results that were at best confined to the coastal villages. The sight of American airmen eating tomatoes in the fields they were decontaminating led to comments that the Americans were known to be crazy anyway. When a shipment of tomatoes from the Palomares warehouse—they had been picked before the accident—was sent to the sailors aboard the cruiser *Boston*, a Camp Wilson wag insisted that they were cast overboard on the sea side and described the whole operation as the Boston Tomato Party. General Montel and his officers made a point of eating shrimp in the bars along Garrucha's main street, but this did little to bring buyers rushing to purchase the local catch.

More serious measures were required, and General Montel proposed to Captain General Muñoz Grandes, the chief of the Spanish High Staff, that the government undertake to buy or

finance the tomatoes and beans that were already in the ware-
houses and those still unpicked in the fields outside the zero zone.
The Ministry of Commerce and the Supply and Transport Commission were charged with the purchasing operation, which began
on February 17, exactly one month after the Palomares accident,
but when the trucks arrived in the area it developed that the
people were reluctant to pick the tomatoes. The men in the immediate Palomares neighborhood assumed that the United States
would pay them for the tomatoes under the claims policy. Others
were discouraged by the rock-bottom prices for Almería tomatoes
since *radioactividad* had taken hold and were reluctant to take
chances with possible contamination.

General Montel's first task, therefore, was to persuade the people of the region to pick their own tomatoes. He achieved it by
threatening the farmers with the danger of losing their markets
in future years if they stayed out now. The buyers, on the other
hand, succumbed to the profit motive. Because the government
was reselling the tomatoes cheaply—it had paid the farmers the
pre-accident market price—the importers finally forgot *radioactividad* and took the crops. After ten days of this, normal commercial operations began to resume. But until the last vestiges of
the Americans' nuclear weapons had been removed from Palomares, the uncertainties—and a bit of the "psychosis"—would go
on living with the village.

And as time went on, ironies of fate became even more pronounced in the Almería region. Whereas Palomares, Villaricos,
and to some extent Garrucha were suffering from the after-effects
of the nuclear accident, Vera was flourishing. Boarding-house
owners, storekeepers, and taxi drivers were enjoying a bonanza
with the invasion of the military, civilian scientists, and hordes of
newsmen. The town accepted the Americans willingly and with
a sociological interest that visiting American tourists usually reserve for "natives." Colored airmen and GIs were the first Ne-
groes most of the Vera people had ever seen and they were studied
with polite curiosity. An old man who had worked in a Philadelphia shipyard forty years earlier often joined Americans for

a beer in the evening at La Estación to force back to life his long-forgotten command of English. He displayed almost a proprietary attitude about the Americans, sometimes telling his envious Spanish friends with deliberate casualness, "Oh, I know these people. Why, I can speak their language." And on a Saturday afternoon, after the market, a little girl said to her father, "Daddy, let's go to Palomares and look at the Americans."

In Palomares, Colonel White and his specialists were completing the decontamination work as February drew to its end and March began on the optimistic note of the finding of the bomb's tail plate ashore and the Alvin's discovery of the underwater track.

As Dr. Langham had observed, the lengthy search for the missing weapon was attracting worldwide attention and letting the Air Force proceed with the decontamination of Palomares in relative peace and away from the limelight. About March 1 the first fields were being returned to their owners and reopened for farm work, as the plowing of the contaminated areas proceeded at a fast clip. Because the planting for the next crop would normally start in the first few days of April, it was crucial to turn the fields back to the farmers to avoid disrupting another agricultural cycle in Palomares. As each of the 854 individual plots was declared free of plutonium contamination, a special certificate signed by General Wilson, General Montel, and a representative of the Spanish Nuclear Energy Board was handed to the owner. These were the first certificates of radioactive decontamination ever issued in the nuclear age.

On March 3 the decontamination was terminated and a survey by Air Force and JEN monitors produced uniform zero readings throughout the Palomares countryside. Only at the two bomb craters, marked with large squares of white cloth, was there still work to be done. This was where highly radioactive soil had been scraped from the surrounding ground and awaited shipment to an atomic cemetery.

The first idea, acceptable to the Spaniards, was to bury the radioactive soil in deep pits. But then both the Spaniards and the Americans had second thoughts. From a technical point of view, there was the theoretical danger that a seismic movement might cause fissures in the pits and provoke a seepage of the plutonium wastes. And, politically, the United States government flatly informed Madrid, it did not want to have an "atomic monument" in Spain. To bury the plutonium soil in Palomares would invite hostile propaganda for years to come.

The final solution was to ship the contaminated soil and vines to a tract of land near the AEC's Savannah River plant near Aiken, South Carolina. There they would be buried in slit trenches that serve as the AEC's atomic cemetery for industrial radioactive wastes and soils occasionally brought from Nevada test sites. That Spanish soil should go for burial to the banks of the Savannah River was another of the historical coincidences surrounding the Palomares accident. In 1540 Spanish explorer Hernando de Soto, in quest of gold and silver, crossed the Savannah River as he moved north from what today is Georgia to South Carolina. Now, 426 years later, in the midst of the nuclear age, other emissaries from Spain were to touch the banks of the Savannah.

To ship the 1750 tons of radioactive soil and vines, the United States government ordered the designing and manufacture in Italy of 5500 special steel drums, each with a 55-gallon capacity. The drums were to be shipped from Naples to Palomares to be loaded aboard a Liberty-class freighter, and Seabees from Task Force 65 immediately proceeded to build a short jetty into the sea from the Camp Wilson beachhead. As soon as the drums arrived, they were trucked to the two crater sites to be filled with the contaminated dirt scraped from the hillsides. Most of the work had to be done at Site No. 2, where a full-fledged TNT explosion had occurred in the cracked bomb, spraying the plutonium particles over a wide area. Twenty-eight airmen, working four-hour shifts from 7 a.m. until 10 p.m. under portable lights, filled the drums in three and a half days of furious activity at Site No. 2. Altogether, 4879 drums were filled at the two crater sites as the men worked with shovels and bare hands to pack the contaminated soil.

Subsequently Colonel White's troopers filled in the crater pits and replaced the contaminated soil scraped away from the hot areas around the two bomb sites. The new soil was bought from Palomares farmers at the south end of the village and carted over to Rabbit's Rise and the Black Head hills. Low whitewashed fenceposts and barbed wire were installed along the Palomares roads where the Air Force bulldozers had earlier torn out the cactus and esparto-grass hedges to open the way for radiological teams and bomb searchers. True to its word, the United States had restored Palomares to its physical condition before the bombs fell out of the sky on January 17. Dr. Langham, who supervised from Madrid the scientific aspects of the decontamination operation, was to say later that in the whole Palomares radiological experience "no major fundamental lessons were learned or any new or unusual circumstances encountered except, in this case, it was the real thing involving real people."

But people, of course, were the crucial aspect of the Palomares episode. It was the first instance of radioactive contamination of an inhabited area in peacetime since the onset of the nuclear age, raising the fundamental question of how a peaceful village is affected by an invasion of hydrogen bombs literally coming out of the blue. Aside from the immediate economic impact and the disruption of the villagers' lives for several months, the effects of this invasion could not be adequately measured the moment Colonel White's men finished the job of decontaminating Palomares and putting everything back in place.

Medically, as Dr. Langham was to remark, it could be assumed that some of the villagers did inhale a certain amount of alpha activity. But, he added, "the probability that anyone inhaled enough to hurt him is small indeed" even though "theoretically, there is a probability of a malignancy being caused" in the tissues of people who breathed in the alpha particles. That an outside chance did remain that such plutonium-induced malignancies might develop in time in the organism of any Palomares villager was a reality that the Spanish JEN also had to accept. For this reason the Spanish government made it known that it would not let the claims case against the United States be closed for at least fifteen, but possibly as many as thirty, years—the maximum period in which cancer from alpha inhalation may conceivably develop.

On the psychological level, the effects of the bombs on the Palomares inhabitants were just as elusive at this juncture. There could be no question that the events beginning with the January 17 accident had deeply affected the villagers, but only time could throw light on the extent and the ultimate nature of this disruption. As the band of the Sixteenth Air Force, expressly flown from Torrejón for the occasion, paraded through Palomares on Sunday, March 6, to mark the end of the decontamination operations, everything was outwardly back to normal. Shepherds were again out in the fields with their flocks and sheepdogs. Farmers were trickling back to the fields, and less than fifty yards from Site No. 3, an elderly man was once more driving his little red tractor over the parched Palomares earth. The children sent away by their parents in the panic of the first week had returned home, and the schools had reopened. Down the steep incline of the road below the spot where the third bomb had blown up, a little boy ran, holding the line of a kite that fluttered in the air.

But there were the intangibles and the imponderables. Ana Navarro, the wife of Eduardo Navarro Portillo, still refused to spend her nights at their house next to Rabbit's Rise. She slept at her daughter's home at the other end of the village and came over every morning to tend to her domestic chores. "I can't sleep here," she told a visitor. "It makes me nervous. There's something strange now about my home." Pepé López, the storekeeper who kicked the bomb, came back to his house on the other side of Rabbit's Rise, but he too was uneasy. He complained about feeling poorly, even though Spanish and American doctors had given him a clean bill of health. In the Palomares bars the men laughed when they heard on the radio the jazzy rendition of "La Bomba Yeh-Yeh," the rock-and-roll tribute to the events in their village. But the laughter was weak, a bit forced. And in all the conversations the common denominator was uncertainty and continuing bewilderment over what had befallen Palomares.

In this sense, then, it still seemed impossible for the United States to restore Palomares to its original condition.

International political and propaganda pressures continued to bear down on the United States, greatly helped by the official secrecy over the Palomares events still maintained by Washington. During February the Communist radio stations kept up their barrage of charges that the United States had dangerously contaminated the whole Almería coast and the adjoining portion of the Mediterranean. The people of Palomares may have known that the Communists' claims were wildly exaggerated, but the rest of the world had no way of knowing it. It was exposed to inevitably inadequate—if not downright inaccurate—newspaper reporting from Palomares, while the United States insisted on holding back the truth, which was infinitely better than the half-truths and accusations being bandied about.

By the middle of February the Soviet government resolved to jump openly into the controversy to see what could be fished out of the troubled Palomares waters. On February 14 the Soviet Peace Committee, a chapter of the World Peace Council, issued a declaration demanding a ban on all peacetime flights of aircraft equipped with nuclear weapons. On February 16 the Soviet Foreign Ministry handed United States Ambassador Foy Kohler a long *aide-mémoire* charging that the Palomares event was a violation of the 1963 nuclear-test-ban treaty. Far-fetched as it may have seemed, the Soviet Union took the position that the danger of radioactive contamination stemming from the accident was a result of a "flagrant contradiction" of United States obligations under the agreement. The Soviet memorandum failed to explain why an accident of this type should be regarded as a deliberately planned nuclear test—the kind that was forbidden in the 1963 pact—and it went on to claim that the possible radioactive contamination of the Mediterranean by the lost bomb would constitute a violation of the 1958 convention on freedom on the high seas. The next day Semyon Tsarapkin, the Soviet delegate to the

United Nations Disarmament Conference, read the memorandum to a conference meeting in Geneva.

The Soviet memorandum was evidently a propaganda maneuver, but the United States and Spain, still bound by their self-imposed policy of total secrecy, contented themselves with rejecting the Moscow charges and restating the obvious fact that no nuclear explosion had occurred in Almería. The Spanish government volunteered the comment that "no radioactivity was registered in the fish of the Almería zone or in any other zone, nor was there radioactivity in the water or on land there."

These official reactions did little to clarify the Palomares situation for a confused public. The Spanish statement was also inaccurate, inasmuch as there *was* radioactivity in Palomares from the two cracked bombs. But the latest Soviet propaganda effort did have the salutary effect of forcing a reconsideration of Washington's public-information policy, which Ambassador Duke had been clamoring for for a full month. Discussions were opened with the Spanish government on how best to face the public-opinion problem, including the fact that up to that moment neither Washington nor Madrid had admitted officially that a hydrogen bomb was actually missing. The fiction that General Wilson and Admiral Guest were merely searching for aircraft debris was wearing uncomfortably threadbare.

And the way in which this fiction was being forced on newsmen —and therefore on world opinion—was verging on the ridiculous. Some of the most inane dialogue since *Alice in Wonderland* or George Orwell's Newspeak echoed on the beaches of Palomares as reporters and Air Force information officers engaged in increasingly frustrating persiflage.

"Skip" Young, and later his two Air Force replacements, had standard answers to the question, repeated hundreds of times daily, as to whether any progress was being made in locating the bomb. A typical conversation would go like this:

REPORTER: "Tell me, any sign of the bomb?"

AIR FORCE SPOKESMAN: "What bomb?"

REPORTER: "Well, you know, the thing you're looking for. . . ."

AIR FORCE SPOKESMAN: "You know perfectly well we're not looking for any bomb. Just looking for debris."

REPORTER: "All right, any signs of the thing that you say is not the bomb?"

AIR FORCE SPOKESMAN: "If you put it that way, I can tell you that there is no sign of the thing that is not the bomb. . . ."

And so it went for days, for weeks.

For newsmen to report with even a degree of accuracy what was one of the year's great stories was an impossible and maddening undertaking. They could stand on the beaches with binoculars, watching the dives and the surfacings of the white Alvin and the red Aluminaut, but neither the Air Force nor the Navy would tell them what was happening. Inevitably, then, rumors flew thick and fast. When the Navy removed a string of marker buoys from one spot, bulletins went out that the bomb had been found or that the search had been abandoned, depending on the reporter's interpretation.

And there were bans on movements, making the reporters' work even more exasperating. Guardia Civil troopers blocked the path to Villaricos so that newsmen could not come close to the Decca main navigation station. On certain days newspapermen were kept out of the village of Palomares altogether. On other days Spanish plainclothesmen prevented them from talking with the villagers. Typically, a very polite policeman would interrupt a conversation to ask, "Do you have written permission from General Montel to speak to this man?"

Finally the situation became so grotesque that it began to dawn on both Spain and the United States that things could not go on in this fashion.

But before the two governments could act in concert, Dr. Otero Navascués, the president of the Spanish Nuclear Energy Board, took matters into his own hands. In the early afternoon of March 1, the Spanish news agency Cifra distributed a long interview in which Dr. Otero Navascués told virtually all there was to tell of the Palomares situation. He said, quite accurately, that not a single case of radioactive contamination "worthy of that name" had occurred in Palomares. But he did acknowledge the existence of a radioactivity problem when he announced that JEN scientists were in Almería taking all the necessary steps to assure that "no risks *remain* to public health." Dr. Otero Navascués disclosed that seventeen JEN officials were engaged in efforts to define "the zones affected by plutonium and uranium-235 scattered as a result of the accident." Many newspaper readers abroad already knew of the scattering of nuclear materials in Palomares, but this was the first time an official admission had been made in Madrid or Washington.

The JEN president went on to report that 6 hectares of land had presented a radioactive contamination of 60,000 counts per minute, a fact that until then had been guarded in deep secrecy. He told Cifra that contaminated soil would be shipped to the United States and offered assurances that nowhere in Palomares did the radioactive count exceed the maximum permissible body burden. This too was an accurate statement.

Finally, Dr. Otero Navascués produced the last fragment of truth about Palomares. "There remains the problem," he said, "of the search for the fourth bomb, which the Americans have very great interest in finding because it is extraordinarily modern. Hence the presence in the area of military personnel."

It was never made quite clear whether Dr. Otero Navascués had spoken with the approval of the Spanish government or entirely on his own. But the whole story was now before the public, and the United States had no choice but to go along. The next day the administration confirmed everything Dr. Otero Navascués had said in Madrid and added some information of its own. It conceded that the Palomares bomb was the first nuclear weapon to be lost in twenty years of flights by atomic-armed aircraft. Defense Department specialists then apprised Washington newsmen of the details of the scattering of plutonium and uranium in Palomares by the two damaged bombs and discussed with them at length the mechanisms that had made nuclear explosions impossible.

Now, six weeks after the event, it was finally official that the

United States had misplaced a powerful hydrogen bomb in the Palomares area. But once it was admitted that the weapon was indeed somewhere in or near Almería, new public assurances seemed required that this situation posed no danger to the population, the fish, and the ships at sea.

It was Ambassador Duke, the athletic American diplomat, who devised a highly original method of convincing the world at large that, bomb or no bomb, the Mediterranean waters off Almería were not radioactive. Since a dramatic demonstration seemed to be in order, Duke conceived the idea of organizing a Palomares swimming party led by himself and including as many members of his family and embassy staff as could be drafted for it. To make the project a joint United States–Spanish enterprise, the Ambassador persuaded Information and Tourism Minister Manuel Fraga Iribarne to go swimming with him. This alone was something in the nature of a diplomatic coup, for Spanish cabinet ministers tend to be somewhat less given to public sportive displays than their American counterparts. They do not mind being photographed partridge-shooting around Toledo, deep-sea fishing off La Coruña, or playing golf at the Sotogrande Club near Algeciras. These sports are considered dignified in Spain and are frequently practiced by Generalissimo Franco, but the notion of a bathing-suit exhibition in Almería must have struck the ministers as a rare one. However, Fraga was not only the Minister of Information and Tourism—the two areas in which the Palomares incident had created most problems—but also a modern-minded man with a touch of humor. He agreed to Duke's proposal, and the date of March 8 was chosen for the Palomares swim-in. It would be a splash heard round the world.

The gathering place for the expedition was the brand-new government tourist hotel at Mojácar, the Parador de los Reyes Católicos. It was so named because the Catholic Monarchs, Ferdinand and Isabella, had their bivouac in that general vicinity in June of 1488, as they completed the reconquest of the Mediterranean coast from the Moors. The old Moorish hilltop fortress-town of Mojácar, towering over the shore and dominating the countryside as far as Vera and Villaricos, was the Moors' last stronghold in the region, and the Catholic Monarchs had laid siege to it. The Spanish siege was the latest of many attacks on Mojácar, which had originally been settled by the Phoenicians in the days of the coastal silver prosperity, under the name of Murgis Akra. The name was corrupted to Mucacra just before the start of the Christian Era, and the Moors, arriving early in the eighth century, called it Mojácar in Arabic. In 1488 Mojácar surrendered without a fight to the Catholic Monarchs after a dramatic meeting between its Governor, Alavez de Moxacar, and the royal emissary, Captain Garcilaso de la Vega. According to old chronicles, Alavez told Garcilaso:

"I am just as Spanish as you are. The members of my race have lived for seven hundred years in Spain, and you tell us, 'You are foreigners, get back to the sea.' In Africa an unhospitable coast awaits us, which will surely say, like you, and certainly with greater right than you, 'You are foreigners, cross the sea from whence you have come and return to your land.' Here we are, between two coasts which deny us our bread, neighborliness, and shelter. Is this human? I never fought against the Christians. Tell that to your King and Queen. Allah is my witness. Therefore I believe that the right thing is to treat us as brothers, not as enemies, and to allow us to continue working our lands, those of our fathers and our grandfathers, and to give pasture to our flocks. If, as their fame goes, Isabella and Ferdinand unite goodness in their hearts with their virtues, I trust in Allah that they will attend to our request. We, for our part, promise fidelity to the Catholic Monarchs. If not, my people will do what they should do. I, before surrendering as a coward, will die as a Spaniard. May Allah preserve you."

Garcilaso conveyed the message to his King and Queen. Isabella then told him to tell Alavez, "We accede to his request after hearing his noble reasoning; that we offer our friendship and we trust that he will know how to correspond to the mercy that we grant him with good will." She added, "May God preserve him and all his people."

For nearly five centuries the bond between the Christians and the Moors of Mojácar was preserved. As the Americans and the Spaniards arrived at the foot of the Mojácar hill for their encounter with nuclear history, the white town was still a relic of Moorish presence on the Mediterranean coast. Much of it had been rebuilt in recent years to accommodate a community of Spanish writers and artists, but the mood was unmistakably Moorish in the winding narrow streets and in the old church where at dusk the Catholic mass was said in the Mozarabian rite, the heritage of the blending of the two cultures.

The guests began gathering at the *parador* below Mojácar in the late afternoon of Monday, March 7. Most of them had flown from Madrid to San Javier. The men then took helicopters to Palomares, while the wives and the children were brought over in embassy sedans. The affair was like a regular family outing, and there was a picnicky air about it. Ambassador Duke came with his wife, Robin, and the two children from his previous marriage, Marilú, eleven, and Darío, eight. General Donovan was there with his wife, Peggy, and their son, Eric, eleven. Other embassy staff members, with or without wives, and newspaper correspondents made up the American group. The children of Information Minister Fraga, Maribel and José Manuel, joined the party during the evening, though their father was not due till the day of the swim-in.

Presently it developed that Duke was planning not just one but at least two swims the next day in what obviously was a very chilly Mediterranean Sea. He announced that the first swim would be at nine o'clock the next morning and retired for the night. A little late, at 9:35 a.m. on Tuesday, March 8, the first nuclear beach party in history got under way.

Like the Pied Piper, Angier Duke marched briskly down from

the hotel to the brown sand beach, followed by easily one hundred embassy staff members and wives, children, television and newsreel cameramen, sound men, newsmen equipped with microphones and pens and pencils, hotel officials, and fascinated Spaniards-at-large. The Ambassador wore a dark red robe over his bathing suit, rubber-soled sneakers, and a rubber cap over his thinning hair. Reaching the waterline, Duke dramatically shed his robe and sneakers but kept his cap on. Then, in the manner of Henry IV of France at the battle of Ivry crying, "Follow my white plume," the Ambassador charged into the cold blue water at the head of his contingent. A crucial decision had to be faced and instantly made by members of his staff: whether loyalty to the President of the United States and his Ambassador to Spain required a plunge in cold seawater at nine o'clock in the morning early in the month of March, when the outside temperature stood at 58 degrees Fahrenheit. Would, for example, the efficiency reports on those reluctant to swim along with Angier Biddle Duke reflect their lack of enthusiasm for this proposition and adversely affect their careers, showing them not to be real swingers? The decision was unanimous, and within seconds the gentle surf was peopled with dozens of splashing and shouting diplomats proving to the world that the Mediterranean was not radioactive. A dignified exception was Robin Duke, who settled for watching her husband's swim-in from the beach, fully dressed. But there were unscheduled entries too, such as the son of *The New York Times* correspondent in Spain, a determined gentleman of nine named Tony, who rushed into the water as his parents busily watched Ambassador Duke's maritime progress.

This progress included the feat of being interviewed while swimming. The interview was carried out by Harry Dibelius of ABC News, who had the longest cord on his microphone and could splash out farther than the other TV and radio reporters. The questions were as memorable as the answers: QUESTION: "How does it feel, Mr. Ambassador?" ANSWER: *"Great, great. Just fine!"* Emerging from the surf, Duke announced happily that the water off Almería was not as cold as was the water at Jones Beach when, as Long Island Parks Commissioner, he used to inaugurate the swimming season with Robert Moses on Memorial Day.

It was a part of Duke's poise that he cavalierly brushed aside the glass of cognac proffered on a silver tray by a white-gloved and liveried hotel waiter who stood on the beach to comfort the swimmers. The others, including non-swimmers, gratefully accepted the cognac and stood around sipping it and commenting on the spectacle they had just witnessed. The morning beach party suddenly turned into a cocktail party.

Next on the program was a visit to Camp Wilson. The Ambassador and General Donovan spent an hour with General Wilson and Admiral Guest, discussing the status of the search. Information Minister Fraga and Air Minister Lieutenant General Lacalle presently joined them for the briefing. What Wilson and Guest had to tell the Spanish officials was not greatly encouraging and it could be summed up by the fact that the United States still did not really know where the missing hydrogen bomb was. As Ambassador Duke had plunged into the Mediterranean that morning, the Navy was just trying out new techniques. Thus the Alvin was shifted from her deep dives in the Alpha One area, where she had been attempting to locate again the track found on March 1, to the shallower waters close to shore, in order to give Guest a better idea of the underwater aircraft debris pattern. The best the American commanders could tell the Spanish visitors was, as General Wilson put it, "We're trying our damnedest, and that's the best we can do."

From Camp Wilson the American and Spanish officials drove on to Palomares to address the villagers. There everything had been prepared beforehand, from the speakers' stand in the rutted main square to the carefully lettered posters and signs. The entire population of Palomares, along with friends and relatives from the whole comarca, filled the square. Never before had Palomares seen so much movement and officialdom. The signs held up by the people of Palomares and the surrounding towns and hamlets told well the story of this corner of Almería, in terms both of obvious official inspiration and of spontaneity.

"FRANCO: YOU SAVED US IN THE WAR—SUPPLY US WITH WATER IN PEACETIME!" read one poster. "VERA NEEDS SIX KILOMETERS OF HIGHWAY TO PALOMARES," said another poster. And a sign said, "WE HAVE BLIND FAITH IN THE JUSTICE OF YOUR DECISIONS." By the speakers' stand, a large poster announced: "WILSON'S TROOPS HAVE BEEN CORRECT WITH PALOMARES."

Then speeches ensued, probably the first time that official rhetoric had echoed in the main square of Palomares. Minister Fraga told the villagers that the central government would now look after them, that efforts would be made to turn this part of Almería into a major tourist center, and that telephone service would be extended to Palomares from Vera. There was courteous applause in the midst of very tangible skepticism in the quiet reactions of the village people.

"First we want the Americans to pay us damages and then the government to do something about the water problem here," said a grizzled farmer. He pulled his black beret down over his forehead and said, "*Hombre,* it is water I need for my bean field, not the promises of a telephone. Anyway, I've got nobody to call."

From the main square the official motorcade swung past Father Navarete's crossroads church and turned into the Villaricos road, going east. A half-mile down the highway the cars reached the turn-off at Eduardo Navarro's house and stopped there. General Wilson and Colonel White led Ambassador Duke to the site of what had been the crater dug by the explosion of the TNT in Weapon No. 3. This site was a monument to the Air Force's efficiency in covering up its nuclear tracks. Nothing amiss was to be seen there. A spanking new retaining wall rose at the foot of the Rabbits' Rise hillock at the spot where the hydrogen bomb had dropped and shattered. Freshly plowed contours were etched sharply over the surrounding fields where six weeks earlier the brown-black cloud of alpha-ray-emitting plutonium particles had sprayed its contamination. A tractor was working on a nearby field. A shepherd, leading his flock of sheep and black goats, stopped on a knoll overlooking the bomb site to watch the excitement. Eduardo Navarro and his wife Ana, both formally dressed in black, were brought forward to meet the American Ambassador. Duke inquired solicitously if all seemed to be back to normal in the fields. Eduardo Navarro replied matter-of-factly, "We'll see when we plant again in April."

At Camp Wilson it was now high noon and the sun was shining warmly. For once, there was no wind. Suddenly there was a flurry of movement at the Spanish Air Force headquarters tents at the west end of the beach, and Information Minister Fraga emerged in his bathing suit, marching with determination toward the water. Ambassador Duke, who had just returned to Camp Wilson from inspecting the bomb site, wasted no time. He burst into the tent used by the Navy's underwater demolition teams and, after tearing off his dark suit, got into a swim suit borrowed from a frogman from New York. Then he caught up with Fraga at the waterline, and the two dignitaries plunged together into the Mediterranean. Spanish and American aides instinctively took off their clothes too, piled them on the sand, and went splashing in their bathing suits or underwear. The big landing craft used by frogmen for their operations was beached at the spot of the swim-in.

Back at the Catholic Monarchs' *parador* at the foot of Mojácar, Ambassador Duke rose at the ceremonial lunch to become the first and only United States official publicly to speak at any time with seriousness to the Spaniards about what had happened in Palomares and its implications. Said Duke: "Here in this part of a nation whose history stretches back beyond the written word, great events are taking place, the portent of which has a meaning for all mankind. A tragedy which occurred in this area on January 17 has brought us face-to-face with a set of realities which has turned the eyes of the world upon this coast and its community of Palomares."

He covered the aerial collision, the contamination problem, and the search for the still missing hydrogen bomb. Then the American Ambassador undertook to spell out the meaning of the nuclear age for the people who had just been visited by it. He said:

The people of Palomares are like the people of the world, interested and concerned, involved, questioning but determined to face the realities of a changing world. None of us can discern our future in the atomic age we live in, but we do know that it is an age with which we must come to terms. The perils and dangers of it have been brought to us by the need to respond to the challenges to the values of our civilization, the values and the culture which the Western world represents. We are outraged at the fact that so much of the energy and imagination and resources of mankind must be devoted to facing this challenge, but there is no foreseeable alternative. It is a part of the set of realities we are learning to live with.

The Spanish government officials in the *parador's* dining room nodded understandingly at the Ambassador's words. They knew about the realities of the nuclear age and the reasons why Spain had entered into a nuclear alliance with the United States. But the villagers were not there at the lunch to listen to Duke. Not the Ponces, the Navarros, the Castros, the De la Torres, and all the others who still questioned why this nuclear age had to come to Palomares.

The impact of the Duke-Fraga swim-in on the world opinion was indeed tremendous. It made the front pages everywhere and, presumably, convinced doubters that the Mediterranean was free from radioactivity. But in the end it was *The Times* of London that put everything into perspective. It said in its leader:

American diplomats are used to demonstrating that American wines are drinkable by drinking them. It is a new extension of their duty to show that waters are safe by bathing in them. And what hostages to fortune the Palomares bathers now are. They must keep exuberantly fit during the weeks to come. If they want to sneeze, they must check it. If they feel off colour, they must conceal it. They have undergone ordeal by water, and time must elapse before the innocence—not of them, but of the missing bomb—is conclusive. At the same time, Mr. Duke has set a precedent which some of his colleagues are likely to take a rather jaundiced look at. Supposing a bomb is reported missing in Norway? In the winter? Perhaps in such cases the job could be suitably left to the Naval Attaché.

On Wednesday, March 9, Admiral Guest offered the press a guided but extremely close-mouthed tour of his task force. As the official Navy log put it that day, "The routine of the search was broken by the visit of 80 newsmen who were given an unclassified briefing and tour of the search area by boat."

Guest, wrapped in his brown leather coat against the wind, was aboard LCU-1492, which picked up the American, Spanish, and other European newsmen at Camp Wilson for the cruise around the task force territory. It was a sunny, breezy morning, and as the landing craft sailed toward the flagship *Boston* and the high-probability area Alpha One, Palomares shrank to the dimensions of a white splotch on the horizon, the mountains of Sierra Cabrera towering over the whole coast.

In the three hours the world press spent with Admiral Guest, the Cubmarine, the Alvin, and the Aluminaut went through demonstration dives and surfacings. Fifteen ships bobbed on the waves, strung out for miles along the coast and out around Alpha One. Guest, chain-smoking cigarettes, provided a running commentary on the techniques employed in the search and told the newsmen that as of that day his men had recovered 175 pieces of aircraft debris from the sea bottom.

But, speaking later aboard the *Boston,* the admiral frankly admitted that "this is not a short, quick operation." He said, "We may be here for a considerable period before we accomplish our mission." At that point, of course, the search was stalemated by the Alvin's inability to find again the torpedo track, because of poor tracking, visibility, luck, or all three. Guest again emphasized the difficulties of the underwater terrain—the ravines that went deeper than 3600 feet, the coral reefs and rocks that led sonar equipment astray—and the frustrating surface weather with winds that hit 65 knots and more. A newsman asked, "Are you ever going to find what you're looking for, Admiral?" Guest clenched his teeth. "You bet your life we are, son," he answered.

Later in the day General Wilson, also chain-smoking, held a briefing in his command post on the situation ashore. He recounted the 6 weeks of search on foot by the airmen's teams and the 450 search missions flown by the helicopters over the Palomares hills and coasts.

"We are now getting into diminishing returns," he said.

The general did not say so to the visiting newsmen, but he was ready to recommend to the Department of Defense that the land search for the lost hydrogen weapon be discontinued. He was satisfied that the bomb was not in any of the high- or low-probability areas ashore; the incessant crisscrossing of the grids by the flights seemed to leave no doubts about it, and now Wilson believed the time had come to face the reality that the weapon simply had to be in the Mediterranean.

iv

March 10 and March 11, two days distinguished by foul weather, were used by Guest to have some maintenance work done on the Alvin and the Aluminaut. The Alvin, for example, had already made fifteen deep and long dives, and the engineers and the pilots thought that some checking up might be in order. The white Alvin and the red Aluminaut were loaded on the *Fort Snelling,* the landing ship docks with the aft floodable deck, and taken to Cartagena, where work on the two submersibles could be done more comfortably.

On Saturday, March 12, the *Fort Snelling* returned to the Alpha One search area with both the Alvin and the Aluminaut. The Alvin was again ordered to go down the steep underwater canyons where the torpedo-like track had been spotted by Valentine Wilson twelve days earlier. This was the Alvin's sixteenth consecutive dive in nearly a month off Palomares. For well over 7 hours, the 22-foot-long submersible had been slowly sailing in and out of narrow gullies at depths between 2500 and 3000 feet. The underwater pressure at that depth was a tremendous 1500 pounds per square inch. Because of low visibility and the consequent danger of being caught in narrow culs-de-sac or slashed by overhanging rocks on entering and leaving the gullies, some of which were only 60 feet wide, Pilots Valentine Wilson and Marvin McCamis had to keep the Alvin's speed down to 1 knot or less.

It was now nearly eight hours since the Alvin had dived, and her batteries were running low. She was about to start surfacing when Wilson, running the submersible practically over the edges of the crevices, thought he saw a familiar-looking furrow. The track had unmistakably been made by something like a torpedo—or a hydrogen bomb. Wilson and McCamis followed it briefly, but now their batteries were really down to the danger point. They reported the location of the track to their surface control ship, a minesweeper. Admiral Guest, aboard his flagship *Boston*, received the word that the track had been found again. Turning to an aide, he said, "Let's keep this to ourselves. No point arousing hopes again."

And then the track was lost once more. Despite the use of pingers and transponders—transmitter-like devices to mark the positions of objects on the sea bottom—the furrow could not be found again when the Alvin went down on Sunday, March 13. For one thing, oceanographic ship *Mizar* with all her underwater tracking equipment and her links to the shore Decca navigational system was working far away in area Alpha Two. As Alvin's chief pilot Rainnie complained again, there was "poor surface tracking." Aboard the *Boston* the loss of the track was accepted philosophically. The only accomplishment that day was the unloading by the SS *Alma Victory* of over 5000 empty steel drums at Camp Wilson for the contaminated soil.

On Monday, March 14, everything seemed to be going as badly as possible, which was the state of affairs to which Task Force 65 was becoming accustomed after close to two months of frustrations. There were high winds and high seas, which prevented the Alvin from resuming her search for the now mythical furrow. The Aluminaut was out of commission for the day with a frozen hatch trunk drain valve. The Decca Hi-Fix navigational system, without which none of the precision underwater hunting could be properly conducted, went off the air for ten hours because of electronic problems. The only seemingly constructive accomplishment that day was the shifting of the *Mizar* from the Alpha Two area offshore to Alpha One, where, it was fervently hoped, the Alvin might again spot the tantalizing underwater track.

At Camp Wilson, Colonel Shepard, the tireless "field marshal" of the land bomb hunt, was leaving Palomares for Washington, to present formally General Wilson's recommendation to the Defense Department that the search ashore be abandoned. The Air Force specialists on the scene were now convinced that everything humanly and technically possible had been done to locate the bomb and that, quite obviously, it just was not to be found ashore. Shep Shepard arrived in Washington late in the evening, when, because of the six-hour time difference, the dawn of Tuesday, March 15, was already coming up off Palomares.

Just as Colonel Shepard was going to sleep in Washington, the Alvin was starting on her nineteenth dive, once more in the southern portion of the Alpha One area. Valentine Wilson and Marvin McCamis were at the controls. The minesweeper *Ability* (MSO-519) acted as the Alvin's surface control ship. Chief Pilot Bill Rainnie was aboard the *Ability,* manning the underwater telephone to his submersible. This time the *Mizar* too was standing electronic guard over the Alvin's dive. Admiral Guest was still aboard the *Boston,* but he was just then preparing to shift his flag to the USS *Albany,* a sister cruiser that had come from the Sixth Fleet to relieve the first flagship after more than a month of search duty.

Ashore, General Wilson, clad in his gray flying suit, was calling the day's first staff meeting in his tent. It was a raw and chilly morning and for all hands it promised to be another interminable day at Palomares station.

In fact, March 15 was a day that began in the usual disastrous fashion. To start things off, the minesweeper USS *Notable* lost her towed ocean-bottom-scanning sonar sled in 250 feet of water when, for no clear reason, the cable snapped. Then the Cubmarine, which had just gone down 400 feet with Jon Lindbergh, had to make an emergency surfacing after its flotation bag was accidentally inflated. Captain Cliff Page, the task force's chief of staff, sighed and took this news fatalistically. "What's next?" he inquired.

Shortly before noon Valentine Wilson and Marvin McCamis maneuvered their white submersible into a 20-foot-wide gully and then slid down a 70-degree slope that looked to them exactly like that canyon side where twice before they had sighted the furrow. They had begun their dive at 9:20 a.m., and since about eleven o'clock the Alvin had been hedge-hopping over the bottom obstacle course. At 2600 feet, squinting to see their way in visibility that was less than 8 feet despite the powerful searchlights, the Alvin's pilots spotted the track again. But instead of following the furrow down the slope, as they had done on the two previous occasions, Wilson and McCamis backed the Alvin *up* the steep slope.

Inching up the incline, they suddenly came upon a billowing gray parachute, clearly covering an elongated object. Wilson quickly checked the depth. It was 2550 feet. They might have found the elusive bomb, but the two pilots instantly realized the ghastly problems of its recovery. The waterlogged parachute and the object behind it were perched, terribly precariously, atop a 20-foot-wide ledge protruding from a 70-degree slope of soil that was pure ooze and, as one of the pilots put it, made one think of freshly poured concrete.

The time was high noon.

Valentine Wilson picked up the underwater telephone and shouted to Bill Rainnie aboard the *Ability* that he had just located a "rusty object." The task force code for the bomb was "Instrument Panel" and for parachute it was *benthos,* the Greek word for the sea bottom. But in the excitement of the find, the pilot confused the codes. Rainnie, just as excited, shouted back, "You found the bomb." There was a pause, and Wilson replied, "No, I found the parachute."

From the *Ability,* Rainnie flashed the code "Instrument Panel" to Guest aboard the *Boston.* The Admiral's reaction was to think that if the bomb had indeed been found, the Navy had better make damned sure it did not vanish again. An unprecedented underwater operation was then set in motion to stand guard over the object

—now officially named Contact No. 261—until its position was properly plotted and recovery operations could begin.

The only craft that could dive deep enough to stand guard over the bomb was the Aluminaut. But at that moment the red submersible was aboard the *Fort Snelling* having her faulty drain valve repaired and her batteries recharged. The Alvin could stay under water for six or seven hours, but Guest could take no chances that the bomb would again become misplaced, as had happened twice with the furrow track. "Get the Aluminaut in the water," he ordered.

It took five hours to ready the Aluminaut for the dive. Meanwhile Wilson and McCamis circled the Alvin twice around the parachute, mainly to shoot Polaroid photographs. There was a strong underwater current, and sometimes the parachute's 100-foot shroud billowed out and sometimes it clung as a wet dress clings to a woman's body. The Alvin's batteries were now running down rapidly, and the pilots decided to wait for the Aluminaut in darkness and without motion. Turning sideways, they wedged the submersible between two faces of the steep canyon, cut all power, and waited, knowing the elusive bomb was almost within grasp, if they could only get at it.

At 5:00 p.m. the Aluminaut broke the water for her dive as the frogmen on the escort rubber boats cast off the lines. At 6:44 p.m., six hours and forty-four minutes after the Alvin had spotted the parachute, help arrived. The Aluminaut, vectored from the *Mizar* three-dimensionally, the way an aircraft flying blind is directed by an air controller, swooped down to the bottom, coming to rest twenty-five feet from the Alvin at the mouth of the gully. To the Navy and its deep-submergence people this was a historic moment, quite aside from the bomb problem. It was the first rendezvous ever by two submersibles in "deep inner space"—at a half-mile depth—and to submariners it was comparable to the docking of two Gemini craft in outer space.

The deep inner space encounter was now accomplished, and the Alvin surfaced after having spent close to twelve hours in the deep

Mediterranean canyons. There was no longer any fear of losing the parachute and the bomb, because the Aluminaut was fitted with an electronic "pinger" which responded to question-asking signals sent down from the *Mizar*. With it, the *Mizar*'s underwater detection equipment and the Decca Hi-Fix navigational system could practically pinpoint the bomb at its 2550-foot resting place. The Aluminaut was ordered to stay with the bomb until the Alvin could have her batteries recharged and return to the bottom to begin recovery operations.

Now the question was what the waiting world was to be told about the Alvin's find. Admiral Guest, who naturally had notified his Navy superiors and the American embassy in Madrid of the "very promising but not conclusive" Contact 261, proposed total silence. He argued angrily with aides and civilian scientists in his cabin aboard the *Albany,* his new flagship, that he was not going to make any public announcements until he was absolutely positive that the hydrogen bomb actually rested behind the parachute. Guest, living up to his bulldog reputation, insisted on confirming photographs that the Alvin had taken but that had not yet been analyzed.

Tensions, long in the making, were now beginning to emerge between the Navy personnel and the civilian scientists and, in fact, between the American military and American government civilians in general. One immediate point of tension occurred between the Navy and the embassy in Madrid. Because it was discovered that the word of the Alvin's success earlier in the day had trickled out in Washington and in West Germany, where Air Force channels obviously were not leak-proof, Ambassador Duke in Madrid felt that a formal announcement should be made as promptly as possible. He was concerned both with Spanish public opinion, which had already waited two months to have the hydrogen bomb removed from the nation's coastal waters, and with Communist propaganda, which was still getting fair mileage from Palomares. Duke therefore proposed to hold a late evening news conference at the embassy to give as much information as was available. Phone calls went out to newsmen, who began gathering at the Duke residence after midnight. But the Navy, and specifically Admiral Guest, violently opposed the announcement, and in the end Duke had no choice but to accept the technical judgment of the on-scene military experts. At two o'clock in the morning of Wednesday, March 16, the newsmen were informed that there would be no ambassadorial press conference and no announcement after all. Once more the public-information aspects of United States operations in Spain were suffering because of the inability of the military and civilians to agree on a course of action. Since it now was widely known that the Alvin had made a find—almost certainly had spotted the hydrogen bomb—the official United States silence had some of the grotesque character of the earlier days when it was steadfastly denied that a nuclear weapon was missing anywhere.

In midmorning on Tuesday, March 15, Colonel Shepard appeared at the Pentagon to make his presentation on behalf of General Wilson for abandoning the land search for the bomb. It was midafternoon in Palomares, and just then Admiral Guest was flashing the Chief of Naval Operations in Washington that the Alvin had spotted the parachute at 1200Z (Zebra time or GMT). As Shep Shepard began his meeting with the Navy-Air Force-AEC technical advisory group, word reached the conference room of the Palomares discovery. The men looked at one another, and an admiral said to Colonel Shepard, "I guess we don't have to worry about land search any more." Nonetheless, it was agreed that the Air Force would maintain the land hunt activities for a few more days, until the identification of Contact 261 was positive beyond the slightest doubt. For Colonel Shepard the Washington trip was the most successful aborted mission in his military career. He folded his maps and caught the first plane back to Spain. The Palomares duty would not last long.

Off Palomares, Admiral Guest was facing the "now what?" phase of SALVOPS. The 1.5-megaton hydrogen bomb had apparently been found after nearly two months in the water, and this, of course, was a great success for the Alvin and Guest and everybody connected with the task force. But instantly political—and Navy—pressures began emanating from Washington and Madrid to have the bomb retrieved. Most people assumed that now that the weapon had been located it should be no great problem to bring it up to the surface and be done with the whole Palomares episode. Even Francisco Simó, the Aguilas fisherman, renewed his proposals in press interviews (for which he charged cash from television networks and news magazines) that the Navy simply let him cast his shrimp lines over the side of the *Manuela Orts* and, *por Dios,* he would fish out the bomb in no time flat. Simó's offers made headlines in the Spanish newspapers, but the Navy had now somewhat less admiration for him, since the bomb contact had turned out to be a good mile from the spot where he claimed to have seen the "half-man" go down. As Admiral Guest put it later, "Mr. Simó did not locate the bomb, sir. Mr. Simó was very, very helpful to us in establishing the area."

What was at hand for Task Force 65, then, was the brutal task of recovery at depths never before tested operationally by existing retrieving equipment and in nightmarishly difficult and treacherous underwater terrain.

At 4 p.m. on Wednesday, March 16, the Aluminaut surfaced after spending twenty-two hours at the bottom, bird-dogging the bomb, making sure that currents or sudden soil slides did not change its position. The Alvin, her batteries recharged and her crew well rested, prepared to go back to the bomb, this time to take a very light messenger line to be attached to the parachute's canopy. Meanwhile Admiral Guest ordered that routine operations continue for the benefit of the watchers ashore, in order to prevent premature disclosure that, in the words of the task force's log, "even a promising contact had been located." Actually, the Alvin's photographs from the day before were quite clear, showing a large parachute covering an "object." There could be little doubt that the "object" was indeed the bomb, but out of a sense of naval discipline or superstition, or both, nobody on the task force ever referred by name to the weapon until it was actually brought to the surface.

At 6:10 p.m. the Alvin dived down to 2550 feet, carrying an 8-centimeter-circumference polypropylene line attached to a 4-foot fluked stake. The *Mizar* at the same time planted an anchor at the end of a nylon line in the mud some 45 feet from the bomb. As the Alvin's Bill Rainnie remarked later, this was "a neat trick in 758 meters of water." The Alvin, with Wilson and McCamis at the controls, now hooked a grapnel into the shrouds of the parachute, using its 64-inch mechanical arm. This arm, controlled by switches inside the submersible, is a grip that operates like a thumb and middle finger. A vast improvement on the human wrist, the Alvin's "wrist" could rotate 360 degrees in either direction. It was capable of operations as complex as tying a bow-tie with a chopstick.

While the Alvin was attaching the grapnel to the parachute and fixing sonar transponders to the canopy, a reference buoy was planted on the surface about 300 yards southwest of what the Navy still described as "Contact 261." The *Mizar* took position over the bomb, and everybody stood poised for the recovery. But the lost bomb was not to give up that easily to the hunters. It still had plenty of fight left.

V

As the raw days of March dragged on without bringing the recovery any nearer fruition, and as nerves and tempers frayed in Madrid, Palomares, and Task Force 65, the uncanny notion occurred to some of the men involved in the operation that the lost hydrogen bomb might have a will of its own. And this uncannily metaphysical notion went on to suggest that, once having freed itself from man's control, the nuclear weapon now was determined to remain lost deep under water forever, beyond man's reach and amidst the primeval elements. This was the kind of unfunny and strained joke that was being made over late drinks in the bar of the Mojácar *parador* where the submersibles' crews and a few of the civilian experts would gather between dives when the weather had again turned bad, or over beers at La Estación's counter before the few remaining Air Force officers there turned in for the night.

Admiral Guest, of course, was far too pragmatic and far too short-tempered at that stage of the operation to engage in such intellectual games. He knew where he had the bomb and he knew that at least one grapnel hook was driven into the bomb's parachute canopy. From the moment the Alvin located Contact 261, the admiral marshaled all the resources of the task force to make the raising of the weapon possible and successful. Impatient as he was, and impatient as were his naval and civilian superiors in Washington, Guest was determined to proceed with the greatest self-discipline and patience in attempting the recovery. He was painfully conscious of the dangerously precarious position in which the bomb lay on the steep incline, he was conscious of the speed and force of the underwater currents, and he was conscious of everything that could still go catastrophically wrong if one false move were made. And he would have been less than human if he had not also taken into account what would happen to his own career if he failed after being so close to success.

As he told the story later, "We worked to the limit of the endurance of our submersibles in order to attempt a recovery on this weapon." The Alvin and the Aluminaut dived whenever weather permitted, after the March 15 spotting of the parachute, to set the stage for actual recovery. More hooks had to be driven into the gray canopy, and more pingers and transponders installed to establish a perfect tracking and navigational system. Then the problem arose of how to lift the 5000-pound bomb and the heavy waterlogged parachute strapped to it, from the narrow gully through the resistance of nearly 2600 feet of water, without tearing the lift lines and losing the weapon, perhaps for good, in one of the unfathomably deep crevices at the bottom of the canyon. A nuclear bomb and a parachute, resting in the most peculiar and difficult of positions, could not be fished out as casually as a man brings up a fish or even a treasure trove from the bottom.

While Admiral Swanson's technical advisory group in Washington had offered Guest a wide variety of instruments, ranging from a hydrazine rig whose hyponitrous acid would provide the buoyancy to lift the bomb, to all kinds of spindles, none of them would be workable at nearly 2600 feet. As Guest said, "The depth was too great. Nobody had ever recovered anything before at this depth or of this weight."

So, Guest said, "We did the next best thing." This was designing and constructing in the workshop of the destroyer-tender USS *Cascade* a special and monstrous-looking rig that Guest named the Poodle. The Poodle, put together by Jon Lindbergh and Ray Pitts of Ocean Systems, and Lieutenant Commander Moody, consisted of four long pointed spider-like steel legs that could sink firmly into the bottom's ooze. At the end of a 40-foot nylon line hanging from the Poodle there was a 1250-pound anchor designed to stabilize the whole weird contraption. From the anchor spread three 300-foot nylon lines equipped at the ends with grappling hooks. The idea was for the grappling hooks to bite into the parachute's canopy and thus provide an even-leverage hoist. Additionally, the Poodle had a camera and was festooned with electronic pingers and transponders tuned to the frequencies of the Alvin and the Aluminaut. In a sense, then, the Poodle was both an underwater winch and a fixed navigational beam on which the two submersibles could home when needed. The navigational accuracy was, of course, essential.

On Thursday, March 17, while the Poodle was being fashioned aboard the *Cascade,* both the Alvin and the Aluminaut had an enforced rest because high winds and seas had again hit the recovery area. But another type of work could be carried out in Palomares. The *Lieutenant George W. G. Boyce,* a Navy Victory ship, arrived offshore and barges began loading aboard her the steel drums with plutonium-contaminated soil for the voyage to the Savannah River burial ground. This was, incidentally, two months to the day after the air collision over Palomares, but nobody was in the mood to remember or commemorate it.

On Friday, March 18, the *Mizar* attempted to lower a heavy nylon line to the parachute along the thin polypropylene messenger line that the Alvin had taken down two days earlier to a point 40 feet from the weapon. But this motion pulled the fluked stake out of the bottom, and the *Mizar* lost contact with the target area. The Aluminaut was promptly dispatched to the bottom but could not track the parachute. The visibility was virtually nil. The next step was for the *Mizar* to lower the Poodle with its heavy anchor and the three 300-foot recovery lines. At 4 p.m., however, the *Mizar*'s underwater tracking system broke down and it took five hours to repair it before the delicate Poodle-lowering operation could be resumed. At 9 p.m. the Alvin went down to grab the recovery lines with its mechanical arm and try to fix them to the parachute. For seven tense hours the *Mizar* and the Alvin attempted to place the Poodle in position and take the lines to the bomb. In the early hours of Saturday, March 19, the wind rose again in the west and the seas became so high that, despite his superior seamanship, Captain G. Fladerer could not hold the *Mizar*'s position accurately. At 5:30 a.m. the Alvin surfaced to announce that the bomb and the parachute appeared to have slid 20 feet down the slippery slope.

This was rather shattering news for Admiral Guest. The slide suggested that at the slightest movement the bomb and the parachute could really tumble down the 70-degree slope and drop into the deep gulch that was known to exist at the foot of the canyon slope, some 3000 feet deep. If this happened, the chances for recovery might have become so difficult as to border on the impossible. The mouth of this gulch was believed to be no more than 10 feet wide, ruling out the possibility that even the Alvin could squeeze herself inside to proceed with salvage operations. Nobody was quite sure how deep this gulch was, and dispirited officers sat at dawn wondering if a method could be devised for blasting the gulch if the bomb actually did fall into it. But of course nobody had ever done any underwater blasting at such depths, and there were immediately some second thoughts about detonating explosives around a nuclear weapon.

While word of the bomb's slide somehow reached one or two newsmen in Madrid, both the embassy and the Navy decided to take no public cognizance of this event. Instead, late on March 19, they jointly issued a communiqué which seemed to be designed to prepare the public for the worst, if the worst happened. The communiqué said:

> With regard to the unidentified object and a parachute at a depth of some 2500 feet about 5 miles off the shore from Palomares, Rear Admiral William S. Guest, the Task Force Commander, has advised that because of the extremely steep slope at the sea bottom on which the object and parachute are resting, he proposes to attempt first to move them to a more favorable recovery area. If

successful, this course of action will lessen the risk of having the object fall from its present precarious position into much deeper water. When the object is positively identified, an appropriate announcement will be made.

The immediate problem, of course, was to see to it that the bomb and parachute, now 2520 feet deep, would at least stay where they were. Just to get them back to their original ledge would be tantamount to getting them to what Guest had described as a "more favorable recovery area." But things were getting still tougher. Thirty-five-knot winds and heavy swells rose late on March 19 and continued on March 20, preventing new dives by the Alvin and the Aluminaut. The minesweeper USS *Salute* lost her towed vehicle carrying the ocean-bottom-scanning sonar. The fleet tug *Luiseno* parted her anchor cable. The oiler *Nespelen* lost her whaleboat. Admiral Guest became more taciturn than ever.

For the next three days there was nothing for Guest to do except alternate his silences with curses addressed to the foul weather. From the afternoon of March 19 until the morning of March 23, a Wednesday, the Mediterranean *mistral* blew too hard to allow any search operations. All the men of Task Force 65 could do was wonder if the bomb was still where the Alvin had last seen her.

On the morning of March 23 the Alvin prepared to dive, but a ballast-system problem delayed her a few hours. Finally she went down during the afternoon to begin one of the most nerve-racking episodes in the whole recovery operation. At first things went well. Rotating her mechanical arm, she succeeded in placing two pingers and a transponder on the parachute. The bomb at least had stayed in the same place. Then the submersible pulled back to let the *Mizar* lower the Poodle anchor and a lift line about 80 feet from the parachute. The Poodle sat down on the slope, and the Alvin advanced again to grab one of its lift lines and try to hook it to the parachute. Then, inexplicably, the Poodle fell over on its side, its two other lines fouled, and there was nothing the Alvin could do to attach any of the three lines or to extricate the collapsed recovery contraption. In the end, the Alvin had to surface because her batteries were exhausted. Despite all the sophisticated tracking systems, the operation was still underwater blind man's buff as far as the control crews on the surface were concerned.

The next day, Thursday, March 24, there was no choice for Guest but to proceed with the recovery attempt. The Alvin dived again at noon and, despite poor visibility, immediately found the parachute. It promptly attached the Poodle's free line to at least six parachute risers. But at that point, probably owing to currents, the parachute began to billow and Guest concluded it would be extremely dangerous for the Alvin to remain any longer in the vicinity. In other words, the Admiral felt he could not risk the submersible and her crew in any further attempts to attach the Poodle's other lines to the parachute. He ordered the Alvin up and she surfaced at 7:30 p.m. The submersibles' pilots reported that it was absolutely out of the question to untangle the Poodle's other lines and, as Guest put it later, "I had to make a decision to take the weapon." The only way to do it was to lift it on the single nylon line that the Alvin had succeeded in attaching to the canopy.

The lift was hooked to the *Mizar*'s winch, and at 8 p.m. the hoisting operation began. It was a clear, pleasant evening off Palomares, and the men were again optimistic that success might be just around the corner. The *Mizar*'s tracking system told Guest that the bomb and parachute had been lifted from the side of the gully into open water and that they were moving up along with the heavy Danforth anchor. The men held their breaths. For a full hour the nylon line was slowly reeled in on the *Mizar*'s winch. Then, at 9:15 p.m., the line took a sudden heavy strain and went awesomely slack. It had snapped, and the bomb with its parachute had dropped somewhere into the black depths of the Mediterranean canyons. Aboard the *Mizar* there were sudden silence and incredulity. Then an elderly chief petty officer said, "It just looks like this bomb don't want to be rescued."

On this black day for the bomb hunters of Palomares there was one touch of silver lining: the *Boyce* had finished loading the

244 / **The Bombs of Palomares**

drums with the radioactively contaminated soil. This represented the end of the long period of trying to restore Palomares to its pre-nuclear-accident condition. General Wilson issued a statement to announce the finish of the radioactivity problem in the village. He said:

> The loading of the last barrel marks the completion of the soil removal portion of our search and recovery operations. Approximately 4900 barrels or around 1100 tons of soil have been transported to the USNS *Boyce* for shipment to the United States. The *Boyce* will sail for the United States later today. I think we have achieved our goal of leaving the Palomares area in the same condition it was in prior to the accident. We will now commence phasing down our camp. However, considerable support will be required for the continuing operation by the Navy.

Indeed, Camp Wilson began shrinking instantly. The big tents that for over two months had housed hundreds of troops were dismantled. The radiological-decontamination shack disappeared. The Air Force Post Exchange was taken down and shipped back to Torrejón, leaving behind only a big blue truck that sold cigarettes, gum, and Wilson corned beef. But in his command tent General Wilson sat and waited for the outcome of the dramatic sea search. It was the Air Force's hydrogen bomb that the Navy was attempting to recover.

Friday, March 25, turned out to be the real Black Friday for Task Force 65. The Aluminaut dived first thing in the morning to try to establish electronic contact with the pingers and transponders the Alvin had hooked onto the parachute, or plain sonar contact with the two objects. But she failed in both endeavors. The Aluminaut's pilots told the *Mizar* that there was no sign of either Douglas or Robert. Douglas was the code name for the parachute, after Admiral Guest's eleven-year-old son. Robert, his fourteen-year-old, had given his name for the code for the bomb.

The Alvin, which again had ballast-system difficulties, could not dive until 6:30 p.m. But she too sent back disturbing news. What seemed like an underwater silt tempest virtually eliminated

naked-eye visibility. The pingers and transponders were not responding. It was becoming increasingly clear not only that the
Mizar had failed to lift the bomb the previous evening because
the nylon line was slashed by either the Danforth anchor or a
granite outcropping, but that the weapon and the parachute were
again actually lost. The Alvin pilots suggested that a bottom slide
caused by the lifting attempt had buried the bomb and parachute
somewhere within the underwater slime and that the pingers were
not responding because they too were deep in the mud. The silt
cloud seemed to support this conclusion. In a sense, then, the sea
hunters were back to the situation that had obtained before
March 1, when the Alvin had first spotted the bomb's furrow.
For reasons that can only be described as utterly mysterious,
Admiral Guest chose this Black Friday to issue a guardedly optimistic communiqué. The announcement said:

> Admiral William S. Guest, Commander Task Force 65, advises
> that operations for the recovery of the object with attached parachute
> are proceeding satisfactorily. These operations must necessarily be
> accomplished slowly and cautiously due to the precarious position
> of the object on a steep slope and the great depths involved. At first,
> weather conditions with high winds and choppy seas continued to
> periodically hamper current efforts. The limited endurance of the
> submersibles being employed and the necessity to recharge their bat-
> teries after each dive are primary factors which, with weather, con-
> trol the tempo of our activity. Everything possible is being done
> to expedite recovery and identification of the object under these
> circumstances.

On the afternoon of Saturday, March 26, the Alvin submerged
in the vicinity of the bomb's original location. But, in the words
of the task force's log entry, she "confirmed that the target was
no longer there." The most urgent question, of course, was the
whereabouts of the bomb. Yet the Alvin's observations that day
only added to the mystery and confusion. The little submersible
reported having seen "clear tracks upslope" and "a confusing
multitude of vehicle tracks in other directions." In the absence
of better evidence, the searchers surmised that the bomb and
parachute were lost somewhere inside the slope's mud but at a

point higher than where they had originally rested. This assumption at least had the advantage of not raising immediate fears that the bomb had tumbled into a deep gulch below the slope.

Admiral Guest's reports on the failure of the lifting attempt on March 24, and the subsequent loss of the bomb, reached Madrid at once. The task force daily provided the embassy and the JUSMAAG with "Sitreps," brief situation reports on each day's operations, and the American officials in turn kept the Spanish government informed. It was probably inevitable under the circumstances that the highlights of these reports would filter down to American newsmen in Madrid and, accordingly, the word of the bomb's loss appeared in such publications as *The New York Times* within twenty-four hours of the event. Since it was patently impossible in the light of these reports to maintain the fiction enunciated in the Navy's communiqué of March 25 that the operations were proceeding "satisfactorily," Admiral Guest issued a new statement in the afternoon of Sunday, March 27. This announcement was as follows:

> Commander Task Force 65 advises that, in a first attempt to recover the object with parachute attached in the waters off Palomares, Spain, the lift line parted as a result of having become caught in and cut by the fluke on an anchor which was part of the recovery rig. The object and parachute are still in the same area, but have moved from the position at which they were originally located, making the next recovery attempt even more difficult and lengthy.

It was one more instance of the chronic inability of the military authorities to conduct a satisfactory public-information program. As had happened so many times during the Palomares crisis, the truth was being forced out of the military by journalistic enterprise, with all the drawbacks of initial inaccuracies and confusion. It was hardly a secret in Madrid and Palomares that both the Navy and Air Force were highly exercised over what they regarded as unauthorized leaks to the press, and at least some of the senior military officers suspected civilians at the embassy of collusion with the newsmen.

But an even more serious difference over information policy between the American military and civilian officials centered on the plans for the day when—at least so it was hoped—the missing hydrogen bomb would again be located and retrieved. Ambassador Duke, who had to concern himself with the Spanish and international political aspects of the Palomares situation, soon became aware of the problem of United States credibility. Communist propaganda, along with skeptics elsewhere, was already strongly suggesting that the United States might very well solve its bomb-hunting problem by simply announcing that it had recovered the hydrogen weapon but offering no proof. Duke reasoned, therefore, that to recover the bomb and ship it home without displaying it for the benefit of world public opinion could have disastrous political effects in the long run. His Palomares swim-in to demonstrate, with all deliberate drama, that the United States had not radioactively contaminated the Mediterranean waters had been the first step in assuaging Spanish fears. Now it seemed vital to Duke to make it incontrovertibly clear, when the occasion arose, that the United States had really removed the bomb from the vicinity of the Spanish coast, and thus write finis to the whole Palomares incident.

Accordingly, Duke passed his views on to the State and Defense Departments, recommending that the hydrogen bomb be shown to the world press immediately after recovery, in some form consonant with military security. The first Washington response was a directive to the effect that such a display could be held, *if feasible*. Duke then charged William A. Bell, the embassy's information attaché, with the task of evolving plans for press coverage and obtaining the operational approval of General Wilson and Admiral Guest.

Bell, a veteran newsman and information specialist, went to Palomares on March 26, with a letter signed by Ambassador Duke naming him the coordinator of the project. From the outset, however, Bell ran into Guest's flat refusal even to let him come aboard the *Albany* to discuss the matter and Wilson's reluctance to be drawn into the embassy's "credibility" project. Guest claimed he was too busy to receive the personal emissary of the American Ambassador, and he dispatched a junior naval information aide to meet Bell at Camp Wilson and tell him just that. As for General Wilson, he informed Bell that both Guest and he concurred in the view that there should be no public display of the recovered hydrogen bomb for reasons of military security. He said that the words "if feasible" in the Washington directive killed the whole project because in Guest's and his opinion such a display simply was not feasible. Bell took cognizance of these military views and returned to Madrid to report to Duke. The Ambassador, as it turned out, had his own ways of dealing with such conflicts of opinion. But of course the bomb at this stage had been neither recovered nor even located again.

vi

The long week that followed the realization that the bomb had been lost was used by Guest in two basic ways.

One was to keep the Alvin, the Aluminaut, the *Mizar*, and the minesweepers equipped with the ocean-bottom-scanning sonar combing the bottom in the area where the parachute and bomb had last been seen. It stood to reason that they could not have gone too far—even with the powerful bottom currents—and Guest was convinced that with time, diligence, and superior tracking efforts, the elusive weapon would be discovered once more. He could not discount, on the other hand, the possibility that the bomb had fallen into some impenetrable gulch or that the currents had dragged it some distance from the first slope. Still, his instinct was that the bomb and parachute were still in the same area. Both the Alvin and the Aluminaut made long dives every day between March 27 and April 1. The Alvin was assigned a contour search below the old bomb position, resuming the technique of circling the farmer's cowpath. The Aluminaut and the minesweeper USS *Salute* worked the flatter areas upslope from the canyon. The *Mizar* surveyed the moderate slopes with her underwater detection equipment.

The other way Guest used the final week of March was to prepare CURV, the latest addition to his underwater arsenal, for recovery operations. CURV, whose initials stand for Cable-Controlled Underwater Research Vehicle, was an experimental torpedo-retrieving apparatus developed by the Naval Ordnance test station at Pasadena, California. Weighing a ton and measuring 6 feet high, 5 feet wide, and 13 feet long, CURV was designed to locate its target with sonar, identify it with underwater television and a 35-millimeter movie camera, and shoot its electronic claw at the torpedo to secure a lifting line for its hoisting to the surface. In test operations for fourteen months, it had recovered forty torpedoes off Pasadena. If anything could retrieve the hydrogen bomb, the Navy believed, it was the CURV, and the *Mizar*'s unsuccessful attempt on March 24 drove this point home even more tellingly.

Actually, the Navy had planned to send CURV to Admiral Guest some time ago, except that its original maximum depth capability was only 2000 feet. When it developed that the Palomares bomb was somewhere between 2000 and 3000 feet, it became necessary to adapt CURV to the new circumstances. Working around the clock, the Ordnance test station specialists increased its range to 2800 feet and successfully tested it at the Pasadena torpedo range on March 25. The next day CURV and its five-man operating crew were flown from California to San Javier and then taken on to Cartagena. On March 27 the USS *Petrel*, a 2000-ton submarine rescue ship, sailed to fetch CURV, and on Tuesday, March 29, this strange contraption joined the task force.

On Friday, April 1, the *Petrel* took CURV to the area where Guest hoped the bomb was hiding and lowered it to the bottom in an experimental dive. The monster worked very well; all it needed now was the parachute and the bomb to sink its claw into.

On April 2, a Saturday, Bill Rainnie, the chief pilot, and Marvin McCamis once more took the Alvin to the bottom to continue the contour search around the canyon they now knew so well. Coming down the lower section of the slope, now dropping at a 35-degree incline, the Alvin nearly drove into the big gray shroud covering the hydrogen bomb. The weapon's latest resting place was at a depth of 2800 feet—it had slid down 250 feet the day the *Mizar*'s line snapped—and it was 120 yards south of its former perch. But the bomb and parachute were just as precariously perched as the first time, and the slope, as Guest remarked later, was as slick as glass. Rainnie calmly said, "Instrument Panel, Instrument Panel," into his telephone and placed an electronic transponder on the bottom to fix the weapon's new location. Nine days had elapsed since the bomb's second disappearance, and now Guest felt that he had almost won the long battle.

But there was no time to be wasted. The bottom currents, which had already dragged the bomb 120 yards to the south, were running strong and Guest was not about to take any more chances. The Aluminaut was again summoned for guard duty, as on March 15, and once more the two submersibles held a deep-inner-space rendezvous. The Alvin, her batteries now running low, surfaced. The red Aluminaut spent twenty-two hours on the bottom, guarding the bomb, and it was the afternoon of Sunday, April 3, when the Alvin came back to relieve her. Now the Alvin attached two pingers to the parachute's canopy and placed a transponder next to it. Then, using her mechanical arm, the little submersible tried to push the shrouds away to peek under the parachute. Guest wanted to make absolutely sure that it was the hydrogen bomb nesting behind the canopy. But the bomb fought back one more time and the attempt failed.

On Monday, April 4, the two submersibles took a day off. Sea conditions had suddenly worsened, and Guest decided to use the time to give the Alvin and the Aluminaut some of the required maintenance. The *Petrel* brought CURV to the spot for one final experimental dive before the recovery operations were set in motion. Monday night the task force had its last good night's sleep before the long drama finally was to run its course.

Now it was the morning of Tuesday, April 5, and as far as Admiral Guest was concerned this had to be it. He had spent seventy-two days off Palomares, planning, fighting the weather, enduring frustrations, and putting together the most competent and sophisticated surface-and-submarine search and recovery naval force ever assembled by the United States. He had recovered over three hundred objects from the sea floor—airplane wings and matchbox-sized devices—and he had found the hydrogen bomb and lost it and found it again. At long last everything was in place, the stage was set, the equipment was ready, and the actors stood poised for action.

From the *Albany*'s bridge Guest ordered Lieutenant Commander Max A. Harrell, the skipper of the *Petrel*, to inch his ship toward the spot from which CURV was to dive to the parachute and the bomb to initiate the recovery operations, the long-awaited Plan Charlie. Harrell, a South Carolinian with a born gift for seamanship and vast deep-water diving experience, moved the *Petrel* into position and anchored her. The electronic technicians at CURV's control console on the deck of the submarine rescue vessel made the final adjustments. CURV was lowered 2800 feet to the bottom, and its high-resolution sonar guided it directly to the pingers on the parachute canopy. About twenty feet above the parachute, CURV's three electrical motors were stopped and the vehicle hovered over its target at a 45-degree angle. Two high-power mercury vapor lights illuminated the parachute so that CURV's underwater television could transmit the view of the operation to the controllers aboard the *Petrel*. The crew on the surface was satisfied and CURV's hydraulically operated extra-large claw shot down to hook the grapnel end of a ⅝-inch nylon line into the apex of the shroud's canopy. Then the claw was detached from CURV and the metallic monster surfaced, bringing up the other end of the nylon line, which was immediately attached to a floating buoy. Now Guest knew he had the parachute and the bomb secured to the recovery rig and the first phase of the immensely delicate operation was completed.

But he was not yet home free. Once before, on March 24, he had had the hydrogen bomb and the parachute on a lifting line, and the cable had snapped before he could get it moved more than a few feet up. Besides, both his March experience and his knowledge of tension dynamics indicated that the 5000-pound bomb and the water-filled parachute weighing probably another

20,000 pounds could not be hoisted on one line. It would be certain to break. The combined weight of Contact 261 had to be distributed more evenly—at least one more line was required—and before a second attachment could be attempted the Alvin would have to be sent down to report precisely on the location of the target. It might have moved again in the last twenty-four hours.

By late afternoon the work of bringing up CURV and the buoyed line was completed. Shortly after 8 p.m. the Alvin plunged into the increasingly choppy Mediterranean for another look at the parachute and the bomb. It took her well over an hour to reach the bottom at the normal rate of descent. Reaching the 2800-foot level, where the parachute had been seen two days earlier, the submersible reported by underwater telephone that the target was no longer there. It seemed to have moved away in the last thirty hours, Valentine Wilson told Bill Rainnie, who was controlling the Alvin from the *Petrel*'s deck. The word was immediately flashed to the *Albany*. Guest, frantic and furious, jumped into his launch to rush over to the *Petrel* with his whole staff. Divers and photographers were ordered to move from their vessels to the submarine rescue ship. The Admiral knew that the parachute and the bomb were still attached to the floating buoy by CURV's nylon line, but if the whole heavy package was drifting away the cable could snap and the weapon could vanish for good this time. Though 300 feet of CURV's tether—the coaxial electric cable—had been added to the monster's principal 2800-foot line, even this length of rope could prove to be catastrophically short in a sudden new drift.

Cursing through clenched teeth and lighting one cigarette from another, Guest began making plans for an emergency recovery, even on one line, at the risk of abandoning his careful time schedule. Just then the Alvin came back on the telephone to report that she had seen the weapon. It had dropped 50 feet down and moved 300 feet west-southwest, Valentine Wilson said. And he added, "It is still moving with the current."

Guest, checking his underwater charts and the bottom-contour map, realized at once that if the drift continued west the bomb and the parachute would go down to 600 fathoms—3600 feet. If they slid south and downward, or even descended in steps, they would wind up in a valley over 700 fathoms, or 4200 feet, deep. In either event, not only would the nylon line snap but it would be completely beyond the capability of CURV or any other piece of equipment in United States possession to attempt recovery again in the foreseeable future. And in the meantime the weapon might get lost once more. It was a grim moment of crisis.

Guest turned to Captain Harrell and told him to move the *Petrel*, with CURV aboard, 300 feet, to the bomb's reported new position. This at least lessened the drag on the nylon line. As he later recalled these tense minutes, Guest said, "We decided that we had to go down and try to get another line on the weapon before the weapon moved further away and out of the reach of the CURV vehicle."

He ordered CURV prepared for a second line-securing dive, despite the night's darkness, pointing out to Max Harrell that if the bomb moved more to the south it would drop into the deep uncharted chasm below. Harrell passed the orders on to the CURV technicians. It was now cold and windy on the *Petrel*'s deck, but the men, caught up in their concern and excitement, seemed unaware of the worsening weather. Deckhands brought steaming cups of coffee to them.

Just then another crisis erupted, this one jeopardizing not only the bomb's recovery but possibly men's lives. Bill Rainnie picked up the underwater telephone on the *Petrel* to hear Valentine Wilson's voice telling him that the Alvin was caught inside the billowing shrouds of the parachute. The submersible was imprisoned in the chute and could not move. As Wilson explained it in quiet tones, the Alvin had been attempting to sail 300 feet west toward the bomb from the spot where it had been during the last dive. Coming downslope with a visibility of only 6 feet, the pilots suddenly saw the parachute's great billowing shape. Wilson threw the engines into reverse, but it was too late and the submersible's momentum drove her right into the tangled chute and its harness lines. The wet cloth covered the Alvin's portholes, and Wilson and McCamis found themselves both blinded and paralyzed by the parachute. To Guest, this was an "exceedingly dangerous situation," as he realized that the two pilots' lives hung in the balance. There was no equipment aboard the *Petrel* or any other ship of Task Force 65 capable of freeing the Alvin from the chute and bringing it up to the surface. If only the submersible's propellers had been caught in the chute, it would have been possible to detach them automatically and let the craft soar up to the surface. As it was, however, the Alvin was completely immobilized at the bottom, and only luck and her pilots' seamanship could now save them. To open the hatch and leave the ship at nearly 3000 feet would have meant instant death for the men in the crushing pressure of those depths.

For fifteen agonizing minutes Wilson and McCamis fought for their lives as Guest and Rainnie stood helplessly by the underwater telephone on the *Petrel*'s deck. Rainnie and Wilson exchanged occasional monosyllabic comments, but there was no real advice that could be given from topside. Finally, Wilson, steering blind, succeeded in pushing the shrouds aside sufficiently to find a small opening in the enveloping parachute cover. He nose-dived through the aperture and with a deft right turn brought the Alvin from under the canopy.

"I'm clear now, Bill," he told Rainnie with total casualness and resumed his tracking operation around the weapon. He had been inches away from ramming the bomb itself, with unpredictable consequences. Before surfacing some two hours later, long after midnight, the Alvin had provided Guest with precise tracking information to assist him in the fastening of the second line.

Wednesday, April 6, dawned with the red-eyed crews preparing to send CURV to the bottom on her second mission. Guest too had stayed up all night on the *Petrel*'s bridge, and now he was pressing for quick action. With the weapon dangerously drifting away toward the deep chasms, there was not a minute to be wasted. His brown leather coat thrown over his black knitted shirt with the two-star insignia, the admiral stood tensely over his charts and telephones. For breakfast he gulped down some hot black coffee and opened a new pack of cigarettes.

A few minutes before 8 a.m., CURV was lowered overboard and vectored down toward the parachute. But now strong winds were coming up from the west, seemingly intent one more time on protecting the bomb from returning to man's fold. As CURV neared the bottom, the sky was slate-gray, the wind was blowing at 22 knots, and 5-foot waves were rocking the ships. It was absolutely essential that the *Petrel* be held in position while CURV attempted to hook the second line onto the parachute. Otherwise, Guest warned his officers, the bomb might be tripped again over the slope—because the line was either too slack or too taut—and vanish once more. Max Harrell somehow managed to keep the *Petrel* almost motionless despite the winds, waves, and currents, for hours on end. Plotting by the Decca equipment showed that the 251-foot-long *Petrel* never deviated from her fix by more than 15 or 20 feet, which by all accounts was a remarkable feat of seamanship and ship-handling.

By 10 a.m., CURV had fastened the second line to at least six parachute shroud lines. On its way up, CURV brought the nylon line to be buoyed off. To forestall surprises, Guest assigned two ships to stand guard over the buoys. Things were finally looking up for the task force. The bomb's parachute was now being held fast by two tough nylon lines, reducing somewhat the danger that the underwater currents might again steal the weapon away from the hunters. Still, Guest figured that more cables were needed to stabilize the bomb and the parachute before the hoisting could begin. But at this point he had to face the reality that his crews had not slept in more than thirty hours and were rapidly becoming fatigued. Guest's own system could seemingly run on nerve alone, but the sleepy, yawning men could not perform exacting and delicate tasks as precisely as the recovery operation required. Though he was quite worried about a continued bottom drift of the bomb, Guest ordered a rest until eight o'clock that evening. But he, Commander Harrell, and most of the *Petrel* crew stayed up all day, preparing for the next night.

High seas and winds, however, prevented the admiral from resuming operations at 8 p.m., as he had planned. The curse of foul Mediterranean weather just would not leave the task force. And with each minute and hour that passed, Guest fretted more about the weapon's whereabouts and possible drift movements. Finally, a few minutes after midnight, the winds abated slightly and orders were given to cast CURV overboard with the third line. It was already Thursday, April 7, and Guest felt time was beginning to run out on him. It had taken two days to attach two lift lines to the parachute, and the weapon's past behavior indicated that it would not remain obedient much longer. Hadn't someone said the other evening, half in jest, that this accursed hydrogen weapon had a life and a mind of its own and simply did not wish to be found?

At 1:30 a.m., as a few house lights still flickered ashore in Palomares five miles away, CURV splashed into the water on her way down to shoot the grapnel line into the chute. Guest's eyes were riveted to the television screen on the control console aboard the *Petrel*. Sixty minutes elapsed. Then ninety minutes. Suddenly, at 3:15 a.m., the screen went dead. It took the CURV operators and Guest only a few seconds to understand that because of low visibility the whole recovery rig had plowed right into the billowing parachute. CURV's motors became entangled in the shroud, and it could not move. The whole machine had become snared by the treacherous bomb's parachute and now it was completely in irons. Unless CURV was freed, Guest could forget about attaching the third lift line to the canopy. The thought crossed the admiral's mind that he should "thank our lucky stars that CURV was an unmanned vehicle instead of a manned vehicle" —the Alvin's entrapment on Tuesday had been enough of a scare—and then a second thought, that it was a "hopeless situation." The bomb's parachute and CURV held each other in a weird embrace, as if in some legend of the deep, and there was no way of tearing them apart. For two full hours CURV's operators, along with Guest and Max Harrell, tried everything in the book, and out of the book, to free the underwater rig.

In every man's life there is a moment for a great command decision and Guest's moment came precisely at 5:15 a.m. on Thursday, April 7. Realizing that CURV could not be sprung loose, that the hydrogen weapon was in a very precarious position, and that it might drift away forever at any moment, Admiral Guest took a deep breath and said very quietly to his aides, "We've got to take the weapon now."

Guest called it later a "precipitous decision." And, in a sense, it was just that. He was going to attempt to bring up the bomb and the parachute on only two nylon lines—precisely the move he had hoped to avoid—and CURV on her electrical tether. It was flying in the face of every known theory of tension dynamics and in the face of the fundamental theory of probabilities, but in truth Guest no longer had a choice. It was now or never.

Shortly before six o'clock in the morning, with the Mediterranean still shrouded in darkness, Guest ordered the tireless Alvin to dive to the bottom to track the pingers on the parachute so that the men aboard the *Petrel* would know what was happening under the sea during the lift. All the preliminaries were completed, and now was the moment of truth—that peculiar Spanish concept of the decision between life and death.

At 7:02 a.m., as the sky in the east turned a pink and golden-blue hue, the winches on the *Petrel*'s two aft booms began to turn. For Admiral Guest it was the most critical, tense, and life-shortening instant since his arrival off Palomares on January 23. This was the moment of the greatest danger that the nylon lines would snap and the bomb would not come away from the bottom. While each of the two especially designed and braided ⅝-inch nylon lines had a strength equal to 10,800 pounds—a total of 21,600 pounds—Guest had to face a set of known adverse facts and whole series of complete intangibles. For one thing, he was aware that within 100 feet of the bottom and 100 feet of the surface the vibrations on nylon lines reduce their strength by as much as 75 per cent. Then there was the action of bottom currents and surface waves. The imponderables included Guest's ignorance of whether the waterlogged 65-foot-diameter parachute

would deploy fully at the moment of lifting and become a seadrove
—a brake—adding perhaps as much as 20,000 pounds of extra
weight. If that were the case, the combined lifting strength of
the two nylon lines simply would not be enough to raise the bomb
and the chute off the sea floor. As Guest recounted his emotions
later, he said, "I was extremely worried about what was going
to happen to this chute as it came off the bottom and whether it
was going to provide excessive drag far beyond the capacity of
those lines or not."

But that was not all. The 5000-pound bomb was not hanging
down at the end of the shrouds, as it should, but was caught in
the material, roughly one-third of the way up the length of the
chute canopy. Although one of the lifting lines was attached to
the apex of the canopy and the total weight was distributed over
the two lines as well as possible, the whole arrangement of the
bomb and the parachute was not exactly as hydrodynamic and
needle-like as Guest would have liked it. And finally there was the
peril that wet nylon lines can be slashed as easily as the thinnest
thread if they are brought across a sharp abrasive metal edge.
The grapnels holding the lines to the parachute were designed to
avoid just such an occurrence, but Guest had seen a nylon line
slashed once before. In fact, there was not a single factor in the
whole hoisting operation that did not have him worried and almost breathless.

After almost forty-eight hours without sleep and one contretemps—and one near-tragedy—after another, Guest's nerves had
become as taut as the nylon lines slowly bringing up the bomb.
He smoked incessantly as he watched the tensionometers' and
dynamometers' dials and listened to the Alvin's clipped reports on
the upward progress of the weapon and its parachute. At one point
he turned to one of his officers and said, without the slightest ex-
aggeration, "You know, I prefer combat any day to this."

But the Petrel's winches kept grinding slowly and surely, and
the lethal package came closer and closer to the surface. It took
one hour and seventeen minutes for the bomb and the parachute
to reach a point one hundred feet below the surface. It now was

8:19 a.m., the sea off Palomares glistened in the sun, and Admiral Guest was facing his final critical moment.

This was the danger period when the nylon lines again could snap because of the severe vibrations reducing the cables' tensile strength. "They could part on me and away we went again," Guest remarked later. He ordered the winches stopped, and a dozen waiting frogmen splashed from their rubber boats into the water. First the divers cut CURV free of the parachute, working with CURV's strobe light. Then they put two steel straps around the weapon and tied them to a heavy boom cable. This procedure took another twenty-one minutes. Exactly at 8:40 a.m. on April 7, the silvery 10-foot-long 1.5-megaton hydrogen bomb was hoisted aboard the *Petrel*, still wrapped in its parachute. It was just one hour and twenty-eight minutes short of eighty days since the bomb had vanished during the aerial collision over the Spanish village of Palomares.

Guest, his white admiral's cap at a slightly jaunty angle on his head, was among the first to take a close look at the bomb as it lay peacefully on the *Petrel*'s deck and the explosives ordnance experts wearing white stocking-caps began checking it and defusing its electrical TNT triggers. It was the first time since Captain Wendorf's B-52 had taken off from the Seymour Johnson base on January 16 that anyone had actually seen the hydrogen weapon. And the bomb did not seem any the worse for its experiences, except for several shallow dents in its metal skin around the warhead. And considering that it had been in an aerial collision, fire, and explosion, floated 30,500 feet down to the sea, plummeted 2550 feet to the bottom, fallen down twice from rocky ledges, and been harshly handled during recovery after nearly three months in salt water, the weapon was in pretty good shape. In fact, it had acquired an extra piece of metal in the accident. A finlike yellow grille was affixed to its top, a section of the B-52's bomb bay, proving for the benefit of the Air Force specialists that the collision's centrifugal forces had actually torn it out of the aircraft.

Standing over their recovered bomb, the red-eyed, exhausted men exchanged weak congratulations. But they were too dog-tired for any real show of joy. Admiral Guest went over to Max Harrell, the *Petrel*'s skipper, and congratulated him for his fine seamanship in keeping the rescue ship in perfect position for nearly forty-eight hours during the recovery operation. Then he said softly to nobody in particular, "Thank God, we finally did it." And it was all over except for the announcements.

Admiral Guest returned to the USS *Albany*, his flagship, and drafted a secret message to the Chief of Naval Operations in Washington, the Commander-in-Chief of United States Naval Forces Europe in London, the Commander-in-Chief of the United States Sixth Fleet in Naples, the American embassy in Madrid, and the JUSMAAG in Madrid, informing them of the successful recovery of the hydrogen bomb. The terse message, sent at 9:31 a.m., local time (0831Z, or GMT), read:

SECRET
Fm CTF Six Five
ACFT SALVOPS—MED.
1. TARGET ON DECK OF PETREL AND IDENTIFIED AS WEAPON AT 070740Z.
WILL AMPLIFY ASAP.
2. RECOMMEND AMEMB AND HIS PARTY AND PRESS DEPART DOCK AT GARRUCHA BY BOAT FOR ALBANY AT 080900X7 ALPHA GP-4
BT

A separate signal to the Pentagon added: "This mission has been completed."

Guest's message reached the embassy in Madrid at 10:35 a.m., and it was Arch K. Jean, the counselor for administration, who first received it. He phoned Earl Wilson, the information counselor, and Bill Bell, the information attaché, and said, "God, he's got the thing." He did not have to elaborate. The three of them went to the fifth-floor office of William Walker, the chargé d'affaires in Ambassador Duke's absence, to discuss the next step.

Since Duke was in the port of Alicante on the Mediterranean, preparing to board a friend's yacht for an Easter weekend cruise, word of the recovery was flashed to him through official Spanish channels. It caught up with him just as the yacht was sailing out of Alicante. Walker telephoned Angel Sagáz, the North American Department head at the Foreign Ministry, to tell him of the recovery. Then the three men agreed that a press conference should be held at once to make a formal announcement. Bell phoned newsmen all over Madrid to come to an emergency news conference at the embassy's auditorium at noon sharp.

Barely containing his excitement, Bell read the announcement:

> The fourth and final weapon from the January 17 crash near Palomares, Spain, has been recovered today and will be transported directly to the United States. The casing was intact. The weapon was located on March 15 at 2500 feet of water, approximately five miles off shore, by units of Task Force 65. Photographs taken at that time tentatively identified the object as the missing weapon. The recovery of this weapon brings to a close the search phase of the operation. No release of radioactivity into the coastal waters had occurred. All wreckage fragments and associated aircraft material of interest to the accident investigation have now been located and recovered.

Bell still lacked specific details of the recovery, which Guest had promised to send as soon as possible, but he told the newsmen to report at the port of Garrucha the next morning at nine o'clock to witness the display of the retrieved hydrogen bomb. Angier Biddle Duke had won his battle with the military in Palomares for the international credibility of the United States report of the weapon's recovery. He did so through the simple expedient of directly persuading Secretary of Defense McNamara that the interests of the United States would be best served in this manner, and Guest and Wilson were consequently ordered to conform.

vii

April 8 was Good Friday, a solemn holiday in Spain. In the towns and villages of Andalusia, where the Roman heritage has not yet been quite forgotten, Good Friday processions were a major event of Holy Week. Thus, officials and newsmen rushing to Garrucha that morning for the public display of the retrieved American bomb kept running into these processions the whole length of Andalusia. There were traffic-blocking processions in Lorca, Huercal-Overa, Cuevas de Almanzora, and Vera.

In Vera the procession formed in a side street before 8:30 a.m., in preparation for the slow march to the church on the west side of town in the direction of Garrucha. Dark-faced Andalusian peasants formed in two files on either side of the street in their Roman soldiers' attire, with swords and shiny helmets. Others were made up to represent Jews and slaves. Between the two lines were gathered the penitents in long hooded violet robes, tall candles in their hands. Behind the penitents, priests, nuns, and children escorted the effigy of the Virgin. The procession was grave and, in an intangible way, startlingly realistic. When the drums of the Roman soldiers started beating their mournful cadence and the hooded penitents began their solemn progress, the whole scene suddenly seemed to be thrust back nearly two millennia in time. This procession on the day of the Lord's sacrifice was, then, the strange and immediate backdrop for the ceremony, twenty centuries later and five miles away, of the unveiling of the nuclear bomb.

The streets of Garrucha were empty on this religious holiday, but the harbor, snugly hidden behind a curving stone breakwater, was a beehive of twentieth-century bustle. Scores of officials' and newsmen's cars were parked at the dock. Guardia Civil troopers in their green uniforms and patent-leather hats stood guard. United States sailors and young ensigns with walkie-talkies were busily directing the traffic of Navy launches transporting the visitors to the USS *Albany*, the flagship of Admiral Guest.

A warm spring sun was shining over the blue sea as the launches sailed a mile or so to the *Albany*. The red Aluminaut and the white Alvin were bobbing on the wavelets, their crewmen standing topside and smilingly waving at the visitors. There was a holiday feeling in the air, reminiscent of a weekend at the naval academy. Aboard the *Albany*, Captain J. H. Wohler, the flagship's skipper, was greeting the visitors at the rail. Ambassador Duke and his wife, Robin, elegant in a yellow dress and with a yellow parasol, came aboard with General Donovan. The Dukes had just arrived in Garrucha from Alicante aboard the yacht. General Wilson, whose beachhead camp had been closed two days earlier, drove in from the Palomares area with General Montel, the Spanish commander on the scene. Guardia Civil Captain Calín, the man who had taken the situation in hand the day of the accident, was another invited guest. But conspicuously absent from this festive occasion was Francisco Simó, the "Paco of the Bomb," for whom the United States Navy had by now lost the last shreds of enthusiasm. The white houses of Palomares were a pleasant sight in the distance, but somehow the Navy did not think of inviting any of the village people whose lives for nearly three months had become so entwined with America's four nuclear bombs. They no longer seemed to be part of the picture.

Presently Admiral Guest led the way to the *Albany*'s ample stateroom for his scheduled press briefing. Though he had completed the actual recovery of the bomb twenty-four hours ago,

Guest still had not a chance to sleep, busy as he had been with the final arrangements of preparing for the weapon's display, getting it ready for shipment to the United States, disbanding his task force, and drafting reports. Exhaustion was visible in his demeanor, but the "Little Bulldog" was as articulate as ever, savoring his hour of triumph. Speaking from memory, down to the most minute details, and illustrating his points on colored charts, Guest drew up a painstakingly detailed history of his search and recovery mission, then for a full hour answered questions with a patience that surprised his subordinates. Only once or twice did his fatigue show as the Admiral rubbed his eyes and faltered in answering a question. At one point he told a questioner, "I'm sorry I can't remember anything this morning." Finally, as he began to shake on his feet, Ambassador Duke broke in to end the briefing. "Admiral," he said, "you have the thanks of your grateful countrymen, of a grateful host country, and, in fact, the gratitude of the world. Thank you very much."

The company then adjourned to the *Albany*'s starboard deck to view the parade of the hydrogen bomb, the second spectacular of the Palomares search, exactly one month after the Duke-Fraga swim-in. The bomb, looking deceptively harmless, lay on the fantail of the *Petrel* next to a sand-filled blue box, its "coffin," in which it was to be shipped to the United States. The bomb and the coffin together weighed 15,000 pounds, Guest had told the newsmen.

The bomb parade was the first known instance in which a high-powered United States hydrogen weapon had been publicly displayed anywhere in the world. The *Petrel*'s Commander Harrell, still demonstrating his seamanship, first sailed past the *Albany* at some 400 yards, then reversed the engines and backed the vessel to a point 35 yards from the cruiser, so that the bomb could be clearly seen. The only visible security measure was the taping over of serial numbers on its skin. Admiral Guest, General Wilson, General Montel, a representative of the Spanish Nuclear Energy Board, several Navy ordnance men, and armed Marines stood around the weapon in a semicircle like proud but jealous parents.

Later in the day, after the public had departed, the hydrogen bomb was packed in its coffin and transferred to the destroyer-tender USS *Cascade* for the journey to the United States, where the Navy was to turn the retrieved weapon back to the Air Force and the Atomic Energy Commission. The Alvin and the Aluminaut were loaded aboard the landing ship docks USS *Lindenwald* for the trip home. Task Force 65 vanished from the Palomares waters, and Admiral Guest chose, of all the places in Europe, the Torrejón Air Force base near Madrid for a weekend rest. The naval, military, and nuclear phases of Broken Arrow around Palomares had come to an end eighty-one days after the B-52 and the KC-135 collided above the remote Spanish village and savagely introduced it to the atomic age. All that remained were the memories of that extraordinary episode and the mark which history had left indelibly on Palomares and its people.

viii

By mid-April the farmers of Palomares had completed the spring planting with high hopes for an abundant and easily marketable crop of tomatoes, beans, wheat, alfalfa, and oranges. But in the green-shuttered house at the foot of the village Colonel Stulb, the Air Force paymaster, still pored over the claims. Antonio Saviote, the serious farmer who owns the land across the road from Rabbit's Rise, traveled to Madrid to complain to the embassy that none of the damage he had suffered had yet been compensated for. Julio Ponce, the day laborer who measures the infrequent Palomares rainfall and who was the first to rush to the scene of the accident, took the eternally fatalistic Spanish view of the days that had shaken his village. "It all came and went and we're still poor," he said without rancor.

The Palomares families, who had started returning to the Vera market every other Saturday, found that people there still stared at them questioningly. "Oh, you are the bomb people," a storekeeper told Miguel Castro Navarro one day in May. "I must come over some day soon to see what all these bombs have done to you."

So the self-consciousness and the resentments remained in Palomares—some against the still uncomprehended nuclear age and some against the Americans—and the men at Tomás Mula's bar tended to agree that nothing good came out of becoming a world-famous village, a recognized place on the map, and a community with a reputation. "I wonder if things were not really better when nobody knew who we were and where we were," Miguel Badillo said to his friends at the bar. They were feeling a bit cheated, a bit anti-climactic, and they nodded in agreement. "Where do we go from here and what do we do with ourselves now that the world is forgetting us but we can't forget what happened to us?" Miguel Castro asked. "Maybe I should go to Switzerland after all."

In Vera things were anti-climactic too. Fernando Carmona, the thirty-three-year-old owner of La Estación, had moved in three months from a $1500 debt and fears of having to close down to a mortgage-free business and money in the bank. "If I had found that bomb, I would have hidden it so that no one could ever find it," he said. "But now I'm going to start losing money again. After all, the Americans are gone." Juan, his young bartender, put it another way. "I hope the Americans lose another bomb around here, but this time I hope it falls right in the middle of the main street in Vera." Diego Soler, a Vera taxi-driver, planned to buy a new car, after having feared in the pre-bomb days that he would have to sell his 1964 sedan.

In Garrucha, Iluminado Rodriguez Gallardo, a real-estate agent, saw in the bomb a promise of new business to come. After a temporary dip in housing prices and a standstill, he thought that foreign tourists would really discover Almería, now that the bombs had made the province famous. "There is something funny about people," he said. "They like to come to famous places, even if they are famous for cemeteries." Then he thought it over and said, "But whatever happens, you know, things will never be quite the same again here."

For the United States the Palomares accident had the dubious advantage of providing a test for nuclear decontamination and bomb safety. To think so was, to be sure, to look for a silver lining in a situation that could easily have turned into a colossal disaster. And, in the long run, Palomares has posed grave problems of military cooperation with Spain, which no longer allowed nuclear overflights of any type and presumably would use the accident as a bargaining point in the renegotiation in 1968 of the base agreements. The brush with the nuclear age had been too close for comfort.

The Navy, on the other hand, profited handsomely from the Palomares experience. It carried out the first deep-inner-space rendezvous between submersibles. Both Admiral Guest and the deep-submergence experts were convinced that the bomb hunt and recovery operations had advanced United States underwater research by at least five years. Nothing even remotely like Palomares could have been staged under normal conditions.

All things considered, the financial cost of the whole operation was not staggering. The total bill was estimated to run roughly $15 million, exclusive of the value of the two destroyed hydrogen bombs, on which the AEC puts no price tags. The replacement value of the three aircraft—the B-52 and the KC-135 lost in the collision and the C-54 that crashed in Sierra Nevada—was probably less than $8 million. The Navy's bill to the Air Force for finding its bomb was $5,340,000. The Palomares claims payments were not likely to exceed $1 million. The out-of-pocket costs for decontaminating Palomares stood at only $52,000. The cost of the use of ships and aircraft and the salaries of sailors, airmen, and soldiers were not tabulated separately, on the theory that they are constant military expenditures. The men are paid whether they hunt bombs in Palomares or sit in their barracks. Above all, valuable experience was gained in every field.

The principal American actors in the long Palomares drama did not fare badly, and the memories of the men killed in the three aircraft now belong to the history of the nuclear age. Three of the survivors from the B-52—Captain Wendorf, the pilot, and Majors Messinger and Buchanan—are back on SAC duty at the Seymour Johnson base and, presumably, are flying again. Lieutenant Rooney, the young copilot, was routinely assigned to Vietnam. Although the Air Force by July had already completed its investigation of the Palomares air accident and its causes, the conclusions remained secret, in keeping with the normal procedures confirmed by federal courts and the President of the United States.

Whatever the Air Force findings were, the military careers of the B-52 survivors did not apparently suffer in the wake of the disastrous January 17 flights.

Among the other Palomares figures, General Wilson was transferred in May from Torrejón to California as deputy commander of an important air base. General Donovan was named head of the Sixteenth Air Force in Spain, which in the meantime had switched from SAC operations to tactical fighter-bomber squadrons. Colonel White, the Texas county agent, was sent to Omaha to be SAC's director of personnel, wearing a brand-new Legion of Merit. Colonel "Skip" Young, the information officer who disliked newsmen, was reassigned to the United States. Admiral Guest resumed his Naples duties after a spate of Washington speechmaking. Most of the officers and men who distinguished themselves in some way in and around Palomares received military awards. The Air Force alone distributed seventy medals and commendations. Not surprisingly, the Air Force made no mention of the Navy and the Navy none of the Air Force when their respective top men received awards at separate ceremonies. In the same vein, Admiral Guest sat down to write a letter to a New York news magazine to question a story crediting the AEC's Sandia Corporation laboratories and Spanish eyewitnesses with substantial assistance in locating the missing bomb. "Had we adhered to their imprecise estimates, the location of the bomb would have been delayed at least a month and more likely several months," he wrote. "The plaudits for this highly successful operation properly belong to the patriotic civilian and military personnel of Task Force 65."

The civilian scientists rapidly returned to their anonymity and special pursuits. Dr. Wright Langham, the plutonium expert, went back to Los Alamos and his new interest in outer-space radiation. Jon Lindbergh rushed from Palomares to Vietnam, where he spent the summer of 1966 on a secret government assignment. The others were left with memories of the excitement of Palomares.

On the Spanish side, the two naval helicopter pilots received medals from their government. Francisco Simó Orts was given by Ambassador Duke a plaque with President Johnson's profile, but he felt this was insufficient compensation and proceeded to sue the United States for $5 million for his help in finding the bomb. A Madrid daily took a more realistic approach in launching a reader campaign to raise money for a new fishing boat for him. And a Spanish provincial newspaper printed a cartoon in which a perplexed King Neptune watched the hydrogen bomb being taken away from the sea floor as a beautiful siren sadly remarked, "And just as we were becoming a nuclear power . . ."

So all that was left of the Palomares experience of 1966 was the need to set in some sort of perspective the story of the nuclear age's invasion of this peaceful and remote Spanish village, its radioactive contamination, its fears of the lost hydrogen bomb, and the violent disruption of its sheltered life.

One part of this final summary was provided by Dr. Wright Langham, the "bridesmaid" at the dawning of the atomic age in 1945, and the humane custodian of the bombs of Palomares.

Looking back at the impact of Palomares, Dr. Langham told a friend in Los Alamos that he was "emotionally disturbed, frustrated, or just plain annoyed that in twenty years we, as scientists, have been unable to dispel the stigma of Hiroshima and Nagasaki and to get the general public . . . to see the potential radiation hazards of nuclear energy in perspective."

From the dawn of history, he said, every step taken by man to find and harness sources of energy has brought problems along with progress. Except for thermal fusion, Dr. Langham noted, every advance in harnessing energy has been used by men to settle their differences in war. Speaking as a scientist, he then offered the view that "the fault lies not in technical progress, but in human frailty on other fronts."

As far as they went, Dr. Langham's viewpoint and frustration were unquestionably well founded. But the nuclear age and its implications that so dramatically burst forth in Palomares on January 17, 1966, also present us with another aspect.

This is the shattering knowledge that human frailties *are* such that it is possible in this world to lose four hydrogen bombs, radioactively contaminate an innocent village, raise the specter of massive nuclear poisoning, and distort, perhaps forever, the lives of a community of people.

The stigma of Hiroshima, Nagasaki, the *Lucky Dragon,* and now Palomares cannot be dispelled in a world over which hydrogen weapons are carried, or must be carried, day and night. It is possible to hope and it is possible to rationalize, but it is not possible to become free of fear and to accept the situation as a way of life.

The story of Palomares, a nightmare of the nuclear age, must speak for itself.

Bibliography

Books

Alexander, Peter. *Atomic Radiation and Life*. London: Penguin Books, 1965.

Banco de Bilbao. *Renta Nacional de España, 1962*. Bilbao, Spain: Banco de Bilbao, 1964.

Compton, Arthur H. *Atomic Quest*. New York: Oxford University Press, 1956.

Lapp, Ralph E. *The Voyage of the* Lucky Dragon. New York: Harper and Row, 1957.

Laurence, William L. *Men and Atoms*. New York: Simon and Schuster, 1962.

Siret, Louis. *Les Premiers Ages du Métal dans le Sud Ouest de l'Espagne*. Brussels, 1887.

United States Atomic Energy Commission. *The Effects of Nuclear Weapons*, revised edition. Washington, D.C.: U.S. Government Printing Office, 1964.

Periodicals, Transcripts, and Special Materials

CBS Television Network. Transcript of "Lost and Found: One H-Bomb" (program televised March 22, 1966).

Hubbell, John G. "The Case of the Missing H-Bomb." *Readers Digest,* September 1966.

Langham, W. H. "Physiology and Toxicology of Plutonium-239 and Its Industrial Medical Control." *Health Physics* (New York: Pergamon Press, 1959), Vol. II.

274 / **Bibliography**

———. "Physiological Properties of Plutonium and Assessment of Body Burden in Man." Reprint from *Assessment of Radioactivity in Man* (Vienna: International Atomic Energy Agency, 1964), Vol. II.

———. "Potential Internal Radiation Hazards." Extract from Report LA-2400, *Potential Hazards of Weapons Prior to Delivery* (Los Alamos Scientific Laboratory, December 1959).

Langham, W. H.; Lawrence, J. N. P.; McClelland, Jean; and Hempelmann, L. H. "The Los Alamos Scientific Laboratory's Experience with Plutonium in Man." *Health Physics* (New York: Pergamon Press, 1962), Vol. 8.

Newsweek. "An H-Bomb Is Missing and the Hunt Goes On," March 7, 1966.

Rainnie, W. O., Jr. "Alvin—and the Bomb." *Oceanus* (published at Woods Hole Oceanographic Institute), September 1966.

Simmons, Howard. "The Missing H-Bomb." Series of articles in the *Washington Post,* February 1966.

Storms, Barbara. "When the Sky Fell." *The Atom* (published by the Los Alamos Scientific Laboratory), May 1966.

United States House of Representatives. Armed Forces Subcommittee transcript of hearings: "Recovery of Lost Nuclear Weapon in Spain," April 20, 1966.

Files of newspapers *ABC, YA, Arriba, Pueblo, Alcázar,* all of Madrid, January 18 to May 15, 1966.